Bristol Studies in Law and Social Justice

Series Editors: **Alan Bogg**, University of Bristol, UK and
Virginia Mantouvalou, University College London, UK

This series explores the role of law in securing social justice in society and
the economy. The focus is on 'social justice' as a normative ideal, and the
law as a critical tool in influencing (for good or for ill) the social structures
that shape people's lives.

Forthcoming

Climate Litigation and Justice in Africa
Edited by **Kim Bouwer**, **Uzuazo Etemire**, **Tracy-Lynn Field** and
Ademola Oluborode Jegede

Labour Law and Social Justice
The Promise of Relational Autonomy
By **Lisa Rodgers**

Low Paid EU Migrant Workers
The House, The Street, The Town
By **Catherine Barnard**, **Fiona Costello**, and **Sarah Fraser Butlin**

Discrimination, Equality and Health Care Rationing
By **Rachel Horton**

Find out more at
bristoluniversitypress.co.uk/
bristol-studies-in-law-and-social-justice

Find out more at
**bristoluniversitypress.co.uk/
bristol-studies-in-law-and-social-justice**

CLASS AND SOCIAL BACKGROUND DISCRIMINATION IN THE MODERN WORKPLACE

Mapping Inequality in the Digital Age

Angelo Capuano

BRISTOL
UNIVERSITY
PRESS

First published in Great Britain in 2023 by

Bristol University Press
University of Bristol
1–9 Old Park Hill
Bristol
BS2 8BB
UK
t: +44 (0)117 374 6645
e: bup-info@bristol.ac.uk

Details of international sales and distribution partners are available at bristoluniversitypress.co.uk

© Bristol University Press 2023

British Library Cataloguing in Publication Data
A catalogue record for this book is available from the British Library

ISBN 978-1-5292-2294-4 hardcover
ISBN 978-1-5292-2296-8 ePub
ISBN 978-1-5292-2297-5 ePdf

Cover design: blu inc
Front cover image: 123rf/wavebreakmediamicro
Bristol University Press use environmentally responsible print partners.
Printed and bound in Great Britain by CPI Group (UK) Ltd, Croydon, CR0 4YY

FSC
www.fsc.org
MIX
Paper | Supporting
responsible forestry
FSC® C013604

To my wife Greta and daughter Lily

Contents

Detailed Contents

Series Editor Preface

Alan Bogg and Virginia Mantouvalou

Bristol Studies in Law and Social Justice explores the role of law in securing social justice in society and the economy. The focus is on 'social justice' as a normative ideal, and the law as a critical tool in influencing (for good or for ill) the social structures that shape people's lives. This international series is designed to be inclusive of a wide range of methodologies and disciplinary approaches. Contributions examine these issues from multiple legal perspectives, including constitutional law, discrimination law, human rights, contract law, criminal law, migration law, labour law, social welfare law, property law, international and supranational law. The series has broad jurisdictional coverage, including single-country, comparative, international and regional legal orders, and encourages a critical and interdisciplinary approach to legal analysis.

About the Author

Angelo Capuano is Lecturer in Law at Central Queensland University. His published work on discrimination law has been used in court and tribunal decisions in Australia and South Africa, including by the Constitutional Court of South Africa. Outside of academia, Angelo has years of practical experience as a government lawyer, court researcher and judge's associate.

Acknowledgements

I would like to acknowledge the people who have had an impact on my growth and development as a lawyer and as an academic. My first job out of law school as the associate to Justice Peter Gray of the Federal Court of Australia sparked my interest in labour law. I then engaged in the life-changing experience of studying law at the University of Oxford with the financial support of a Rotary International Ambassadorial Scholarship (I was also informed that I was the first person from Melbourne's traditionally working-class western region to win the scholarship since its inception in 1947). After finishing my degree at Oxford, I started researching the concept of 'social origin' discrimination as a PhD student at Monash University under the superb supervision of Professor Marilyn Pittard and Dr Colin Campbell. Outputs from my research soon followed, including: Angelo Capuano, 'Giving Meaning to "Social Origin" in International Labour Organization ("ILO") Conventions, the Fair Work Act 2009 (Cth) and the Australian Human Rights Commission Act 1986 (Cth): "Class" Discrimination and Its Relevance to the Australian Context' (2016) 39(1) *UNSW Law Journal* 84; and Angelo Capuano, 'The Meaning of "Social Origin" in International Human Rights Treaties: A Critique of the CESCR's Approach to "Social Origin" Discrimination in the ICESCR and its (Ir)relevance to National Contexts such as Australia' (2017) 41(3) *New Zealand Journal of Employment Relations* 91.

These articles stimulated my academic interest and I have expanded on them considerably to produce this book, which engages with a number of new legal, technological and workplace developments since the articles were published.

I am thankful for the opportunity to currently work with collegiate and supportive academic colleagues at Central Queensland University.

I would also like to express my love and gratitude to my family. Life threw me a few curve balls, including a ruptured eye, so reaching this stage and being able to write this acknowledgement is elating to say the least. My wife, Greta, has been my rock for many years and she provided much support and made sacrifices so that I could write. My daughter, Lily, fills every day with joy and laughter.

Class and Social Background Discrimination: An Introduction

Introduction

This book has two aspects and aims. First, it aims to unravel the extent to which discrimination in employment based on class and factors reflective of social background is prohibited in Australia, South Africa, Canada and New Zealand, and key differences in the law of each of these jurisdictions. Second, it examines the application of the law to the use of new technology and practices, to expose how their use creates risks of this type of discrimination and to propose how these technologies and practices can be re-imagined to reduce these risks.

The first of the book's aims are achieved in Chapters 2 and 3. Chapter 2 considers whether, and the extent to which, discrimination based on class and factors reflective of social background is prohibited in international labour law as part of the prohibition on 'social origin' discrimination in conventions of the International Labour Organisation ('ILO').[1] Chapter 3 then maps the legal frameworks in four common law countries (Australia, South Africa, Canada and New Zealand) to unravel the extent to which discrimination in employment based on class and factors reflective of social background is prohibited in these countries. The analysis in these chapters reveal that whilst 'class' and 'social background' are not expressly listed as grounds of discrimination in legislation within these jurisdictions, certain listed grounds are understood in terms of class and/ or factors reflective of social background. This includes the grounds of 'social origin' in Australian and South African law, 'social condition' and

---

[1] Discrimination based on 'social origin' is prohibited in two conventions of the ILO. See *Discrimination (Employment and Occupation) Convention, 1958 (No. 111)* ('*ILO 111*'); *Termination of Employment Convention, 1982 (No. 158)* ('*ILO 158*').

'family status' in laws within Canada, and 'family status' in New Zealand law, amongst other grounds.

The second of the book's aims are achieved in Chapters 4, 5, 6 and 7. Chapter 4 examines an employer's use of social media, such as for cybervetting, job advertisement targeting, and terminating an employee's employment for social media posts. Chapter 5 examines automated candidate screening technologies, such as the use of certain algorithms and AI in recruitment. Chapter 6 examines the changing nature of work in the digital age, including certain aspects of platform work in the 'gig economy' and the post-pandemic shift to remote working and homeworking. Chapters 4, 5 and 6 expose how all these practices create significant inequalities and opportunities for discrimination based on class and/or certain factors reflective of social background. These chapters also assess whether, and which of, these practices create risks of discrimination in Australian, South African, Canadian and New Zealand law. Finally, Chapter 7 is solutions focused and it re-imagines workplace practices and policy to propose strategies which may not only reduce these risks but also proactively assist in making workplaces fairer.

Before analyzing the law and applying it to new technologies and practices, it is first necessary to lay the foundation needed to understand the analysis in this book. Chapter 1 provides this foundation through addressing three important questions. Firstly, what is 'class'? This is by no means a simple question to answer because 'class' is a highly ambiguous concept that can be interpreted or measured in different ways by different people. Craig McGregor's observation that 'class theory is a sociological minefield of conflicting analyses'[2] illustrates not only that there is no one settled theory of class,[3] but that these theories conflict with one another. As such, it is important to consider leading class theories to help inform the analysis of the jurisprudence to be discussed in subsequent chapters. Secondly, whilst there are various competing class theories, which of these class theories has most relevance and application in modern workplaces? Thirdly, how might discrimination based on class and factors reflective of social background occur in modern workplaces?

Part II of this chapter addresses the first question by introducing leading theories of class, such as those of Marx, Weber, Durkheim and Bourdieu to articulate possible approaches to class. Rather than being a complete overview of class theory, this analysis will focus on articulating class theories which are most relevant to understanding the ILO, Australian, South African and Canadian jurisprudence analysed in this book.

---

[2]   Craig McGregor, *Class in Australia* (Penguin, 1997), 23.

[3]   See also Henry Paternoster, *Reimagining Class in Australia: Marxism, Populism and Social Science* (2017, Springer International Publishing AG), 258.

Part II of this chapter addresses the second question by using a social-psychological lens, relying on Social Identity Theory ('SIT') to show how humans are prone to discriminate based on a person's class and social background.

Finally, Part III of this chapter addresses the third question by using existing literature to explain the development of a normative framework for understanding class and social background discrimination. It will introduce the distinction between 'formal' versus 'substantive' equality, 'asymmetrical' versus 'symmetrical' definitions of discrimination, and categorical frames of conceiving class and social background discrimination. This will provide an important theoretical basis for understanding subsequent chapters of this book.

I. Theories of class

In September 2021 the accounting firm KPMG announced that it 'aims to see 29 per cent of UK partners and directors come from a working-class background by 2030'.[4] Similarly, in the same month the UK branch of Price Waterhouse Coopers (PwC) reported that its staff with a working-class background are paid approximately 12 per cent less than other staff.[5] The World Values Surveys, which are conducted by an international network of social scientists, reveal that many people around the world accept that 'classes' exist, and they even allocate themselves to a particular 'class' – among 1,813 respondents from Australia 30.5 per cent identified as 'working class', 4.4 per cent identified as 'lower class' and only 2.4 per cent gave no answer,[6] among 4,018 respondents from Canada 19.3 per cent identified as 'working class'

---

[4] KPMG UK, 'KPMG publishes firmwide socio-economic background pay gaps' (Press Release, 9 September 2021) https://home.kpmg/uk/en/home/media/press-releases/2021/09/kpmg-publishes-firmwide-socio-economic-background-pay-gaps.html. Also see KPMG UK, 'Socio-Economic Background Pay Gap Report 2021' (September 2021) ('KPMG Pay Gap Report') https://assets.kpmg/content/dam/kpmg/uk/pdf/2021/09/KPMG-Socio-Economic-Background-Pay-Gap-Report.pdf, 10.

[5] PwC, Diversity Pay Report (accessed 23 September 2021) ('PwC Diversity Pay Report') https://www.pwc.co.uk/who-we-are/our-purpose/empowered-people-communities/inclusion/diversity-pay-report.html. PwC seems to measure 'lower socio-economic background' and not 'working class' explicitly. It relies on the Social Mobility Commission measurement guidance which use the terms 'working class' and 'lower socio-economic background' interchangeably. See Social Mobility Commission, Cross-industry toolkit (accessed 23 September 2021) ('SMC Toolkit') https://socialmobilityworks.org/toolkit/measurement/#data.

[6] World Values Survey Wave 7 (2017–2020; Study #WVS-2017): Australia, 84 (PI: Professor Ian McAllister, The Australian National University); Co-PIs: Professor Toni Makkai and Dr Jill Sheppard, The Australian National University).

and 6.8 per cent identified as lower class,[7] and among 3,531 respondents from South Africa 23.8 per cent identified as 'working class', 42.8 per cent identified as 'lower class' and 4.5 per cent did not know.[8] This demonstrates that in various countries, including Australia, Canada and South Africa, the concept of 'class' and class inequality is an accepted social phenomenon.

What, then, is 'class' and what does it mean to be 'working class' or 'lower class'? This chapter will now provide an overview of leading theories of class, and in doing so it will shed light on various approaches to measuring a person's class.

A. Class as a gradational concept

The concept of class, and what makes up a person's class, has been contested and it is the subject of much debate.[9] Some argue that class structures have dissolved and no longer exist, while others disagree on the scope of the concept of 'class'.[10] One popular way to view class is as a gradational concept, with each class occupying a place in a hierarchy – underclass, lower class, middle class, and upper class, for example.[11] This descriptive view of class attempts to classify levels of social stratification and then fit people within those levels, so it views a class in relation to its social location.[12] This is the approach taken by the World Values Surveys which simply refer to, for example, the 'lower class', 'working class', 'middle class' and 'upper class' without clarifying how class is measured; rather the survey relies on the perceptions of respondents and how they personally measure their 'class' and assign themselves a class location.

1. Class determined by occupation

Another popular way to measure 'class' is to conflate certain occupations into classes which take a gradational form. This is the approach taken by

[7] World Values Survey Wave 7 (2017–2020): Canada, 85 (PI: Professor Guy Lachapelle, Concordia University; Co-PI: Antoine Bilodeau, Concordia University) https://www.worldvaluessurvey.org/WVSDocumentationWV7.jsp. The survey did not collect data on whether participants provided no response.

[8] World Values Survey Wave 6 (2010–2014), 121–2 (PI: Professor Hennie Kotzé, Stellenbosch University) https://www.worldvaluessurvey.org/WVSDocumentation WV6.jsp.

[9] See, for example, Erik Olin Wright, *Approaches to Class Analysis* (2005, Cambridge University Press).

[10] See, for example, Wright, *Approaches to Class Analysis* (n 9).

[11] See, for example, Erik Olin Wright, 'Social Class' in George Ritzer (ed), *Encyclopedia of Social Theory*, 718.

[12] Ibid, 718.

KMPG and PwC when they seek to identify who has a 'working class' background for the purposes of their respective policies, which are referred to above. For both KPMG[13] and PwC parental occupation is an indicator of class background.[14] According to KPMG, 'working class' background in particular is defined as having parents with 'routine and manual' occupations.[15] PwC take a similar approach but refer to guidance of the UK's Social Mobility Commission ('SMC'),[16] which defines 'working class' or 'lower socio-economic' background by reference to '[r]outine and manual occupations'[17] (such as farm workers, labourers), service occupations, 'technical and craft occupations' (such as a tradespeople), and the 'long-term unemployed'.[18]

To distinguish what separates the 'working class' from other classes the SMC (which PwC policy relies upon) and the Bridge Group (which KPMG UK policy largely relies upon) conflate these occupations into a gradational three tiered class hierarchy which reflects that used by the Office for National Statistics[19] – the 'professional' class sits at the top, the 'intermediate' class sits in the middle, and, finally, the 'working' or 'lower' class sits at the bottom.[20] The 'professional' class includes senior managers such as chief executives or finance managers, '[t]raditional professional occupations' (for example, lawyers, medical practitioners, scientists and civil or mechanical engineers) and '[m]odern professional occupations' (for example, teachers, nurses, physiotherapists, social workers, musicians, police officers at or above sergeant

---

[13] KMPG note that they 'use parental occupation as a measure for ... [their] socio-economic background pay gaps, identified by the Bridge Group, and other social mobility experts, as the most robust and reliable indicator'. See KPMG Pay Gap Report (n 4), 8.

[14] PwC Diversity Pay Report (n 5); KPMG Pay Gap Report (n 4), 8.

[15] KPMG Pay Gap Report (n 4), 8.

[16] PwC Diversity Pay Report (n 5).

[17] Social Mobility Commission, 'Simplifying how employers measure socio-economic Background: An accompanying report to new guidance' (Report, updated May 2021) https://socialmobilityworks.org/wp-content/uploads/2021/05/Summary-rep ort-on-measurement-changes_FINAL-Updated-May-2021.pdf, 13.

[18] SMC Toolkit (n 5).

[19] See Office for National Statistics, 'SOC 2020 Volume 3: the National Statistics Socio-economic Classification (NS-SEC rebased on the SOC 2020)' https://www.ons.gov. uk/methodology/classificationsandstandards/standardoccupationalclassificationsoc/soc2 020/soc2020volume3thenationalstatisticssocioeconomicclassificationnssecrebasedonthe soc2020#understanding-soc-2020.

[20] See Bridge Group, 'Who gets ahead and how? Socio-economic background and career progression in financial services: a study of eight organisations' (Report) ('Bridge Group Report') https://static1.squarespace.com/static/5c18e090b40b9d6b43b093d8/t/5fbc3 17e96e56f63b563d0f2/1606168962064/Socio-economic_report-Final.pdf, 25; KPMG Pay Gap Report (n 4), 8; Social Mobility Commission, 'Cross-industry toolkit' (accessed 29 September 2021) https://socialmobilityworks.org/toolkit/measurement/.

rank and software designers).[21] The 'intermediate' class includes '[m]iddle or junior managers' (for example, office managers, retail managers, bank managers, restaurant managers and warehouse managers) and '[c]lerical and intermediate occupations' (for example, secretaries, personal assistants, clerical workers, etc).[22]

Using occupation to measure class may have gained recent traction[23] but this way of viewing class is nothing new, and it resonates with the work of French sociologist Emile Durkheim. Grusky and Galescu argue that Durkheim unwittingly developed 'a class analysis grounded in the technical division of labor'[24] and he 'anticipated' a 'micro-class model'.[25] Durkheim, they argue, contributed to class analysis on multiple fronts, including by providing 'a positive micro-level story about the "small classes" (i.e., *gemeinschaftlich* occupations) that are destined to emerge at the site of production and shape individual values, life chances, and lifestyles'.[26] This 'micro-level story' captures the 'predicted rise of social organization at the local occupational level'.[27] In his book *The Division of Labor in Society*, which was first published in 1893,[28] Durkheim predicted that the main organizational form layered or 'intercalated' between the individual and the state will be 'occupational associations' (or groups).[29] According to Durkheim, people in these occupational associations or groups could develop 'informal ties or bonds' and the associations themselves established and administered a system of ethics, resolved conflicts between members and with other associations, and served 'as elemental representative bodies in political governance'.[30]

This approach therefore conflates occupations into classes with the result that class location is measured purely in occupational terms or by reference to occupational associations. There is an inherent problem with defining class by reference to occupation for the purposes of discrimination law. This is because, if class is defined in terms of occupation alone, all people within

---

[21] See, for example, Bridge Group Report (n 20), 25.

[22] See, for example, Bridge Group Report, (n 20), 25.

[23] See also Tony Bennett, David Carter, Modesto Gayo, Michelle Kelly and Greg Noble, *Fields, Capitals, Habitus: Australian Culture, Inequalities and Social Divisions* (2020, Taylor & Francis).

[24] David B Grusky and Gabriela Galescu, 'Is Durkheim a Class Analyst?' in Jeffrey C Alexander and Philip Smith (eds), *The Cambridge Companion to Durkheim* (2005, Cambridge University Press), 325.

[25] Grusky and Galescu, 'Is Durkheim a Class Analyst?' (n 24), 323, 324.

[26] David Grusky and Gabriela Galescu, 'Foundations of a neo-Durkheimian class analysis' in Erik Olin Wright, Approaches to Class Analysis (2005, Cambridge University Press), 55.

[27] Grusky and Galescu (n 26), 56.

[28] Emile Durkheim, *The Division of Labor in Society* (translated by George Simpson, 1960, The Free Press of Glencoe Illinois), vii.

[29] See Durkheim (n 28), 28; Grusky and Galescu (n 26), 56.

[30] Grusky and Galescu (n 26), 56.

an occupational group (for example, lawyers, accountants, or teachers) will each exhibit the same class identity. If all employees or applicants for a job within a sector have the same occupation and therefore class identity, class would not be a distinct characteristic of each individual but rather it would be a common feature of all the individuals within the occupational group. In this setting it may be impossible to show discriminatory treatment based on a characteristic which is shared by everyone, or almost everyone, who works or applies to an employer.

B. Class as a relational concept

To better understand the concept of class, and what factors are indicative of a person's class beyond occupation, it is important to provide an overview of three important class theories, those of Karl Marx, Max Weber, and Pierre Bourdieu. These theories use class to explain inequality by defining class in terms of a person's relationship with 'resources', thus they view class as a complicated relational concept rather than a simple gradational concept (both the Marxist and Weberian traditions reject a gradational view of class).[31] Whilst Marx, Weber and Bourdieu view class in terms of a person's relationship with 'resources', for reasons which will be outlined here and elaborated upon below they each take a different view of what, or how, 'resources' shape class. For both Marx and Weber class is shaped by a person's relationship with income producing assets[32] which determine whether he or she has opportunities in life, dominion over others, or is exploited by others. As such, for them, the 'resources' which shape class are economic. Bourdieu adopts a much broader view of the 'resources' which create life opportunities and takes into account not only economic factors but also various non-economic factors.[33] This chapter will now explain in greater detail the key differences in the way Marx, Weber and Bourdieu view class.

It is important to emphasize here that this book will not provide an exhaustive overview of class theory. Rather, in keeping with the focus of the book, it will merely provide an overview that is relevant to the analysis in subsequent chapters.

1. Marxist tradition: class shaped by relationship with means of production

In 1848 Marx authored *The Communist Manifesto* with Freidrich Engels, the same year of various revolts against monarchies which spread from Sicily

---

[31] Wright, 'Social Class' (n 11), 718, 719.
[32] See Erik Olin Wright, *Class Counts* (Cambridge University Press, 2000), 27–8.
[33] Wright (n 11), 'Social Class', 719.

to France, Germany, the Austrian Empire and Italy.[34] Marx and Engels observed that society was increasingly 'splitting up' into two classes hostile to one another, the 'bourgeoisie' on the one hand, and, the 'proletariat' on the other.[35] Whilst Marx and Engels identified that classes had existed in the social orders of ancient Rome (which had 'patricians, knights, plebians, slaves'[36]) and the Middle Ages (which had 'feudal lords, vassals, guild-masters, journeymen, apprentices, serfs'[37]), they argued that successive industrial developments gave rise to new classes. First, they argued that the closed guilds of the feudal industrial system (which had a monopoly on production) were replaced by manufacturing to meet growing market demand, and so the guild-masters were replaced by the manufacturing middle class.[38] Second, when manufacturing could not keep up with demand, the manufacturing system was replaced by modern industry powered by steam and machinery and led by the industrial millionaires, the bourgeois.[39] In this setting, and as just noted, Marx and Engels identified two classes:[40] the bourgeoisie who own the 'means of production' on the one hand, and, the proletariat who sell their labour[41] to, and are exploited by, the bourgeoisie[42] on the other. 'Means of production' refers to the subjects of labour such as raw materials and instruments of labour such as machinery in a factory.[43] As such, to put it simply, Marx viewed factory owners and captains of industry as the bourgeoisie class and the people who worked for them as the proletariat class. These two classes were therefore defined by their relationship to the means of production, and their role in the economic order.

2. Weberian tradition: class shaped by level of market capacities

Unlike Marx whose analysis of class was central to his theories, the Weberian tradition of class analysis is 'largely based on Weber's few explicit, but fragmentary, conceptual analyses of class'.[44] Weber had worked on *Economy and Society* up to his death in 1920, and the three completed chapters and a

---

[34] Encyclopaedia Britannica, 'Revolutions of 1848'.

[35] Karl Marx and Freidrich Engels, *The Communist Manifesto* (2018, Lerner Publishing Group Inc, United States; originally authored in 1848), 2.

[36] Ibid, 1.

[37] Ibid, 1.

[38] Ibid, 2.

[39] Ibid, 2.

[40] Ibid, 1.

[41] Ibid, 8.

[42] Ibid, 10.

[43] See Diana Stukuls Eglitis, 'Means of Production' in George Ritzer (ed), *Encyclopedia of Social Theory*, vol. 1 (Sage Publications Inc, 2005), 493.

[44] Wright (n 11), 'Social Class', 720.

fragment of the fourth were published in a February 1921 instalment (which is Part 1 of the book *Economy and Society*).[45] In the February 1921 instalment of *Economy and Society* Weber wrote that a person's class position is the 'typical *Chance*' ('provision with goods', 'outer social standing', 'inner personal fate') that flows from the 'extent and nature' of the person's power over 'goods, education, and skills (*Leistungsqualifikationen*)', and the extent to which they have value in creating income and revenue.[46] Put more simply, for Weber class is determined by one's power over resources which affect market-derived income (which Weberians refer to as 'market capacities'), and such income in turn affects the life chances or opportunities available to a person or their children.[47] The causal component of life chances are therefore a person's 'economic interests in the possession of goods and opportunities for income … under conditions of the commodity or labor markets'.[48] When people have this causal component of life chances in common Weber refers to this as a 'class', that is a group of people with the same 'class situation'.[49] They are not themselves 'communities' but rather 'represent possible, and frequent, bases for communal action'[50] because their economic interests are aligned.

Both the Marxian concept of 'means of production' and the Weberian concept of 'market capacities' are similar concepts which capture income producing assets.[51] As such, a common thread in Marxist and Weberian class theories is the way access to, or control over, such resources (for Marx the 'means of production' and for Weber 'market capacities') create inequality which contributes to one's class identity. However, it is important to emphasize here, as noted above, that a key distinction between Marxist and Weberian thought is *how* control over these resources creates inequality to, in turn, shape class. For Marx, the bourgeoisie's ownership and control over the means of production permits them to *oppress* workers, the proletariat. For Weber, the level of a person's wealth and income determines his or her 'life chances'[52] or opportunities.

3. Bourdieu: class shaped by reference to economic, social and cultural capital

Whilst both Marx and Weber view a person's control over income producing assets as central to shaping his or her class, the French sociologist Pierre

---

[45] Max Weber, *Economy & Society: A New Translation* [1921] (2019, Harvard University Press, edited and translated by Keith Tribe), vii.

[46] Weber (n 45), 450.

[47] Wright (n 11), 'Social Class', 720; Wright, *Class Counts* (n 32), 27–8.

[48] Max Weber, *Economy and Society* [1924] (1978) cited in Wright, 'Social Class' (n 11), 720.

[49] Ibid.

[50] Max Weber, *Economy and Society* cited in Wright, *Class Counts* (n 32), 28.

[51] See Wright, *Class Counts* (n 32), 27–8.

[52] Wright, 'Social Class' (n 11), 720.

Bourdieu takes this a step further. For Bourdieu, life opportunity is not only determined by a person's economic resources but also his or her level of various non-economic resources.[53] Bourdieu's class theory, as will now be explained, built upon the relational concept of economic capital evident in the theories of Marx and Weber, and extended it to social capital, cultural capital and symbolic capital.[54] That is, for Bourdieu, a person's class is determined not only by the person's access to economic capital (for example, money, property[55] and buying power), but also other forms of capital such as social and cultural capital.[56]

Social capital refers to relationships available to a person which can be used as a resource or advantage. For Bourdieu, social capital is:

> the aggregate of the actual or potential resources which are linked to possession of a durable network of more or less institutionalized relationships of mutual acquaintance and recognition – or in other words, to membership in a group – which provides each of its members with the backing of the collectivity-owned capital, a 'credential' which entitles them to credit, in the various senses of the word.[57]

'Social capital' therefore refers to the resources which are available to a person through their relationships with others. It is therefore a source of advantage over other people who do not have the benefit of such relationships.[58] Social capital can also be inherited and its inheritance may be symbolized by a famous family name, because the inheritor is 'known' and therefore does not need to

---

[53] Wright, 'Social Class' (n 11), 719–20.

[54] See Bridget Fowler, 'Pierre Bourdieu on social transformation, with particular reference to political and symbolic revolutions' (2020) 49 *Theory and Society* 439, 440. For a discussion of the concept of symbolic capital, see Pierre Bourdieu, 'Symbolic Capital and Social Classes' (2013) 13(2) *Journal of Classical Sociology* 292, 296–7, 299–300.

[55] Pierre Bourdieu, 'The Forms of Capital' in JG Richardson (ed), *Handbook of Theory and Research for the Sociology of Education* (Greenwood Press, 1986) 241, 243.

[56] Pierre Bourdieu, *Distinction: A Social Critique of the Judgement of Taste* (Richard Nice trans, Harvard University Press, 1984) [trans of: *La distinction: Critique sociale du jugement* (first published 1979)] 114; Bourdieu, 'The Forms of Capital' (n 55), 241–58; Pierre Bourdieu, 'What Makes a Social Class? On The Theoretical and Practical Existence of Groups' (1987) 32 *Berkeley Journal of Sociology* 1. This approach to class was also adopted by Mike Savage and Fiona Devine when measuring class for the 2013 Great British Class Survey. See *How Do You Identify New Types of Class?* (3 April 2013, BBC Science) http://www.bbc. co.uk/science/0/22001963; Mike Savage et al, 'A New Model of Social Class? Findings from the BBC's Great British Class Survey Experiment' (2013) 47 *Sociology* 219.

[57] Bourdieu, 'The Forms of Capital' (n 55), 248–9.

[58] See Alejandro Portes, 'Social Capital: Its Origins and Applications in Modern Sociology' (1998) 24 *Annual Review of Sociology* 1, 7.

make the acquaintance of people.[59] Economic capital can make it easier for a person to acquire social capital and cultural capital.[60]

Cultural capital is a complex idea, and it can comprise of: (1) objectified cultural capital; (2) institutionalized cultural capital; and (3) embodied cultural capital.[61] These three forms of cultural capital can be explained as follows:

1. Objectified cultural capital refers to 'cultural goods' such as 'pictures, books, dictionaries, instruments, machines, etc' that do not only reflect a person's buying power but their ability to understand and appreciate those cultural goods and draw profits from the use of such cultural capital.[62]
2. Institutionalized cultural capital refers to the formal recognition of a person's cultural capital by institutions, such as in the form of qualifications or credentials.[63]
3. Embodied cultural capital includes 'dispositions of the mind and body'[64] that may be acquired or cultivated through socialization and upbringing, such as accents or mannerisms, tastes, lifestyles, skills, cultural skills, knowledge, habits, attitudes, cultural traditions, personal character, ways of thinking etc.[65] Bourdieu viewed it as the conversion of 'external wealth' to 'an integral part of the person, into a habitus' which is not transmitted instantaneously (such as an inheritance for instance) but over time[66] and for the most part unconsciously.[67] Put another way, it captures how a

---

[59] See Bourdieu, 'The Forms of Capital' (n 55), 250–1. Prime examples are members of the Windsor family in the United Kingdom, the Murdoch and Packer families in Australia, and the Bush and Trump families in the United States of America.
[60] Bourdieu, 'The Forms of Capital' (n 55), 252–4.
[61] Ibid, 243.
[62] Ibid, 246–7.
[63] Ibid, 247–8.
[64] Ibid, 243.
[65] See, for example. Bourdieu, *Distinction* (n 56), 12, 27, 54, 70, 220, 260–95; J Lynn Gazley et al, 'Beyond Preparation: Identity, Cultural Capital, and Readiness for Graduate School in the Biomedical Sciences' (2014) 51 *Journal of Research in Science Teaching* 1021, 1023; Christiana Tsaousi, '"What Underwear Do I Like?" Taste and (Embodied) Cultural Capital in the Consumption of Women's Underwear' (2014) *Journal of Consumer Culture* 1, 3–5 http://joc.sagepub.com/content/early/2014/04/07/1469540514521084.abstract; Soo-yong Byun, Evan Schofer and Kyung-keun Kim, 'Revisiting the Role of Cultural Capital in East Asian Educational Systems: The Case of South Korea' (2012) 85 *Sociology of Education* 219, 219–20; Alem Kebede, 'Cultural Capital' in Ronald L Jackson II and Michael A Hogg (eds), *Encyclopedia of Identity* (Sage Publications, 2010) vol 1, 161, 163; M Print, 'Social and Cultural Capital in Education' in Sanna Järvelä (ed), *Social and Emotional Aspects of Learning* (Elsevier, 2011) 276, 279.
[66] Bourdieu, 'The Forms of Capital' (n 55), 244–5.
[67] Gerbert Kraaykamp and Koen van Eijck, 'The Intergenerational Reproduction of Cultural Capital: A Threefold Perspective' (2010) 89 *Social Forces* 209, 210.

person's environment (for example, from their family and upbringing) gradually shapes and may become internalized within a person over time.

Cultural capital can be acquired informally, such as when parents transmit cultural capital to children by acting with their 'embodied sensibilities'[68] or influencing a child's pronunciation of words that indicates their 'class' or origins.[69] It can also be acquired formally through economic capital when 'wealthy parents send their children to prestigious schools'[70] and thus the children also acquire cultural capital from the people with whom they associate at school – their teachers, classmates or other parents.

Whilst Weber refers to *Leistungsqualifikationen* (power over goods, education and skills[71]) as a resource that opens up life chances and is thus relevant to class formation, as explained above this concept is used by Weber to capture those skills and qualifications that have income producing capacities. As such, it is narrower than the concept of cultural capital which is identified by Bourdieu (which captures broader aspects of culture and education that are not just directly related to creating an income).

For Bourdieu, therefore, and as explained above, a person's economic, social and cultural capital can shape and be criteria of class identity, this will now be elaborated and built upon.

II. The problem of class and social background discrimination

Although the concept of 'class' has been the subject of much intellectual thought for well over a century, the problem of *discrimination* on the basis of 'class' has only relatively recently caught the attention of writers and others, particular those from Australia[72] and the UK.[73]

There is growing evidence that class discrimination or classism is a serious problem in modern workplaces. 'Classism' is defined as 'unfair treatment of

---

[68] Kebede (n 65), 163.

[69] Kraaykamp and van Eijck (n 67), 210.

[70] Kebede (n 65), 163.

[71] Weber, *Economy & Society* (n 45), 450.

[72] See, for example, Angelo Capuano, 'Giving Meaning to "Social Origin" in International Labour Organization ("ILO") Conventions, the Fair Work Act 2009 (Cth) and the Australian Human Rights Commission Act 1986 (Cth): "Class" Discrimination and Its Relevance to the Australian Context' (2016) 39(1) *UNSW Law Journal* 84; Margaret Thornton, 'The elusiveness of class discrimination' (2012) 24(3) *Legaldate* 7, Margaret Thornton, 'Equality and Anti-Discrimination Legislation: An Uneasy Relationship' (2021) 37(2) *Law in Context* 12.

[73] See, for example, Geraldine Van Bueren QC, 'Inclusivity and the law: do we need to prohibit class discrimination?' (2021) *European Human Rights Law Review* 274 https://www.biicl.org/documents/138_inclusivity_and_the_law_-_ehrr_article.pdf.

people because of their social class',[74] which may include bias, prejudices, inequalities and structural barriers that could lead to discrimination.

An analysis of the career paths of 16,500 KPMG partners and employees over a five-year period, published by KPMG UK in December 2022, showed that socio-economic background (as defined by parental occupation when they were 14) is 'the biggest barrier to progression', in particular from graduate through to director levels.[75] The research confirmed that those from lower socio-economic backgrounds are likely to progress more slowly than average, and this problem is compounded for women from such backgrounds.[76] Parental occupation was used as a marker for socio-economic background because of its connection with life opportunities,[77] which could include a range of economic, social and cultural or educational opportunities.

A PwC survey of 32,517 people from 19 countries[78] commissioned in February 2021 found that 13 per cent of workers reported 'discrimination on the basis of social class or background'.[79] In Australia, a 2020 Diversity Council of Australia ('DCA') survey of over 3,000 workers found that 'class' was most strongly linked to inclusion at work and that it was, together with First Nations background, disability status, sexual orientation, gender identity and religion, most strongly linked to exclusion (for example, discrimination, being ignored, not getting the same opportunities as others in the workplace).[80] Further, there is evidence that class-based biases may be inherent in hiring processes.[81] In the UK, recent government attention towards 'levelling up' the country through addressing geographical inequalities[82] and observation of a 'class pay gap' (whereby people who move

---

[74] MacMillan Dictionary https://www.macmillandictionary.com/dictionary/british/classism.

[75] KMPG, 'Social Mobility Progression Report 2022: Mind the Gap' (Report, December 2022), 7, 11 ('*2022 Social Mobility Progression Report*').

[76] *2022 Social Mobility Progression Report*, 12.

[77] See *2022 Social Mobility Progression Report*, 7.

[78] The 19 countries were Australia, Canada, China, France, Germany, India, Japan, Kuwait, Malaysia, The Netherlands, Poland, Qatar, Saudi Arabia, Singapore, South Africa, Spain, United Arab Emirates, United Kingdom and the United States.

[79] PwC, 'Hopes and fears 2021: The views of 32,500 workers' (Survey) https://www.pwc.com/hopes-fears#content-free-1-c5f8.

[80] Brown et al, 'Class at Work: Does Social Class Make a Difference in the Land of the "Fair Go"?' (Sydney, Diversity Council Australia, 2020), 11.

[81] See Michael W Kraus, Brittany Torrez, Jun Won Park and Fariba Ghayebi, 'Evidence for the reproduction of social class in brief speech' (2019) 116(46) *Proceedings of the National Academy of Sciences* 22998.

[82] UK Government, 'Levelling Up the United Kingdom' (Presented to Parliament by the Secretary of State for Levelling Up, Housing and Communities, 2 February 2022) https://assets.publishing.service.gov.uk/government/uploads/system/uploads/attachment_data/file/1052708/Levelling_up_the_UK_white_paper.pdf.

up professional groupings 'earn significantly less than people who were born into those professional groupings') provides further evidence of classism.[83]

This research by the DCA and the SMC, however, each adopt an overly simplistic view of 'class'. Whereas the DCA takes into account wealth, income, formal education/qualifications and occupation,[84] the SMC measures class in purely occupational terms (as explained above in this chapter). Both of these views of 'class' miss important species of capital which Bourdieu identified in his work as being formulative of class, namely social capital, objectified cultural capital, and embodied cultural capital.

This chapter will now argue that Bourdieu's theory of class is likely to be the most helpful in understanding the problem of classism as well as class and social background discrimination in Australia, South Africa and Canada. First, using a social-psychological lens, it will rely on in-group and out-group bias studies to explain the human propensity to discriminate based on factors such as class and social background. Second, it will engage in an analysis of Australia, South Africa and Canada to show that the factors to which Bourdieu referred as indicative of class – the species of economic, social and cultural capital – are often the subject of what social-psychologists would refer to as 'out-group hate'. As a result of this analysis, it will be argued that in Australia, South Africa and Canada Bourdieu's class theory is highly relevant and applicable to the problem of discrimination (as well as vilification, abuse, bullying, etc) on the basis of 'class'.

A. Are humans hardwired to discriminate based on class and social background?

The concept of discrimination has interested social psychologists for many decades.[85] In the 1970s, social psychology, spearheaded by experiments conducted by Henri Tajfel and colleagues, began to make great strides in understanding the tendency in humans to discriminate.[86] This understanding stemmed from Tajfel's work on in-group bias, which will now be explained.

---

[83] See Social Mobility Commission, 'Changing Gears: Understanding Downward Social Mobility (Research report, November 2020), 6, 10. See also Sam Friedman and Daniel Laurison, *The Class Ceiling: Why it Pays to be Privileged* (2019, Bristol University Press). Recent empirical research from Australia has also found that even where organizations with 'advanced positions on diversity' had gender and culturally diverse leaders these leaders had similar privileged class attributes as their 'white/male colleagues': See Carl Rhodes, Alison Pullen and Celina McEwen, 'Leadership Diversity Through Relational Intersectionality in Australia: Research Report' (Research Report, 2023, The University of Technology Sydney), 15, 19. This further supports the argument that a 'class ceiling' in employment exists for those from disadvantaged backgrounds.

[84] Brown et al, 'Class at Work' (n 80), 6–7.

[85] Marilynn B Brewer, *Intergroup Relations* (Open University Press, 2nd ed, 2003), 43–67.

[86] Ibid, 43–45.

14

1. 'In-group favouritism' leads to discrimination against 'out-group' members

One of Tajfel's experiments[87] found that even when subjects were randomly assigned to meaningless groups,[88] when subjects had to make a distinction between members of their group (the in-group) or members of the other group (the out-group) 'they discriminated in favour of the ingroup'.[89] Interestingly, this 'in-group favouritism' appears to have been based on group membership alone. The groups were not competing 'for a limited resource',[90] and they had 'no prior meaning' to the participants[91] nor any history of long-term rivalry, conflict or hostility.[92] The 'in-group favouritism' did not seem to be motivated by any personal interest,[93] there was nothing to be gained personally from engaging in the discrimination,[94] and the subjects were identified by a code number (and thus their identities were anonymous).[95]

Social psychologists were surprised that the subjects in Tajfel's experiment treated other subjects differently based purely on their membership to a group.[96] Before the Tajfel experiments, social psychologists thought discrimination resulted from 'existing prejudice and hostility that developed over time in the course of intergroup relations'.[97] Now, Brewer writes, 'we know that intergroup discrimination can be produced by mere categorization into separate groups, in the absence of any history of intergroup contact or conflict'.[98] The 'pattern of discrimination' known as 'in-group favouritism' 'has been found' in many other studies,[99] and it may be relevant in employment contexts. One study by Lewis and Sherman found that there may be an inclination to prefer qualified in-group members over-qualified out-group members.[100]

---

[87] See Henri Tajfel, 'Experiments in Intergroup Discrimination' [1970] *Scientific American* 96, 99–101.

[88] Ibid, 99.

[89] Ibid, 101.

[90] Saul Kassin, Steven Fein, Hazel Rose Markus, *Social Psychology* (Wadsworth, 9th ed, 2014), 176.

[91] Brewer (n 85), 45.

[92] Kassin, Fein, Markus (n 90), 176; Brewer (n 85), 45.

[93] Tajfel (n 87), 101; Brewer (n 85), 45.

[94] See Brewer (n 85).

[95] Tajfel (n 87), 99.

[96] Brewer (n 85), 45.

[97] Ibid.

[98] Ibid.

[99] Kassin et al (n 90), 176–177. See also Brewer (n 85), 45. Brewer writes that, since 1970, 'this finding has been replicated in many experiments using different types of allocation matrices and different bases of group categorization'.

[100] Amy C Lewis and Steven J Sherman, 'Hiring you makes me look bad: Social-identity based reversals of the ingroup favoritism effect' (2003) 90(2) *Organizational Behavior and Human Decision Processes* 262, 267. Lewis and Sherman observe that '[w]hen there was a

Tajfel proposed that people tend to divide the world into 'us' (in-groups) and 'them' (out-groups), a theory known as Social Identity Theory ('SIT').[101] Categorizing people into 'in-groups' and 'out-groups' is facilitated by a mental process known as social categorization, without which the world will likely appear 'overly complex and confusing'.[102] Tajfel and Turner argue that a result of dividing the world into in-groups ('us') and out-groups ('them') through mental categorization is that the in-group will discriminate against the out-group to enhance their self-image, thereby showing in-group favouritism[103] and a sense of 'positive distinctiveness' (the view that 'we' are better than 'them').[104] Discrimination in favour of an in-group can also be viewed as discrimination against an out-group because '[m]any researchers have contended that altruistic behavior toward the in-group is the mirror image of spiteful behavior toward the out-group, such that these two behaviors are the two sides of the same coin'.[105]

---

match between the requirements of the job and the traits possessed by both applicants, participants showed ingroup favoritism, with over 86 per cent selecting the qualified ingroup member over the equally qualified outgroup member'. See further Brewer (n 85), 69–72.

[101] There are many 'dimensions' which people use to categorize themselves and others into a group, and to divide the world into 'us' *versus* 'them'. '[D]imensions that people can use to categorize themselves' include 'race', '[g]ender, age, profession, ethnicity, status, country of birth, sports team, social group and education'. See Pascal Molenberghs, 'The Neuroscience of In-Group Bias' (2013) 37(8) *Neuroscience and Biobehavioural Reviews* 1530, 1530. Also see Rengin Firat and Steven Hitlin, 'Morally Bonded and Bounded: A Sociological Introduction to Neurology' in *Biosociology and Neurosociology*, Will Kalkhoff, Shane R Thye and Edward J Lawler (eds) (2012), 186–7; Michael Argyle, *The Psychology of Social Class* (Routledge, 1994), 224–6.

[102] Pascal Molenberghs and Samantha Morrison, 'The Role of the Medial Prefrontal Cortex in Social Categorization', (2014) 9(3) *Social Cognitive & Affective Neuroscience* 292.

[103] See Henri Tajfel and John Turner, 'The Social Identity Theory of Inter-Group Behavior' in S Worchel and WG Austin (eds) *Psychology of Intergroup Relations* (1986), 16. Also see Molenberghs (n 101), 1530–5. Out-group members may be preferred but this tends to occur when the candidate is likely to fail, and this in turn seems to reinforce in-group bias. See Amy C Lewis and Steven J Sherman, 'Hiring you makes me look bad: Social-identity based reversals of the ingroup favoritism effect' (2003) 90(2) *Organizational Behavior and Human Decision Processes* 262, 267. Neuroscience studies also seem to support SIT, and the position that people prefer members of their in-group. See Molenberghs (n 101), 1532.

[104] Michael A Hogg, 'Social Identity Theory' in Peter James Burke (ed) *Contemporary Social Psychological Theories* (2006), 120.

[105] Toshio Yamagishi and Nobuhiro Mifune, 'Social Exchange and Solidarity: In-Group Love or Out-Group Hate?' (2009) 34 *Evolution and Human Behavior* 229, 230 citing Henri Tajfel and John Turner, 'An integrative theory of intergroup conflict' in WG Austin and S Worchel (eds), *The social psychology of intergroup relations* (1979), 33–47; Henri Tajfel and John Turner, 'The social identity theory of intergroup behavior' in S Worchel and WG Austin (eds), *Psychology of intergroup relations* (1986), 7–24; JC Turner, MA Hogg, PJ Oakes, SD Reicher and MS Wetherell, *Rediscovering the social group: A self-categorization*

2. Mental categorization into 'in-groups' and 'out-groups'

Given that in-group favoritism may lead to discrimination against members of out-groups, how might people categorize into groups in the real world outside controlled conditions of an experiment?

An 'in-group' tends to be mentally represented by 'prototypes', which represent the criteria most emblematic of a group identity and its distinctiveness from other groups. Prototypes have been described to be 'complex fuzzy sets of interrelated attributes (behaviors, beliefs, attitudes, customs, dress, and so forth) that capture similarities within groups and differences between groups'.[106] According to Hogg, 'prototypes capture similarities within the in-group and accentuate differences between our group and a specific out-group'.[107] People within groups are able to distinguish between themselves and others by how well they match the prototype, and it seems that some people may match the prototype more than others.[108] Through social categorization, a person is seen through the lens of a prototype and measured against that prototype or assigned prototypical attributes and is thereby depersonalized or stereotyped.[109] This helps people to determine who they might 'like' or 'dislike':

> The more ingroup prototypical people are, the more you like them. Furthermore, because within one's group, there is usually agreement over prototypicality, prototypical members are liked by all – they are 'popular'. Likewise, less prototypical members are 'unpopular,' and can be marginalized as undesirable deviants. Outgroup members are

---

theory' (1987). Brewer writes that while '[i]ngroup love is not a necessary precursor of outgroup hate … the very factors that make ingroup attachment and allegiance important to individuals also provide a fertile ground for antagonism and distrust of those outside the ingroup boundaries'. See Marilynn B Brewer, 'The Psychology of Prejudice: Ingroup Love and Outgroup Hate?' (1999) 55(3) *Journal of Social Issues* 429, 442. In the context of employment, where an employer hires a person because that person is a member of the employer's 'in-group', then, clearly, this will mean that job candidates from the 'out-group' will experience unfavourable treatment and adverse discrimination (that is, not getting the job).

[106] Michael A Hogg, 'Social Identity Theory' in *Encyclopedia of Identity* (Sage Publications, 2010), 749.

[107] Ibid, 749. For Hogg prototypes 'are stereotypes of a particular group, and [o]ne way to think of a group prototype is what comes immediately to mind if, for example, one were to say to you, "French," "Republican" or "terrorist"'.

[108] Michael A Hogg and Deborah J Terry, 'Social Identity Theory and Organizational Processes' in Michael A Hogg and Deborah J Terry (eds), *Social Identity Processes in Organizational Contexts* (2001), 6.

[109] Michael A Hogg, 'Social Identity Theory' in Peter J Burke (ed), *Contemporary Social Psychological Theories* (2006), 118.

effectively un-prototypical of the ingroup and so are liked less than are ingroup members.[110]

Some people may therefore prefer certain prototypes which reflect familiar characteristics ('us') and discriminate against a prototype which reflects alien characteristics ('them').

B. Social categorization, out-group discrimination and disadvantage based on Bourdieu's species of capital: examples from Australia, Canada and South Africa

Whilst social psychology provides evidence of the way humans are hardwired to discriminate based on group-membership alone, to what extent is this discrimination likely to be based on criteria of class? This chapter will now turn to engage in a conceptual analysis of Australia, Canada and South Africa, to point to examples of social categorization and out-group discrimination which appear to be based on Bourdieu's species of capital (particularly cultural capital).

The Canadian scholar Wolfgang Lehmann refers to the potential for working-class students who attend university to become 'cultural outsiders' or have 'outsider status'.[111] Lehman and Taylor also refer to the way 'working class' students who transition to university may feel like a 'fish out of water' in that particular 'field' (a term coined by Bourdieu).[112] Whilst it has been observed that working-class students may undergo certain habitus transformation[113]

---

[110] Michael A Hogg, 'Social Identity Theory' in *Encyclopedia of Identity* (Sage Publications, 2010), 750.

[111] See Wolfgang Lehmann, 'Working-class students, habitus, and the development of student roles: a Canadian case study' (2012) 33(4) *British Journal of Sociology of Education* 527, 530.

[112] Wolfgang Lehmann and Alison Taylor, 'On the role of habitus and field in apprenticeships' (2015) 29(4) *Work, employment and society* 607, 615. Whether a person's cultural capital is a source of disadvantage depends on the extent of the disparity between that person's cultural capital and the one which dominates a field, thus where there is significant disparity the person may be a 'fish out of water' and not easily 'fit' in that field. On the other side of the coin, whether cultural capital is a resource for advantage depends on whether that particular form of cultural capital is the dominant one in the 'field' in which people are operating, and thus allows a person with that capital to more easily navigate and 'fit' in that field (and be a 'fish in water') (See Pierre Bourdieu interviewed in Loic JD Wacquant, 'Towards a Reflexive Sociology: A Workshop with Pierre Bourdieu' (1989) 7(1) *Sociological Theory* 26, 43; Trevor Gale and Stephen Parker, 'Retaining students in Australian higher education: cultural capital, field distinction' (2017) 16(1) *European Educational Research Journal* 80, 89). Whilst many working-class students may be a 'fish out of water' in the university field, 'working-class cultural capital' may be dominant and therefore advantageous in other fields (such as in blue-collar trades and services, for example). See also Abigail Marks et al, 'Feminized cultural capital at work in the moral economy: Home credit and working-class women' (2023) *Gender, Work & Organization* 1, 4–5, 13.

[113] Lehman (n 111), 533.

such as through the development of cultural capital, dispositions and tastes,[114] Lehmann's work underscores the importance of cultural capital as a marker of 'working-class' categorization in the university field:

> Many adults with working-class backgrounds who have achieved social mobility remember their time at university as a period of profound confusion that includes feelings of inferiority vis-à- vis their well-traveled, better read, privately educated, well-spoken, articulate, and generally more privileged peers (and faculty). They speak of academic struggles, false starts and restarts, chance encounters with faculty, and an often circuitous trajectory toward academic success. These stories highlight the importance of cultural capital (Bourdieu 1986) for the ease with which those who possess it navigate university life and the symbolic violence felt by those whose cultural capital does not live up to the expectations of academia.[115]

This illustrates how cultural capital is therefore integral to shaping a person's perceived social categorization (that is, who they consider to be 'us' and 'them' in elite fields such as universities). Lehmann's study of working-class university students shows that as people engage in the process of habitus transformation whilst at university through cultivating cultural capital,[116] they exhibit signs of undergoing a transformation in class associations and feel relief about escaping the cultural 'backwardness' of their upbringings.[117] Although some forms of cultural capital can be acquired to permit habitus transformation (such as being better read, travelling or developing certain tastes), other forms of cultural capital (as argued above 'working-class cultural capital' may be advantageous in certain fields) are more difficult to transform and they may be with someone for life (such as a working-class accent, manner of speech or certain dispositions of the mind and body cultivated from upbringing).

Lehmann's work demonstrates not only that cultural capital is used as a marker for people to assess how in-group prototypical people are but it (or lack thereof) may also be a source of disadvantage in certain fields. Although classism can be directed at anyone (even the relatively privileged), it does seem that those from working-class or disadvantaged backgrounds will most likely bear the brunt of classism in employment. This is supported by the reality that, to attempt upward social mobility, it is people from working-class and disadvantaged backgrounds (not advantaged backgrounds) who must

---

[114] Wolfgang Lehmann, 'Habitus Transformation and Hidden Injuries: Successful Working-class University Students', (2013) 87(1) *Sociology of Education* 1.

[115] Ibid, 3.

[116] Ibid, 7, 8, 11.

[117] Ibid, 11.

access fields in which they may be 'fish out of water' (such as universities and professions). Added to this is the higher level of stigma and ridicule which seems to be directed at disadvantaged and working-class identities (and their 'cultural backwardness'). The extent to which cultural capital serves as a marker for in-group love and out-group hate is reflected in pejorative terms or perceptions in Australia, Canada and South Africa, which will now be explained.

1. Australia

In Australia people claim to be victims of 'classism' or prejudice based on their perceived class[118] and 'social, economic and cultural inequalities are rising'.[119] This author has directed attention to the classed nature of social categorization and the extent to which 'out-group' members with distinct economic and cultural capital are subject to ridicule and stigma:

> the stigmatised nature of lower-class status in Australia … [is] evidenced by the common use of pejorative terms which are used to describe people who appear to exhibit characteristics that are consistent with lower-class identity. These pejorative terms include 'bogan' (or its derivatives 'barry', 'bennie', 'boonie', 'chigger' or 'Ravo', [citation omitted] 'Charlene', 'Charmaine', 'cogger', 'feral', 'bevan', 'bevchick', 'bog', 'booner', 'charnie bum', 'gullie', 'mocca' and 'scozzer', all of which are defined in similar terms as a 'bogan'), [citation omitted] 'cashed up bogan', 'dero', 'pov' or 'povo', 'ocker', 'yobbo', 'feral', 'westie', 'wog', 'shitkicker', 'dole bludger' and 'no-hoper'. Many of these are, it can be argued, examples of working-class stereotypes that are 'held up to middle-class ridicule' [citation omitted] – quite distinct from the more positively viewed middle–upper class 'yuppie' or 'hipster'.[120]

Categorization into these groups tends to be based on the extent of the person's perceived economic and/or cultural capital, particularly embodied cultural capital (the way a person speaks, dresses, and that person's tastes).[121]

---

[118] See Sarah Scopelianos and Kara Jensen-Mackinnon, 'Classism in Australia is 'real'. Meet the crusaders calling it out' (ABC News, 17 June 2021) https://www.abc.net.au/news/2021-06-17/rn-this-working-life-the-influence-of-class/100170956; Virginia Trioli, 'He was a Xavier boy, and he's lodged in my memory of my first experience of Australia's great class divide' (ABC News, 19 June 2021) https://www.abc.net.au/news/2021-06-19/xavier-boy-memory-australias-great-class-divide/100223742.

[119] Steven Threadgold and Jessica Gerrard (eds), *Class in Australia* (2022, Monash University Publishing), 4.

[120] Capuano, 'Giving Meaning to "Social Origin"' (n 72), 85.

[121] Ibid, 120–123.

The 'bogan', which is associated with 'tastelessness',[122] is perhaps the most well-known among these groupings. Paternoster, Warr and Jacobs write that 'the figure of the bogan conveys the contemporary complexity of class' and '[i]t is a product of a public reckoning with the value of work, intellect and cultural distinction'.[123] Their research also suggests that the term 'bogan' may reflect distain for the poor and the making of moral judgements.[124]

2. Canada

In Canada, people may face discrimination because they have a regional accent (for example, aboriginal people from northern Ontario or people from Newfoundland may speak with regional accents[125]) cultivated from where they grew up in Canada. These accents reflect a person's social background, but they may also have a classed dimension. Newfoundland & Labrador English, which is also known as 'drawl' or 'Newfie talk', is associated with the lower class and is often the subject of ridicule and comedy.[126] Within Newfoundland & Labrador the term 'skeet' appears to be used to identify people who do not meet the expected standards of consumerism,[127] thus it is a way of categorizing people by reference to the extent of, to use Bourdieu's words, their consumption of cultural goods. Additionally, the use of the term 'hoser' across Canada to describe lower class people,[128] who are identified as such based on their behaviours, tastes, perceived low intelligence and lack of education,[129] further reflects the way cultural capital helps shape group categorization. In Canada generally welfare recipients are stigmatized, whilst in Quebec the 'sufficiently common' expression 'B.S.', which is short for

---

[122] Henry John Paternoster, Deborah Warr and Keith Jacobs, 'The enigma of the bogan and its significance to class in Australia: A socio-historical analysis', (2018) 54(3) *Journal of Sociology* 429, 442.

[123] Ibid, 442.

[124] Ibid, 443.

[125] See, for example, Ontario Human Rights Commission, 'Language-related grounds of discrimination: ancestry, ethnic origin, place of origin, race' (accessed 28 June 2022) https://www.ohrc.on.ca/en/policy-discrimination-and-language/language-related-grounds-discrimination-ancestry-ethnic-origin-place-origin-race.

[126] Sandra Clarke, *Newfoundland and Labrador English* (2010, Edinburgh University Press), 135.

[127] See, for example, CBC, 'Why don't skeets know they're skeets?' (Video interview, 12 September 2016) https://www.cbc.ca/news/canada/newfoundland-labrador/why-dont-skeets-know-theyre-skeets-1.3758774.

[128] See, for example, Derek Denis and Sali A Tagliamonte, 'Language change and fiction' in Wolfram Bublitz, Andreas H Jucker and Klaus P Schneider, *Handbooks of Pragmatics* (2017, Vol. 12, De Gruyter Mouton), 576.

[129] See, for example, Mark Abley, 'Hoser' (The Canadian Encyclopedia, published online 27 June 2019)

'bien-être social (welfare)', is a derogatory way to describe people and it reflects a stereotype.[130]

3. South Africa

In South Africa the intersections between class and race seem to be more pronounced than they are in Australia and Canada, yet cultural capital appears to be a key factor which helps people make class-based group categorizations (whether of white, coloured, or both racial groups).

Social groups include, for example, the white Afrikaner working-class on the one hand, and, Cape Coloured on the other.[131] Afrikaners may be identified by their style of speech,[132] dress sense, choice of clothing, décor and food they serve.[133] Within Afrikaner communities a 'hyperfeminine "nouveau riche" style' has emerged that is 'instantly recognizable' to Afrikaans-speaking South Africans,[134] and it is 'associated in the popular imagination with "aspiring" women from the lower middle-class in cities such as Pretoria'.[135] In contrast, members of the Cape Coloured community may be associated with certain recognizable graffiti, the practice of 'drifting' in cars, wearing 'orange prison garb' and the use of gang hand signs.[136]

Bekker and Levon also refer to the 'cross-cultural and cross-linguistic elements' of both of these groups.[137] They observe that that there are 'phonetic features that are highly stereotypical of Afrikaans-influenced English in South Africa and that generally index a working-class identity, whether white or coloured'.[138]

Like the 'bogan' in Australia, the 'chav' in the UK or 'redneck' in the United States, the term 'zef' (which 'traditionally meant "poor white" or "white trash"' and 'originates from the Ford Zephyr' which was 'popular within white working-class communities during the apartheid period'[139]) has been reclaimed and is used as an in-group identity marker.[140] As such, whether we are referring to social groups in Australia (such as the 'bogan'), Canada (such as the 'hoser' or 'skeet'), or South Africa (such as the Afrikaner,

---

[130] See *R.L. c. Ministère du Travail, de l'Emploi et de la Solidarité sociale*, 2021 QCCS 3784 (CanLII), para [143] ('*R.L.*').

[131] Ian Bekker and Erez Levon, 'Parodies of whiteness: Die Antwoord and the politics of race, gender, and class in South Africa' (2020) 49(1) *Language in Society* 115, 116, 118.

[132] Ibid, 128, 132–133.

[133] Ibid, 125.

[134] Ibid, 128.

[135] Ibid, 128.

[136] Ibid, 132.

[137] Ibid, 121.

[138] Ibid, 132–3.

[139] Ibid, 116.

[140] Ibid, 116.

'zef', or Cape Coloured), various forms of cultural capital are used to socially categorize these groups as either the in-group or the out-group. Relying on the work of Tajfel and others in social psychology (discussed above) people within these groups may, consciously or subconsciously, discriminate against those who are perceived to not belong and thus be in an out-group. In contrast, people who do not identify as belonging to these groups may (again, consciously or subconsciously) discriminate against members of the groups by favouring their own in-group members. Such discrimination may be largely based on cultural capital because, as shown above, this form of capital is a key marker of class-based group identity. For reasons that are explained in Chapters 4, cybervetting and hiring for cultural fit can be arenas in which outgroup discrimination based on class can play out.

Whilst markers of group identity (such as cultural capital) may help people to identify out-group members and so permit them to potentially discriminate, not all discrimination is (consciously or subconsciously) based on any particular reason or characteristic. It may be indirect, or structural, or systemic, thus people who possess certain levels of economic, social and cultural capital may face disadvantage and discrimination even where these species of capital are not known or obvious to discriminators. This chapter will now turn to provide a normative framework for understanding class and social background discrimination, and the different ways this type of discrimination might occur in workplaces. It will therefore set the foundation for understanding the scope for class and social background discrimination in the modern workplace and how this type of discrimination might occur from the technology and practices examined in Chapters 4, 5 and 6 of this book.

III. A normative framework for understanding class and social background discrimination

This part of this chapter will, as just noted, now explain the development of a normative framework for understanding class and social background discrimination. It will explain the distinction between 'formal' and 'substantive' equality, 'asymmetrical' versus 'symmetrical' definitions of discrimination, the differences between 'direct' and 'indirect' (or 'adverse effect') discrimination, and the concept of 'intersectionality', amongst other things. This framework is needed not only to understand the jurisprudence discussed in this book,[141] but also the various ways an employer's use of social media,[142] recruitment algorithms and AI,[143] and remote working policy[144]

---

[141] See Chapters 2 and 3.
[142] See Chapter 4.
[143] See Chapter 5.
[144] See Chapter 6.

involves or creates risks of discrimination based on class and/or factors reflective of social background.

A. Substantive or formal equality, symmetry or asymmetry?

An important question is whether discrimination laws should protect only the disadvantaged, or everyone regardless of their disadvantage. Addressing this question requires a brief introduction to the distinction between important concepts. First, the distinction between formal and substantive equality. Second, the distinction between symmetrical and asymmetrical discrimination laws.

The realization of 'equality' is an important policy goal of discrimination laws because these laws aim to address discriminatory treatment towards people with certain protected attributes. The concept of 'equality', however, is interpreted in different ways. First, the concept of 'formal equality' captures the idea that everyone should be treated equally. Second, and in contrast, in relation to the goal of 'substantive equality' Sandra Fredman draws on relevant discourse to propose a four-dimensional principle:

> to redress disadvantage; to address stigma, stereotyping, prejudice and violence; to enhance voice and participation; and to accommodate difference and achieve structural change.[citation omitted] Behind this is the basic principle that the right to equality should be located in the social context, responsive to those who are disadvantaged, demeaned, excluded, or ignored.[145]

Put simply, the goal of formal equality is to treat everyone the same whereas an important aspect of substantive equality is to address disadvantage and aim to 'reduce the gap between the more disadvantaged and the less disadvantaged'.[146]

A law which prohibits discrimination against the historically or presently 'disadvantaged' (for example, women, people with disability, people experiencing homelessness or poverty) is asymmetrical[147] and may promote the goal of substantive equality. A law which protects all people from discrimination on the basis of a certain attribute, irrespective of the person's 'disadvantage', is symmetrical and may promote the goal of formal equality. For example, in Australia laws which prohibit discrimination on the basis of race (and therefore protect white people and people of colour), sex (and

---

[145] Sandra Fredman, 'Substantive equality revisited' (2016) 14(3) *International Journal of Constitutional Law* 712, 713.

[146] Ibid, 722.

[147] See further Beth Gaze and Belinda Smith, *Equality and Discrimination Law in Australia: An Introduction* (2017, Cambridge University Press), 76–8; Naomi Schoenbaum, 'The Case for Symmetry in Antidiscrimination Law' [2017] *Wisconsin Law Review* 69, 77–8.

therefore protect women and men) and age (and therefore protect people who are young and old) are symmetrical.[148]

The jurisdictions examined in this book adopt different approaches to protected attributes which have been interpreted, or defined, to refer to class. In international labour law, Australian law and South African law the attribute 'social origin' appears to apply symmetrically to achieve formal equality.[149] In contrast, in Quebec, New Brunswick and the Northwest Territories the attribute 'social condition' applies asymmetrically to protect the disadvantaged.[150]

B. Direct versus indirect discrimination

Discrimination can be direct and also indirect. Direct discrimination is perhaps the most obvious way to conceive the act of discrimination. Gaze and Smith explain that direct discrimination:

> occurs when a protected characteristic is used to disadvantage a person, whether consciously, intentionally, because of unconscious bias, or as a result of common practice, making assumptions or using stereotypes to fill gaps in information about a person.[151]

Indirect discrimination is concerned with 'discriminatory effects'.[152] Generally speaking, although definitions differ in different laws,[153] indirect discrimination may occur when practices or conditions, though apparently neutral on their face, have a disadvantaging or disproportionate effect on people with a protected attribute (for example, disability or sex). Some anti-discrimination laws, such as those in Australia, require that the practice or condition also be unreasonable[154] whilst in international labour law the condition or practice must not be 'closely related' to the inherent requirements of the job.[155]

Class discrimination, as Chapters 4, 5 and 6 will show, may occur not only directly (that is, because of a job applicant's or employee's economic,

---

[148] See further Gaze and Smith (n 147), 76; Naomi Schoenbaum, 'The Case for Symmetry in Antidiscrimination Law' [2017] *Wisconsin Law Review* 69; Aileen McColgan, *Discrimination, Equality and the Law* (2014, Hart Publishing), Chapter 3.

[149] See Chapters 2 and 3.

[150] See Chapter 3.

[151] Gaze and Smith (n 147), 22–3.

[152] Ibid, 23.

[153] See Chapters 2 and 3.

[154] See, for example, Angelo Capuano, 'Post-Pandemic Workplace Design and the Plight of Employees with Invisible Disabilities: Is Australian Labour Law and Anti-Discrimination Legislation Equipped to Address New and Emerging Workplace Inequalities?' (2022) 45(2) *UNSW Law Journal* 873, 893.

[155] See Chapter 2.

social or cultural capital, or lack of such capital) but also indirectly in certain circumstances (that is, where an employer imposes a condition or practice which disadvantages people with certain economic, social and cultural capital, or lack thereof [subject to other legal tests, such as those just mentioned in the above paragraph, being met[156]]).

C. Categorical frames of conceiving class and social background discrimination

Discrimination, as Atrey explains, also runs along a continuum – single-axis, multiple, additive, embedded, compound, and intersectional discrimination.[157] This part of this chapter will now briefly explain this continuum, to prepare the discussion for the different ways discrimination is conceived in the jurisdictions examined in this book.

Atrey's analysis has identified a number of variants of single-axis discrimination – 'strictly', 'substantially', 'capacious', and 'contextual' single-axis discrimination.[158] 'Strictly' single-axis discrimination is discrimination which is based solely on a single ground and that one ground is the cause of the discrimination.[159] 'Substantially' single-axis discrimination runs along a single central axis, but acknowledges that other axes may be relevant.[160] For example, in a claim of sex and age discrimination a court would identify that one or the other substantially caused the discrimination. 'Capacious' single-axis discrimination can be understood by reading a single-axis of discrimination (for example, sex) capaciously to include aspects of another axis (for example, age) which disadvantage people which identify with the first axis (for example, women). For example, using this approach a court may find that an older woman has experienced discrimination which is not experienced by younger women or older men.[161] 'Contextual' single-axis discrimination, as the name suggests, uses contextual factors (such as identities or other grounds) to inform the causal relationship between an act and harm in the form of discrimination based on an axis.[162]

If discrimination is conceived as being 'quantitatively' limited to one ground, there is a risk that discrimination which is multi-causal and 'qualitatively' intersectional can be missed.[163] As such, it is necessary to go

---

[156] See, for example, Chapters 2 and 3.
[157] See Shreya Atrey, *Intersectional Discrimination* (2019, Oxford University Press), 78–139.
[158] Ibid, 85–6, 95
[159] Ibid, 86–9.
[160] Ibid, 96.
[161] Ibid, 100.
[162] See Ibid, 106. For an example of contextual framing see the dissenting judgment of Justice Sachs in *Volks NO v Robinson and Others* (CCT12/04) [2005] ZACC 2, especially at [198] and [219].
[163] Atrey (n 157), 95–6.

a step further to consider multiple, additive, embedded, compound and intersectional discrimination. Multiple discrimination is discrimination which is based on multiple grounds which are each treated separately and isolated from one another.[164] For example, on this approach, a claim of *both* race *and* sex discrimination can be proven where discrimination on each ground is argued separately from one another.[165] Put another way, these claims can be seen as multiple single-axis claims which each need to be proven individually.[166] Additive discrimination accepts that discrimination can be based on more than one ground, but goes a step further in recognizing that discrimination is based on the way these separate grounds interact with one another.[167] Compound discrimination is 'where similar patterns of disadvantage associated with different groups are compounded with patterns of disadvantage associated with other groups based on different grounds'.[168] Embedded discrimination, for Atrey, 'considers two or more grounds as coming together to form a separate ground of discrimination'.[169]

Amongst the various ways to conceive discrimination, intersectional discrimination is the most complex to explain. This approach is reflected in South African jurisprudence (discussed in Chapter 3) and it will now be explained with a focus from the South African perspective. In contrast, the legal regimes in Australia and Canada have not developed to the point where they can be regarded as adopting an intersectional approach.[170] As will be explained in Chapter 3 and further below, the intersectional approach to discrimination in South Africa is largely the result of South Africa's transformative constitutionalism which strives to right the wrongs of apartheid.

1. *Intersectional discrimination*

Kimberlé Williams Crenshaw has been described as 'a pioneer and leading scholar on intersectionality'.[171] Crenshaw was dismayed with discrimination law's 'single-axis framework' and 'showed how courts reduced intersectional claims' of discrimination based on multiple grounds (such as race *and* sex) to individual grounds (that is, *either* race *or* sex).[172] Intersectional discrimination therefore contrasts with this single-axis framework and 'other categorial

---

[164] Ibid, 109.
[165] Ibid, 109.
[166] Ibid, 84, fn 113.
[167] Ibid, 84–5.
[168] Ibid, 118.
[169] Ibid, 85.
[170] See Chapter 3.
[171] *Mahlangu and Another v Minister of Labour and Others* (CCT306/19) [2020] ZACC 24, fn 85 ('*Mahlangu*').
[172] Atrey (n 157), 78.

frames of conceiving discrimination'[173] such as, for example, multiple, additive, embedded and compound discrimination.[174]

Intersectionality helps us to understand the *structural* and *dynamic* consequences which result from the interaction between multiple attributes, such as class, sex, gender, race, disability, religion, sexual orientation, etc.[175] Atrey argues that intersectionality is principally comprised of five strands:

> first, it is concerned with tracing both **sameness and difference** in experiences based on multiple group identities; secondly, it is concerned with tracing the sameness and difference in **patterns of group disadvantage** understood broadly in terms of subordination, marginalization, violence, disempowerment, deprivation, exploitation, and all other forms of disadvantage suffered by social groups; thirdly, in order to make sense of these same and different patterns of group disadvantage they must be considered as a whole, namely with **integrity**; fourthly, intersectionality can only be appreciated in its full socio-economic, cultural, and political **context** that shapes people's identities and patterns of group disadvantage associated with them; and lastly, the purpose of this intersectional analysis is to further broadly conceived **transformative** aims which remove, rectify, and reform the disadvantage suffered by intersectional groups.[176]

In the vast literature around intersectionality which has developed, this, Atrey adds, is just one account 'from the point of view of discrimination law' which 'unpicks the strands that have been central to intersectionality in the way it was initially set out by Crenshaw and has been developed by others over the last thirty years'.[177]

For the purposes of this book, then, intersectionality is about using context to detect the nature of disadvantage at multiple axes (for example, race, sex and class) in order to achieve transformational change and remove or address that disadvantage for a certain group. For example, in the case of poor black women who experience disadvantage at the intersection of class, race and sex, disadvantage is *similar* to that suffered by black men (as they are also black) and white women (as they are also women) and poor whites (as they are also poor), but it is also *different* in that they suffer disadvantage not just based on race, sex or class, but as *poor black women*.[178] The various ways of

---

[173] Ibid, 78.

[174] Ibid, 78–139.

[175] Ibid, 33.

[176] Ibid, 36.

[177] Ibid, 36.

[178] See Ibid, 38–9. Atrey discusses the interaction of sex and race, but this author added the dynamic of class in the example for the purposes of this book.

conceiving discrimination (single-axis, multiple, additive, embedded, and compound) do not take into account contextual factors which illuminate the unique nature of disadvantage suffered by, for example, poor black women, thus they may fail to detect discrimination at the intersection of race, sex and class, and, address systemic barriers to usher in transformational change.

In *Mahlangu and Another v Minister of Labour and Others* (*'Mahlangu'*) the majority of the Constitutional Court of South Africa used an intersectional approach to find unfair discrimination.[179] In this case, the court considered whether a section of legislation which excluded domestic workers from the definition of 'employee' (with the result that they could not receive social security benefits under the legislation)[180] was invalid under section 9(3) of the constitution (which prohibits unfair discrimination based on certain attributes).

The majority referred to the transformative purpose of South Africa's constitution to break the ills of the past (such as racism and oppression from apartheid)[181] and noted the usefulness of the intersectional analysis in addressing systematic disadvantage.[182] In the view of the majority, '[i]ntersectionality requires that courts examine the nature and context of the individual or group at issue, their history, as well as the social and legal history of society's treatment of that group'.[183]

Therefore, in considering whether the legislation limited the constitutional right to equality, the court considered the history of social security in South Africa relating to domestic workers and 'the historical disadvantage that Black women have faced as a group'.[184] Apartheid had placed black women at the bottom of the social hierarchy[185] and they were, as a result, required to do the least skilled, lowest paid, and most insecure work.[186] The court observed that the 'case of domestic workers' (most of whom were black women) 'was particularly severe'.[187] Importantly, the court observed that current marginalization faced by domestic workers is therefore historical,[188] and this marginalization endures to the present day.[189] Black women in South

---

[179] (CCT306/19) [2020] ZACC 24.

[180] Mahlangu (n 171), paras [4]–[6].

[181] See Mahlangu (n 171), paras [55], [79], [102], [106].

[182] Mahlangu (n 171), para [89], [191].

[183] Mahlangu (n 171), para [95].

[184] Mahlangu (n 171), para [95].

[185] Mahlangu (n 171), para [96] citing Wing and de Carvalho, 'Black South African Women: Toward Equal Rights' (1995) 8 Harvard Human Rights Journal 57, 60.

[186] Mahlangu (n 171), para [99].

[187] Mahlangu (n 171), para [99].

[188] Mahlangu (n 171), para [100].

[189] Mahlangu (n 171), para [102].

Africa suffered under a 'triple yoke of oppression' which was based on their race, gender and class.[190]

In the context of its analysis of the historical exclusion of domestic workers in South Africa, the court noted that any analogy between domestic workers and other groups of workers also excluded from the legislation in question (members of the South African National Defence Force (SANDF) and the South African Police Service (SAPS)) could not be drawn.[191] Members of SANDF and SAPS also had coverage for death or injury through other schemes whereas domestic workers were in a 'legislative vacuum' with no coverage at all.[192]

With this historical context in mind, the majority observed that domestic workers in South Africa continued to face multiple and overlapping disadvantage, such as racism, sexism and inequality based on gender and class stratification.[193] In the context of these enduring disadvantages, the court observed that the 'overwhelming majority of domestic workers' are black women[194] and that domestic work 'is a circumstance-driven employment decision' which is 'driven by financial need' and due to low salaries '[d]omestic workers remain shackled by poverty'.[195] The majority therefore held that given 'domestic workers are predominantly Black women' their exclusion from the legislation 'indirectly discriminates against them on grounds of sex, gender and race'[196] and limited the right not to be unfairly discriminated against under section 9(3) of the South African constitution.[197]

The equality breach identified by the majority was seen to impact the achievement of 'structural systemic transformation'.[198] Excluding domestic workers from the benefits of the legislation preserved the disadvantages which poor black women experienced during apartheid, and the legislative scheme was therefore an impediment to structural and systemic transformation in South Africa. Declaring the relevant section of the legislation invalid was, for the majority, seen to fulfil the 'transformative mandate' set by the South African constitution, both at the group and individual levels.[199]

---

[190] Mahlangu (n 171), para [96] citing Nolde, 'South African Women Under Apartheid: Employment Rights with Particular Focus on Domestic Service and Forms of Resistance to Promote Change' (1991) *Third World Legal Studies* 203, 204.

[191] Mahlangu (n 171), para [94].

[192] See Mahlangu (n 171), para [94].

[193] Mahlangu (n 171), para [90].

[194] Mahlangu (n 171), para [93].

[195] Mahlangu (n 171), para [104].

[196] Mahlangu (n 171), para [94].

[197] Mahlangu (n 171), para [107].

[198] Mahlangu (n 171), para [105].

[199] Mahlangu (n 171), para [106].

The majority held that the intersectional framework enabled the court to 'shift its normative vision of equality and the 'baseline' assumptions embedded in anti-discrimination law'.[200] The court's contextualization of the experience of domestic workers revealed intersectional and compounding disadvantages based on race, sex, gender and class which domestic workers faced historically and which endure to the present day.[201] As such, the intersectional analysis revealed how the exclusion of domestic workers from the legislation discriminated against a group (poor black women) at the intersection of race, sex, gender and class.

As the analysis in Chapter 3 will show, intersectionality is increasingly being used by South African courts in cases which concern 'social origin' discrimination.

Conclusion

This chapter set out to answer three important questions which are relevant to understanding discrimination based on class and social background, and to provide foundation knowledge needed to understand subsequent chapters of this book.

First, it sought to answer the question 'what is class?'. To address this question, it provided an overview of leading class theories, including those of Emile Durkheim, Karl Marx, Max Weber and Pierre Bourdieu. The chapter traced the development of these class theories, highlighted major differences between them, and explained how Bourdieu's theory builds upon those of Marx and Weber by measuring class not just in economic terms, but by reference to species of capital (economic, social and cultural capital). It also highlighted how the cultivation of certain species of capital (such as embodied cultural capital) interconnects with and relies upon a person's upbringing, family and social background.

Second, having provided an overview of leading class theories, it then turned to ask which of these theories has most relevance and application in modern workplaces. Using a social-psychological lens, this chapter exposed how in Australia, South Africa and Canada social categorization in class-based social groups (and associated risks of out-group discrimination) involves assessing species of capital, particularly cultural capital. Additionally, it directs attention to the way classism might play out in certain fields (such as universities and professions) when those from working-class and

---

[200] Mahlangu (n 171), para [102]. See further Kimberle Crenshaw, 'Demarginalizing the Intersection of Race and Sex: A Black Feminist Critique of Antidiscrimination Doctrine, Feminist Theory and Antiracist Politics' (1989) 1 *University of Chicago Legal Forum* 139, 144–5.

[201] See Mahlangu (n 171), para [102].

disadvantaged backgrounds access them to attempt upward social mobility, only to find they are 'fish out of water' because they lack the cultural capital dominating in those fields. In modern workplaces, workers may therefore be vulnerable to exploitation, adverse treatment or disadvantage because they either lack or do not have the 'right' cultural capital in certain fields. It therefore proposes that Bourdieu's theory of class is likely to be the most relevant and applicable to understanding the problem of class discrimination in modern contexts.

Third, the chapter then turned to consider how discrimination based on class and factors reflective of social background might occur in modern workplaces. It explained different ways of conceiving discrimination, such as direct versus indirect, symmetrical versus asymmetrical, single-axis, multiple, additive, compounding, and intersectional. This discussion highlighted how discrimination may, in addition to being direct, also arise indirectly from structural and systemic barriers which disadvantage people based on class and other attributes.

2

Unravelling the Meaning of 'Social Origin' Discrimination in Conventions of the International Labour Organization (ILO) and its Applications in the Digital Age

Introduction

As noted in Chapter 1, discrimination on the basis of 'social origin' is prohibited by ILO conventions. Article 1 of *ILO 111* prohibits discrimination on the basis of grounds including 'social origin' and article 5 of *ILO 158* prohibits termination of employment on the basis of grounds including 'social origin'. The term 'social origin' is not, however, defined in these instruments.

In 1957 and 1958, when delegates from different countries were debating the meaning of the term 'social origin' in the proposed *ILO 111*, there was much uncertainty from various delegates as to what the term meant[1] or how it would apply in certain countries, such as Canada and Sweden.[2] Approximately 55 years later, when Australian politicians and others turned their attention to the concept of 'social origin' discrimination at public hearings into the proposed *Human Rights and Anti-Discrimination Bill* 2012 (Cth),[3] very little progress had been made in understanding the concept of 'social origin' (and

---

[1] *Record of Proceedings* (International Labour Conference, Fortieth Session, Twenty-Eighth Sitting, Geneva, 25 June 1957), 466.

[2] See, for example, *Discrimination in the Field of Employment and Occupation* (International Labour Conference, Fortieth Session, Geneva, 1957, Report VII(2)), 17–18, 29; *Record of Proceedings* (International Labour Conference, Fortieth Session, Twenty-Sixth Sitting, Geneva, 23 June 1958), 408.

[3] This Bill had sought to consolidate Australia's anti-discrimination laws but was not passed and is not likely to be revived.

'social origin' discrimination).[4] Some Australian senators believed that 'social origin' has an 'almost limitless meaning',[5] is 'vague'[6] and 'almost meaningless'.[7]

This chapter sets out to achieve two main objectives. First, it clarifies the meaning of 'social origin' in ILO conventions to show that, far from being vague or meaningless, the term has a clear meaning in 'jurisprudence' developed by the ILO's supervisory bodies. Second, it explains why ILO jurisprudence matters in domestic contexts, particularly Australia and South Africa.

Part I will explain the ILO supervisory system and the respective roles of two supervisory bodies, the ILO Committee of Experts on the Application of Conventions and Recommendations ('Committee of Experts') and Commissions of Inquiry, in interpreting ILO conventions. Part II will explain the concept and scope of 'discrimination' in ILO jurisprudence, to set the stage for an analysis of discrimination based on 'social origin'. Part III will then analyse the reports of ILO supervisory bodies and the *travaux préparatoires* (preparatory works) of relevant treaty to elucidate the meaning of 'social origin' in ILO conventions, and clarify how this type of discrimination might occur. Finally, Part IV will rely on legal rules of interpretation to explain why this ILO jurisprudence matters in domestic contexts, particularly in Australia and South Africa.

I. The ILO and ILO supervisory bodies

One function of the ILO is to supervise the implementation of ILO conventions and recommendations in member states. This ILO supervisory system has been explained elsewhere[8] but for the sake of the clarity of this chapter, the respective roles and functions of the Committee Experts on the one hand, and Commissions of Inquiry on the other, will now be briefly outlined.

The ILO monitors member states through: (1) regular systems of supervision; and (2) special procedures.[9]

---

[4] See generally Official Committee Hansard, Senate Legal and Constitutional Affairs Legislation Committee, Human Rights and Anti-Discrimination Bill 2012 (Wednesday 23 January 2013, Melbourne), 27, 39, 40, 54, 62, 76; Official Committee Hansard, Senate Legal and Constitutional Affairs Legislation Committee, Human Rights and Anti-Discrimination Bill 2012 (Thursday 24 January 2013, Sydney), 10, 31, 48, 65, 66; Official Committee Hansard, Senate Legal and Constitutional Affairs Legislation Committee, Human Rights and Anti-Discrimination Bill 2012 (Monday 4 February 2013, Canberra), 6, 7, 10, 12.

[5] See *Dissenting Report by Coalition Senators* (opposition to the proposed *Human Rights and Anti-Discrimination Bill*), para [1.18].

[6] Official Committee Hansard, Senate Legal and Constitutional Affairs Legislation Committee, Human Rights and Anti-Discrimination Bill 2012 (Monday 4 February 2013, Canberra), 6.

[7] Official Committee Hansard, Senate Legal and Constitutional Affairs Legislation Committee, Human Rights and Anti-Discrimination Bill 2012 (Thursday 24 January 2013, Sydney), 31.

[8] See Angelo Capuano, 'Giving Meaning to "Social Origin"' (see Chapter 1, n 72), 86–88.

[9] International Labour Organization, *ILO Supervisory System/Mechanism* http://www.ilo.org/global/about-the-ilo/how-the-ilo-works/ilo-supervisory-system-mechanism/lang--en/index.htm.

The Committee of Experts, which is comprised of 20 'eminent jurists',[10] engages in regular systems of supervision through producing findings that can include general reports, 'observations' on the application of conventions in member states, 'direct requests' which are addressed to governments, and, 'general surveys' on the laws and practice in member states.[11]

Special procedures, on the other hand, respond to ad hoc complaints of alleged non-observance with ratified ILO conventions.[12] Member States can file a complaint with the International Labour Office if it believes that another member is not observing any of the ILO conventions which both of them have ratified.[13] Complaints that a member state is not complying with a convention can also be filed by delegates to the International Labour Conference (which can include government, worker or employer delegates[14]) or by the Governing Body[15] (which is the ILO's executive body[16]). The Governing Body may appoint a Commission of Inquiry consisting of three independent members[17] to hear the complaint.[18] Commissions of Inquiry, which 'is the ILO's highest-level investigative procedure',[19] have a perceived

---

[10] International Labour Organization, *Committee of Experts on the Application of Conventions and Recommendations* http://www.ilo.org/global/standards/applying-and-promoting-international-labour-standards/committee-of-experts-on-the-application-of-conventions-and-recommendations/lang--it/index.htm.

[11] International Labour Standards Department, Handbook of Procedures relating to International Conventions and Recommendations (International Labour Organization, 2012), 36–37 [59](k) https://www.ilo.org/wcmsp5/groups/public/---ed_norm/---normes/documents/publication/wcms_192621.pdf; Constance Thomas, Martin Oelz and Xavier Beaudonnet, 'The Use of International Labor Law in Domestic Courts: Theory, Recent Jurisprudence, and Practical Implications' in Les normes internationales du travail: Un patrimoine pour l'avenir (International Labour Organization, 2004), 254.

[12] Thomas, Oelz and Beaudonnet, ibid, 255.

[13] *International Labour Organization Constitution*, Art 26.

[14] International Labour Organization, *About the ILC* https://www.ilo.org/ilc/AbouttheILC/lang--en/index.htm.

[15] International Labour Organization, *Complaints* http://www.ilo.org/global/standards/applying-and-promoting-international-labour-standards/complaints/lang--en/index.htm.

[16] International Labour Organization, *About the Governing Body* https://www.ilo.org/gb/about-governing-body/lang--en/index.htm.

[17] International Labour Organization, *Complaints* https://www.ilo.org/global/standards/applying-and-promoting-international-labour-standards/complaints/lang--en/index.htm.

[18] *International Labour Organization Constitution*, Art 26(3).

[19] International Labour Organization, *Complaints* https://www.ilo.org/global/standards/applying-and-promoting-international-labour-standards/complaints/lang--en/index.htm.

'judicial nature'[20] because they are seen to conduct a 'judicial investigation' and make findings which are based on that investigation.[21]

The Committee of Experts and Commissions of Inquiry therefore interpret ILO conventions in practice[22] because, through regular supervision by the Committee of Experts and special ad hoc procedures such as a Commission of Inquiry, they comment on situations that constitute non-compliance with ILO conventions. Whilst they are not binding[23] or authoritative,[24] interpretations of ILO conventions by the Committee of Experts and Commissions of Inquiry carry significant value and weight.[25]

The below text will therefore analyse the way the term 'social origin' is understood by ILO supervisory bodies to aid the interpretation of the term in ILO conventions. Given the ambiguity of the term 'social origin' in *ILO 111* the preparatory works to the convention will also be consulted to clarify its meaning.[26] Prior to this analysis, however, it would be useful to clarify the concept of 'discrimination' in ILO jurisprudence, to prepare the discussion of 'social origin' discrimination.

II. The concept and scope of 'discrimination' in ILO jurisprudence

Article 1 of *ILO 111* prohibits discrimination on the basis of grounds including 'social origin'. For the purposes of the convention, 'discrimination' includes 'any distinction, exclusion or preference made on the basis of race, colour, sex, religion, political opinion, national extraction or social origin,

---

[20] *Commonwealth v Hamilton* (2000) 108 FCR 378, 390 [44] (Katz J) ('*Hamilton*'), citing *South West Africa (Ethiopia v South Africa) (Preliminary Objections)* [1962] ICJ Rep 319, 427–8 (Jessup J).

[21] Ibid.

[22] Jean-Michel Servais, *International Labour Law* (Wolters Kluwer, 3rd ed, 2011) 85. See, for example, Holly Cullen, 'Does the ILO Have a Distinctive Role in the International Legal Protection of Child Soldiers?' (2011) 5 *Human Rights and International Legal Discourse* 63, 68; Holly Cullen, 'The Collective Complaints System of the European Social Charter: Interpretative Methods of the European Committee of Social Rights' (2009) 9 *Human Rights Law Review* 61, 69.

[23] Claire La Hovary, 'Showdown at the ILO? A Historical Perspective on the Employers' Group's 2012 Challenge to the Right To Strike' (2013) 42 *Industrial Law Journal* 338, 350.

[24] Servais (n 22), 85.

[25] See Part IV of Chapter 2 for a discussion of their value in the domestic jurisprudence of Australia and South Africa.

[26] See *Vienna Convention on the Law of Treaties* (Done at Vienna on 23 May 1969), arts 31–32 ('*VCLT*').

which has the effect of nullifying or impairing equality of opportunity or treatment in employment or occupation'.[27]

Indirect discrimination falls within the scope of the convention.[28] In an observation of the Netherlands, the Committee of Experts noted that *ILO 111* covers both direct and indirect discrimination based on 'social origin'.[29]

According to the Committee of Experts, indirect discrimination occurs when: (1) apparently neutral practices or conditions are applied to everyone, but; (2) they result with unequal treatment or a 'disproportionately harsh impact on some persons on the basis of [protected] characteristics';[30] and (3) they are 'not closely related to the inherent requirements of the job'.[31] An intention to discriminate is not an element of the definition in *ILO 111*.[32]

The Committee of Experts has also clarified that the prohibition on 'social origin' discrimination in *ILO 111* covers not only hiring decisions but 'any circumstance which has the effect of nullifying or impairing equality of opportunity or treatment in employment and occupation'.[33] In *ILO 111* the terms 'employment' and 'occupation' within the meaning of 'discrimination' includes 'access to employment'.[34] This includes 'equal opportunities in selection and recruitment processes'.[35] The Committee of Experts has expressly stated that the 'application of the principle of equality guarantees every person the right to have his or her application for a chosen job considered equitably, without discrimination based on any of the grounds of' *ILO 111*[36] such as 'social origin'. The right appears to apply throughout

---

[27] *ILO 111*, Art 1(1)(a).

[28] See *Equality in Employment and Occupation: General Survey by the Committee of Experts on the Application of Conventions and Recommendations,* Report III (Part 4B) (International Labour Conference, 75th session, 1988) ('General Survey 1988'), para [28].

[29] Observation (CEACR) - adopted 2008, published 98th ILC session (2009), *Discrimination (Employment and Occupation) Convention, 1958 (No 111)* – Netherlands.

[30] *Equality in Employment and Occupation: Special Survey on Equality in Employment and Occupation in respect of Convention No. III, Report of the Committee of Experts on the Application of Conventions and Recommendations,* Report III (Part 4B) (International Labour Conference, 83rd Session, 1996) (*'Special Survey 1996'*), para [26] cited in *Hamilton* (n 20), para [35].

[31] *General Survey on the fundamental Conventions concerning rights at work in light of the ILO Declaration on Social Justice for a Fair Globalization, 2008:* Report of the Committee of Experts on the Application of Conventions and Recommendations, Report III(1B) (International Labour Conference, 101st Session, 2012, ILC.101/III/1B) (*'General Survey 2012'*), 313 [745]. See also *Hamilton* (n 20), para [58].

[32] *General Survey* 2012 (n 31), 313 [745].

[33] Direct Request (CEACR) - adopted 2006, published 96th ILC session (2007), Discrimination (Employment and Occupation) Convention, 1958 (No 111) – Ghana.

[34] *ILO 111*, Article 1(3).

[35] *General Survey 2012* (n 31), 315 [753]. See also *Special Survey* 1996 (n 30), [82]–[83].

[36] *General Survey 2012* (n 31), 316 [754].

the entire recruitment process, from finding (that is, job advertisements), screening, selecting for interview and hiring.[37]

III. 'Social origin' includes class and factors reflective of social background

'Social origin' has a specific meaning[38] that is distinct from other attributes (such as race, ancestry, citizenship, ethnic origin, place of origin[39] and national extraction [which covers 'a person's place of birth, ancestry or foreign origin'[40]]). Thus, to address discrimination on this basis legislators should *explicitly* include 'social origin' as a ground[41] rather than erroneously assume it can be addressed through prohibiting discrimination based on other grounds.

According to the Committee of Experts, 'social origin' discrimination arises when 'an individual's membership in a class, a socio-occupational category or a caste determines his or her occupational future either by denying him or her certain jobs or activities or, on the contrary, by assigning him or her to certain jobs'.[42]

---

[37] *General Survey 2012*, 315–316 [753]-[754]. See also, for example, Observation (CEACR) - adopted 2020, published 109th ILC session (2021), Discrimination (Employment and Occupation) Convention, 1958 (No 111) – Türkiye. See also Direct Request (CEACR) - adopted 2020, published 109th ILC session (2021), Discrimination (Employment and Occupation) Convention, 1958 (No 111) – Fiji; Direct Request (CEACR) - adopted 2001, published 90th ILC session (2002), Discrimination (Employment and Occupation) Convention, 1958 (No 111) – Netherlands; Direct Request (CEACR) - adopted 2007, published 97th ILC session (2008), Discrimination (Employment and Occupation) Convention, 1958 (No 111) – Egypt.

[38] See Direct Request (CEACR) - adopted 2009, published 99th ILC session (2010), *Discrimination (Employment and Occupation) Convention, 1958 (No 111)* – Austria.

[39] Observation (CEACR) - adopted 2010, published 100th ILC session (2011), *Discrimination (Employment and Occupation) Convention, 1958 (No 111)* – Canada. Also see Observation (CEACR) - adopted 2013, published 103rd ILC session (2014), *Discrimination (Employment and Occupation) Convention, 1958 (No 111)* – Guinea.

[40] Observation (CEACR) - adopted 2012, published 102nd ILC session (2013), *Discrimination (Employment and Occupation) Convention, 1958 (No 111)* – Guinea.

[41] See Observation (CEACR) - adopted 2008, published 98th ILC session (2009) – Netherlands; Direct Request (CEACR) - adopted 2020, published 109th ILC session (2021), Discrimination (Employment and Occupation) Convention, 1958 (No 111) – Norway.

[42] General Survey 1988 (n 28), para [54]. Also see General Survey 2012 (n 31), para [802]; Special Survey 1996 (n 30), para [43]. See also Discrimination in the Field of Employment and Occupation (Report VII(1), International Labour Conference, Fortieth Session, 1957), 19.

'Social origin' discrimination therefore occurs when a person faces discrimination based on his or her class,[43] caste[44] or socio-occupational category.[45] 'Social origin' 'has been conceived principally in terms of social mobility',[46] but, in addition to this, the below analysis of the reports of ILO supervisory bodies will show that it is also understood in terms of certain factors that go to social background.

This chapter will elucidate the meaning of 'class' as a constituent element of 'social origin' and which factors reflective of social background appear to fall within the meaning of the ground. It will not consider the concepts of 'caste' and 'socio-occupational category' discrimination for two reasons. Firstly, this book deliberately focuses on the issues of class and social background discrimination because they have particular relevance and topicality in the digital age and the jurisdictions to be analysed (Australia, South Africa, Canada and New Zealand).[47] Secondly, there are a number of works on caste discrimination.[48]

The below analysis will refer to two ways that discrimination based on 'class' and 'social background' is conceived in ILO jurisprudence. First, it will explain how this type of discrimination occurs at the single axis, independent of other characteristics or attributes. Second, it will show the additive and intersectional nature of 'social origin' discrimination and how this type of discrimination, in certain contexts, overlaps or interacts with discrimination based on other attributes or characteristics.

---

[43] See, for example, Direct Request (CEACR) - adopted 2009, published 99th ILC session (2010), *Discrimination (Employment and Occupation) Convention, 1958 (No 111)* – Austria.

[44] Also see Observation (CEACR) - adopted 2011, published 101st ILC session (2012), *Discrimination (Employment and Occupation) Convention, 1958 (No 111)* – Pakistan; Direct Request (CEACR) - adopted 2011, published 101st ILC session (2012), *Discrimination (Employment and Occupation) Convention, 1958 (No 111)* – United Kingdom; Observation (CEACR) - adopted 2010, published 100th ILC session (2011), *Discrimination (Employment and Occupation) Convention, 1958 (No 111)* – Pakistan.

[45] See Article 2, *ILO 111*; *General Survey 1988* (n 28), para [55].

[46] 1989 *Report of the Commission of Inquiry appointed under article 26 of the Constitution of the International Labour Organisation to examine the observance by Romania of the Discrimination (Employment and Occupation) Convention, 1958 (No. 111)* ('*Romanian Commission of Inquiry*'), para [40].

[47] See Chapters 4, 5 and 6.

[48] See, for example, David Keane, *Caste-based Discrimination in International Human Rights Law* (2016, Routledge); Prakash Shah, *Against Caste in British Law: A Critical Perspective on the Caste Discrimination Provision in the Equality Act 2010* (2015, Palgrave); Annapurna Waughray, *Capturing Caste in Law: The Legal Regulation of Caste Discrimination* (2021, Routledge).

A. Class and social background discrimination at the single axis

'Social origin' discrimination occurs at the single axis where the discrimination is based on constituent elements of 'social origin' such as 'class' and/or factors reflective of 'social background'. What, however, does it mean in ILO jurisprudence for a person or employer to discriminate on the basis of 'class' and/or 'social background'? The below discussion will clarify the meaning of these two concepts as constituent elements of 'social origin'. First, it will clarify the meaning of 'class' (as a constituent element of 'social origin') as it appears to be understood by the Committee of Experts and in preparatory works to *ILO 111*. Second, it will show how ILO supervisory bodies have measured 'social origin' by reference to factors that go to social background.

1. Class measured by economic, social and cultural capital

Based on a detailed analysis of the reports of the Committee of Experts, this author has argued that 'class', as a constituent element of 'social origin' in ILO conventions, appears to be understood in a manner consistent with Bourdieu's class theory[49] in that it is measured by reference to economic, social and cultural capital.[50] More specifically, as argued by this author, the Committee of Experts appears to adopt similar criteria to Bourdieu's species of capital when identifying the 'social categories' that attract comment on 'social origin' discrimination in its various reports.[51] For the Committee of Experts, 'social origin' is broader than 'social status'[52] or 'source of income'[53] and not covered by 'economic status',[54] thus the concept captures more than just economic measures of class.

The position that 'social origin' in *ILO 111* is measured by reference to Bourdieu's species of capital also finds support in the preparatory works to the

---

[49] See Chapter 1 for an explanation of Bourdieu's class theory.

[50] See Capuano, 'Giving Meaning to "Social Origin"' (see Chapter 1, n 72), 97–120.

[51] See generally Ibid.

[52] Direct Request (CEACR) - adopted 2011, published 101st ILC session (2012), *Discrimination (Employment and Occupation) Convention, 1958 (No 111)* – Eritrea; Direct Request (CEACR) - adopted 2011, published 101st ILC session (2012), *Discrimination (Employment and Occupation) Convention, 1958 (No 111)* – Zambia; Direct Request (CEACR) - adopted 2010, published 100th ILC session (2011), *Discrimination (Employment and Occupation) Convention, 1958 (No 111)* – Eritrea; Direct Request (CEACR) - adopted 2008, published 98th ILC session (2009), *Discrimination (Employment and Occupation) Convention, 1958 (No 111)* – Ghana.

[53] Direct Request (CEACR) - adopted 2006, published 96th ILC session (2007), *Discrimination (Employment and Occupation) Convention, 1958 (No 111)* – Canada.

[54] See, for example, Direct Request (CEACR) - adopted 2010, published 100th ILC session (2011), *Discrimination (Employment and Occupation) Convention, 1958 (No 111)* – Eritrea.

convention. In preparatory works to *ILO 111* 'social origin' was conceived mainly in terms of social mobility, to address the problem of people being confined to the same occupational level as their parents.[55] Low levels of social mobility, which limited the ability of people to gain employment at different levels to their parents, was observed to result from, amongst other things, 'natural factors' which favoured children of professionals in their preparations for a profession 'such as cultural environment, and moral and economic support during study'.[56] It was also observed that people were given preferences in accessing certain forms of employment based on 'subtle factors' including their 'family name or manner of speech, or the educational establishment which he attended'.[57]

The International Labour Office therefore suggested that 'social origin' be included as a prohibited ground of discrimination and its inclusion 'gave rise to no particular discussions or objections', thus the convention 'includes the expression 'social origin' in the form in which it was originally proposed'.[58] This view of 'social origin', although developed in the late 1950s, is highly relevant to employment in the digital age. This is because cultural environment during upbringing and classed manner of speech continue to disadvantage those from working class backgrounds whilst benefitting those from other backgrounds in accessing employment. The workings of certain AI in recruitment, as the analysis in Chapter 5 of this book will show, provides an example of the way people may face barriers to employment based on these factors. The increased uptake of such technology to make recruitment decisions may therefore serve to automate the development of structural barriers based on class, thus making laws which prohibit 'social origin' discrimination in employment increasingly relevant in the age of recruitment algorithms and AI.

'Class' (and therefore 'social origin') discrimination, therefore, may occur where a person experiences discrimination which is based on his or her economic, social and/or cultural capital (or lack thereof). This may include,

---

[55] International Labour Conference, Seventh Item on the Agenda: 'Discrimination in the Field of Employment and Occupation' (Report VII(1), Fortieth Session, 1957), 19 ('*ILC, Report VII(1), 40TH Sess, 1957*').

[56] *ILC, Report VII(1), 40TH Sess, 1957*, 19.

[57] *ILC, Report VII(1), 40TH Sess, 1957*, 19.

[58] Hector Bartolomei de la Cruz, Geraldo von Potobsky and Lee Swepston, *International Labor Organization: The International Standards System and Basic Human Rights* (1996, Westview Press), 267. See also International Labour Conference, Seventh Item on the Agenda: 'Discrimination in the Field of Employment and Occupation' (Report VII(2), Fortieth Session, 1957); International Labour Conference, 'Record of Proceedings' (Forty-Second Session, 1958); International Labour Conference, Fourth Item on the Agenda: 'Discrimination in the Field of Employment and Occupation' (Forty-Second Session, 1958).

for example, discrimination traceable to class by being based on a person's wealth (economic capital), connections, family resources, and family name (social capital), tastes, hobbies, mannerisms, accent, manner of speech or other dispositions of the mind and body (embodied cultural capital), consumption and appreciation of cultural goods (objectified cultural capital), and/or attendance at a certain high school (institutionalized cultural capital).[59]

2. 'Social origin' may include certain geographic origins or localities

Based on this author's analysis of the reports of the Committee of Experts, 'social origin' may be evident from a person's locality or geographic origins (such as if they live in or come from a traditionally 'working class' suburb).[60] 'Social origin' discrimination may therefore also include excluding people from employment (including recruitment) because they emanate from certain geographical areas.[61]

The problem of 'post-code discrimination', which involves people being excluded from jobs based on where they live, may be an example of discrimination which is based on 'social origin'. As Chapter 4 will show, opportunities for such 'post-code discrimination' are now enhanced with the use of job advertisement targeting tools on social media.

3. 'Social origin' reflected by home and family dynamics, certain relatives and family background

Observing Colombia, the Committee of Experts noted that a phase in recruitment known as 'home visit' was used to ascertain the 'social background' of job applicants and suggested that such investigations into the social background of applicants could result in 'social origin' discrimination.[62] Social background, therefore, may be an indicium of a person's 'social origin'.

What factors reflective of a person's 'social background', however, fall within the meaning of 'social origin'? The below text will analyse reports of ILO supervisory bodies to show that 'social origin' appears to be understood

---

[59] See Capuano, 'Giving Meaning to "Social Origin"' (see Chapter 1, n 72).

[60] Ibid, 115–120.

[61] See, for example, *General Survey 2012* (n 31), 336 [804].

[62] Observation (CEACR) – adopted 2009, published 99th ILC session (2010), *Discrimination (Employment and Occupation) Convention, 1958 (No 111)* – Colombia; Observation (CEACR) - adopted 2011, published 101st ILC session (2012), *Discrimination (Employment and Occupation) Convention, 1958 (No 111)* – Colombia; Observation (CEACR) - adopted 2008, published 98th ILC session (2009), *Discrimination (Employment and Occupation) Convention, 1958 (No 111)* – Colombia.

by reference to certain factors that go to social background, such as home and family dynamics, family and relatives, and the way of life a person has cultivated from upbringing.

(a) 'Social origin' reflected by home and family dynamics

As just explained above, the Committee of Experts noted that the use of the 'home visit' phase in recruitment processes within Colombia permitted investigations into the 'social background' of applicants which could result in 'social origin' discrimination. Aspects of an applicant's social background which are revealed as a result of the 'home visit' phase could therefore be indicative of 'social origin'.

The 'home visit', or *visita domiciliaria*, has been reported to have the aim of verifying, for the purpose of assessing a person's compatibility with an organizational culture, a person's 'household composition', 'socioeconomic status', 'social space distribution', 'family and social environment' and 'personal and family behavior'.[63]

EAFIT University also provides a report on the experiences of interviewees and interviewers of 'home visits' in Colombia. An attorney interviewee claimed that the 'home visit' required the disclosure of 'personal data' as well as information about court, traffic fines, and professional family affairs.[64] A business student interviewee claimed that the 'home visit' had less to do with interviewing her than it did with analyzing space in the home and interviewing her family about her.[65] A specialist in organizational psychology who has conducted 'home visits' explains that the process seeks to understand a person's quality and standard of living, relationships at home and the way that person interacts with family through not only interviewing the applicant but people with whom the applicant coexists.[66] Therefore, determining a person's behavior in his or her family appears to be one main reason for conducting a 'home visit',[67] in addition to adducing a person's identity and

---

[63] ¿Para qué sirve la visita domiciliaria? http://www.dinero.com/negocios/articulo/para-sirve-visita-domiciliaria/43507.

[64] Una visita para conocer el entorno del aspirante http://www.eafit.edu.co/egresados/noticias/2011/Paginas/una-visita-para-conocer-el-entorno-del-aspirante.aspx (accessed 21 August 2014).

[65] Ibid.

[66] Ibid.

[67] Ibid. Also see Casallas Contreras Maria Angelica, Condia Lopez Aura Matilde, Medina Cruz Deisy Angelica, Torres Velasquez Lucelly, 'Caracterizacion de la visita domiciliaria como tecnica de intervencion de trabajo social en instituciones de salud' (Universidad De La Salle, 2006), 24 http://repository.lasalle.edu.co/bitstream/10185/12806/1/62001010.pdf.

personality, family dynamics, economic status, housing status, apparent spending behaviours as well as association (or their family's association) with criminal groups.[68]

The 'home visit' can therefore expose to an employer a person's family identity (and thus its reputation), family structure, wealth or poverty, associations, family dynamics and culture, family issues, clashing personalities or other factors that are readily gained from visiting people's homes and interviewing their family. It seems likely that all these factors may reflect 'social background' and therefore 'social origin', because they are factors which appear to be ascertained by interviewers when they conduct the 'home visit'.

As Chapter 4 of this book will argue, the use of social media in recruitment to 'cybervet' job candidates is a digitized form of the 'home visit' and thus carries similar risks of 'social origin' discrimination.

(b) 'Social origin' reflected by relatives (ancestors, parents and spouses) and family background

Whilst there have been a number of Commissions of Inquiry[69] only one has clarified the concept of 'social origin' discrimination. In the 1989 *Report of the Commission of Inquiry appointed under article 26 of the Constitution of the International Labour Organisation to examine the observance by Romania of the Discrimination (Employment and Occupation) Convention, 1958 (No. 111)* ('*Romanian Commission of Inquiry*'), the Commission found that numerous government acts amounted to discrimination based on grounds including 'social origin'. The Commission's reasoning suggests that, for reasons that will now be explained, a person can experience 'social origin' discrimination where he or she faces discrimination which is based on an ancestor, parent, spouse, or their family background.

The *Romanian Commission of Inquiry* concerned a joint complaint filed with the International Labour Office by thirteen Workers' delegates to the 76th Session of the International Labour Conference.[70] In June 1989 the Governing Body was informed of the complaint[71] which claimed that the communist Romanian government (which was led by Nicolae Ceauşescu

---

[68] Una visita para conocer el entorno del aspirante http://www.eafit.edu.co/egresados/noticias/2011/Paginas/una-visita-para-conocer-el-entorno-del-aspirante.aspx (accessed 21 August 2014).

[69] See International Labour Organization, 'Complaints/Commissions of Inquiry (Art 26)' https://www.ilo.org/dyn/normlex/en/f?p=NORMLEXPUB:50011:0::NO::P50011_ARTICLE_NO:26.

[70] *Romanian Commission of Inquiry* (n 46), para [4].

[71] *Romanian Commission of Inquiry* (n 46), para [4].

until his regime collapsed in December 1989[72]) was not observing *ILO 111*.[73] A Commission of Inquiry was appointed by the Governing Body to consider the complaint.[74] The Commission of Inquiry was chaired by Mr Jules Deschênes[75] and comprised of Mr Francesco Capotorti[76] and Mr Budislav Vukas[77] as members.

Whilst the Commission's reasons are lengthy and concern a number of issues, three separate allegations were particularly relevant to the issue of 'social origin' discrimination under *ILO 111*. These allegations related to: (1) restrictions on access to higher education; (2) applications of employment dismissal law; and (3) restrictions in accessing employment. This chapter will now analyse the Commission's reasoning and findings in relation to each of these three allegations, to clarify how the Commission appears to have understood the ground 'social origin' in *ILO 111*.

(i) Parents and ancestors

One allegation made to the Commission was that a person's access to higher education was, to varying degrees, dependent on not only that person's personal conformity with the communist ideology or political order[78] but also the conformity of his or her parents to that ideology.[79] The Commission observed:

> The criteria of political opinion and social origin were frequently combined. Thus, access to higher education was rendered more difficult, if not impossible, for certain persons, because *their parents*

---

[72] Britannica, 'Nicolae Ceaușescu' https://www.britannica.com/biography/Nicolae-Ceausescu.

[73] *Romanian Commission of Inquiry* (n 46), para [1].

[74] *Hamilton* (n 20), 389 [42] (Katz J).

[75] 'Chief Justice, Superior Court of Quebec. Lecturer in private international law, University of Montreal. Former expert of the Sub-Commission on Prevention of Discrimination and Protection of Minorities of the United Nations Commission on Human Rights.' See *Romanian Commission of Inquiry* (n 46), para [8].

[76] '[P]rofessor of international law at the Law Faculty of the University of Rome (La Sapienza). Former expert on the Sub-Commission on Prevention of Discrimination and Protection of Minorities of the United Nations Commission on Human Rights, and former judge and advocate general at the Court of Justice of the European Communities (CJEC).' See *Romanian Commission of Inquiry* (n 46), para [8].

[77] '[P]rofessor of public international law and Director of the Institute of Comparative Law at the Law Faculty of the University of Zagreb. Member of the Permanent Court of Arbitration. Member of the ILO Committee of Experts on the Application of Conventions and Recommendations.' See *Romanian Commission of Inquiry* (n 46), para [8].

[78] *Romanian Commission of Inquiry* (n 46), para [216], [580].

[79] *Romanian Commission of Inquiry* (n 46), para [580].

[emphasis added] had been members of political parties opposed to the Single Party, and for this reason, had been imprisoned, deported or exiled.[80]

On a strict and literal reading the Commission's reasoning supports the proposition that a person can experience 'social origin' discrimination where he or she is discriminated against because of the political affiliation or opinion of his or her parent.[81] Discrimination on the basis of 'political opinion', on the other hand, may be found where the person (instead of his or her parent) holds a particular political affiliation or view and as a result is dismissed or not promoted.[82] This may explain why the 'criteria of political opinion and social origin were frequently combined' and why the children of critics to the state may have suffered discrimination on the basis of 'social origin', while the critics themselves may have suffered discrimination on the basis of 'political opinion'.

When this reasoning is read with the benefit of context, however, it appears that people in Romania were denied access to higher education not simply because their parents had certain political opinions, but because their parents had engaged in acts that were socially stigmatized or negatively viewed.

In the communist Romanian political and social context non-conformity with the communist ideology resulted not only with personal stigma or guilt, but it also tainted a person's descendants. Where persons were suspected of non-conformity with the ideology or having anti-communist intentions or actions, a 'logic of collective guilt' was imposed and their families were persecuted.[83] Importantly 'Recourse was made to the utilization of aberrant criteria in order to *destroy the opportunities of children from families of "unhealthy background"* [emphasis added], preventing them from studying in higher education'.[84]

---

[80]   *Romanian Commission of Inquiry* (n 46), para [580].

[81]   Ibid. See also Henrik Karl Nielsen, 'The Concept of Discrimination in ILO Convention No. 111' (1994) 43(4) *International & Comparative Law Quarterly* 827, 836–837. Nielsen writes: 'it appears that distinctions, exclusions or preferences made on the basis of the political opinion of a person's ancestors constitute discrimination on the basis of social origin'.

[82]   *Romanian Commission of Inquiry* (n 46), para [580].

[83]   *Speech given by the President of Romania, Traian Băsescu, on the occasion of the Presentation of the Report by the Presidential Commission for the Analysis of the Communist Dictatorship in Romania* (The Parliament of Romania, 18 December 2006) http://cpcadcr.presidency. ro/upload/8288_en.pdf. See also *Romanian Commission of Inquiry* (n 46), para [372].

[84]   Traian Băsescu, Ibid http://cpcadcr.presidency.ro/upload/8288_en.pdf.

It therefore appears that, in this context, a person's non-conformity with the communist ideology was a stigmatized act which 'tainted' their descendants, thus people with such 'tainted' and 'unhealthy backgrounds' were prevented from accessing higher education.

During the relevant period the Romanian state also promoted its version of communist ideology under threat of disciplinary sanction (including terminating contracts of employment).[85] The ruling single party could 'exercise its control over all conditions of employment',[86] and the state was 'virtually the sole employer'.[87] Non-conformity with communist ideology or the single party put workers in 'grave danger of not being re-employed',[88] thus they could be convicted of 'leading a parasitic form of life'.[89] Opposing or resisting the regime could therefore result in not only marginalization, arrest, imprisonment, exile or being sent to labour camps,[90] but also conviction and social stigma as a 'social parasite'.

This context illuminates how, in communist Romania, the children of people who were members of opposition parties would likely have been tainted with an 'unhealthy background', and thus faced restrictions in accessing higher education because of the actions of their parents. Membership to opposition parties was merely one way a parent could 'taint' his or her descendants under the regime. As such, the above reasoning of the *Romanian Commission of Inquiry*, when read with the benefit of this context, supports the view that people can face 'social origin' discrimination where they are discriminated against because their ancestor or parent is socially stigmatized or negatively viewed.

The Commission's treatment of a second allegation, which related to the way dismissal law within Romania was applied, further suggests that 'social origin' is reflected by parents. The Commission referred to section 130(1)(e) of the Labour Code which permitted dismissals for an employee's failure to meet 'occupational requirements'. These requirements were, in effect, not inherent requirements of the given jobs and instead referred to behaviour, political opinions or religious beliefs which went against the

---

85 *Romanian Commission of Inquiry* (n 46), para [12].

86 *Romanian Commission of Inquiry* (n 46), para [580].

87 Katherine Verdery, *National Ideology Under Socialism: Identity and Cultural Politics in Ceausescu's Romania* (1995, University of California Press), 73.

88 *Romanian Commission of Inquiry* (n 46), para [259].

89 *Romanian Commission of Inquiry* (n 46), para [259].

90 *Speech given by the President of Romania, Traian Băsescu, on the occasion of the Presentation of the Report by the Presidential Commission for the Analysis of the Communist Dictatorship in Romania* (The Parliament of Romania, 18 December 2006) http://cpcadcr.presidency. ro/upload/8288_en.pdf. Also see Gheorghe Boldur-Lățescu, *The Communist Genocide in Romania* (Nova Science Publishers, 2005), 136.

norm.[91] For example, dismissal was used by the state (which was effectively the sole employer) as a 'penalty against certain categories of persons'[92] and the Commission relevantly observed that:

> The threat of dismissal has been used frequently to make people adopt the behaviour desired by the authorities, and pressure has been brought to bear on family members. One witness told the Commission that he was threatened with dismissal on a number of occasions if he did not try to convince his mother to cease her activities against the Government.[93]

The Commission concluded that applications of the dismissals provision permitted 'the establishment of exclusions or distinctions based in particular on political opinions or social origin'.[94] In relation to 'social origin', it appears that the Commission seemed concerned about the way the dismissals provision was used and applied to discriminate against workers on the basis of the activities of their parents.

(ii) Family background and way of life cultivated from upbringing

For the Commission of Inquiry, in light of testimony and information it received, discrimination based not only on 'political opinion' and 'religious belief' but also 'social origin' was widespread in Romanian higher education.[95] According to the Commission, the discrimination was permitted by certain regulations such as 'sections 115–123 and 148 of Act No. 28/1978 on education and training'.[96] Sections 115 to 123 of Act No. 28/1978 prescribed that students be given a communist education that was influenced in its design by the Communist Party.[97] Section 148 of that Act prescribed 'the obligations of pupils and students'[98] which required them to assimilate to the communist party's ideology and act 'in accordance with the socialist norms of behaviour in society', amongst other things.[99] Witness testimony demonstrated how this requirement to conform and assimilate with the communist ideology disadvantaged members of the Roma community based on, for reasons that will now be explained, the cultural capital which they acquired in upbringing as a result of being born into Roma families.

---

[91] *Romanian Commission of Inquiry* (n 46), para [374].
[92] Ibid, para [372].
[93] Ibid, para [372].
[94] Ibid, para [374].
[95] Ibid, para [216].
[96] Ibid, para [216].
[97] See Ibid, para [189].
[98] Ibid, para [189].
[99] Ibid, para [189].

First, based on the testimony, the state did not provide members of the Roma community 'with the normal and necessary social conditions to permit the access of members of this minority to education and culture' and teachers mistreated and discredited people from this group.[100] As a result of the social conditions implemented by the state, it seems that Roma children could not cultivate the required education and culture to comply with the requirement to conform. Thus, many of them may have been restricted in accessing higher education due to the circumstances of their upbringing which were brought about by the state. In creating policy which required higher education students to conform with the communist ideology and socialist norms of behaviour, the state was effectively imposing a policy with which many members of the Roma community could not comply as a result of the circumstances of their upbringing and insufficient cultural capital.

Second, based on further witness testimony to the Commission, even if Roma could access higher education, access to such higher education for members of this group 'meant denying their origins'.[101] The Commission, after detailing this and other testimony, then observed that '[t]he instances reported by the witnesses concern the existence of de facto inequalities which mainly affect certain persons belonging to the same ethnic group and having a different way of life from that of their fellow citizens'.[102]

It therefore appears that the requirement for conformity with the communist ideology in order to access higher education also disadvantaged members of the Roma community because, in order to comply with the requirement, they had to deny their origins or way of life cultivated from upbringing. Such way of life seems to reflect not only political or religious beliefs but also embodied cultural capital, such as 'dispositions of the mind and body' acquired from family and parents during upbringing. This may explain why, in the Commission's view, discrimination based on a combination of 'political opinion', 'religious belief' and 'social origin' was widespread in higher education.

(iii) Spouses and other relatives

The Commission's treatment of a third allegation, which related to the system of controlling access to employment and occupation,[103] supports the position that 'social origin' can be reflected by family members other than parents, such as spouses. In addition to allegations that criteria or preferences for employment were based on political opinion[104] or religion,[105] or that

---

[100] Ibid, para [219].
[101] Ibid, para [219].
[102] Ibid, para [220].
[103] Ibid, para [255].
[104] Ibid, para [261]-[266].
[105] Ibid, para [266].

minorities were excluded from employment based on their race, ethnicity or national extraction,[106] witness testimony demonstrated that access to employment was also conditional upon social background. According to one witness, criteria for employment included, amongst other things, having 'good social background'.[107] Other testimony alleged that employment of national minorities (such as Hungarians) in positions which required responsibility (such as a managerial position) 'was often made conditional on his or her having a Romanian spouse'.[108] For the Commission, the available information indicated that 'direct or indirect discrimination is practised against members of certain minorities in the matter of access to employment'.[109] Further, the Commission concluded that '[a]ccess to employment' gave rise to discrimination based not only on political opinion, religion, national extraction or race, but also 'social origin'.[110] This conclusion, in light of the testimony, suggests that a person's social background, and in particular their spouse, may also be indicative of 'social origin'.

The *Romanian Commission of Inquiry*, read as a whole and with the benefit of context, therefore appears to support the view that 'social origin' discrimination may occur when a person experiences discrimination which is based on that person's parent, ancestor, family background, way of life cultivated from upbringing, and/or spouse. The Commission's reasoning often entangles 'social origin' with other attributes (such as political opinion, religion, race, etc) and the above analysis has attempted to provide clarity by disentangling this reasoning to illuminate how 'social origin' is distinct from, but also connected with, these other attributes.

From this discussion, it appears that 'social origin' has a technical meaning that can relate to a person's present situation and it does not seem to be restricted to historical factors. This suggests that the notion of 'origin' in the term 'social origin' does not confine the measurement of a person's 'social origin' by reference to historical considerations or circumstances in the past (such as family history or ancestry), but it may also include a person's present circumstances (such as family, home dynamics, present cultural capital) and relationships (such as parents, family and spouses).

B. The multiple additive nature of 'social origin' discrimination

'Additive' discrimination might occur when a person faces discrimination based on multiple attributes at the same time and 'each type of discrimination

---

[106] Ibid, para [268]–[269].
[107] Ibid, para [265].
[108] Ibid, para [271].
[109] Ibid, para [275].
[110] Ibid, para [285].

can be proved independently'.[111] Fredman calls this 'additive multiple discrimination'.[112]

In *Special Survey* 1996 the Committee of Experts noted 'social origin can also give rise to a presumption of certain political opinions which may work either to the advantage or to the disadvantage of the persons concerned; this can also be seen to be true in the case of religion, race and colour'.[113]

This statement by the Committee of Experts recognizes that a person's 'social origin' – their 'class', for example – can give rise to certain presumptions about that person's political opinion. For instance, a person from a working-class background may be assumed – as they often are – to support unions and workers parties. It may also be possible for this to work in the inverse. For instance, an aboriginal woman engaged in a union march may be assumed to have a particular class or social background because she is aboriginal, a woman, an active union member, or, a woman aboriginal unionist. A person may therefore be assumed to have a certain 'social origin' because of their political opinion. This may mean a person could face multiple additive discrimination based on both 'political opinion' and 'social origin' at the same time.

In certain contexts, attributes (race, colour, ethnicity, national extraction, sex and/or political opinion) may also raise presumptions about a person's 'social origin' – their class and social background. There may therefore be opportunities for multiple additive discrimination based on class, social background and these other attributes. For example, due to the social and economic disadvantages of Australian First Nations Peoples as a group, a First Nations Person may, due to their racial appearance, be presumed to have a particular class or level of economic, social and cultural capital which may be the focus of discrimination.

C. The intersectional nature of 'social origin' discrimination

The Committee of Experts, as the below analysis will show, tends to discuss five attributes in-tandem with its comments on 'social origin': race, colour, ethnicity, national extraction and sex. This multidimensional character of discrimination is evident in feminist arguments that it is impossible to extract 'one dimension of social differentiation (i.e. gender) from its constitutive relationship with

---

[111] Sandra Fredman, 'Intersectional discrimination in EU gender equality and non-discrimination law' (May 2016, Report, European Commission), 7, 27.

[112] Ibid, 7, 27.

[113] Special Survey 1996 (n 30), para [44]. See further N Valticos and G von Potobsky, *International Labour Law* (Kluwer Law and Taxation Publishers, 1995), 120; N Valticos, *International Labour Law* (Kluwer, 1979), 106.

other axes (i.e. "race", class, sexuality, nation)'.[114] In particular, this position is eloquently put in the following paragraph:

> As Avtar Brah (1996: 19) argues, 'structures of class, racism, gender and sexuality cannot be treated as "independent variables" because the oppression of each is described in the other – is constituted by and is constitutive of the other'. In Brah's view, 'it is imperative that we do not compartmentalize oppressions, but instead formulate strategies for challenging all oppressions on the basis of an understanding of how they interconnect and articulate' ([Brah] ibid: 12; see also Brah and Phoenix, 2004; Crenshaw, 1989, 1991; McCall, 2005).[115]

This avoidance of 'compartmentalising oppressions' appears to capture the way that 'social origin' has been discussed by the Committee of Experts (as will be explained below) because, in its various comments, a person's 'social origin' sometimes appears to be interconnected with other attributes – their race, ethnicity, colour, national extraction, sex, age or disability. These attributes may muddle together to create compounding disadvantages. The intersections between 'social origin' and other attributes, such as race, ethnicity, religion and political opinion, are also evident in the reasoning of the *Romanian Commission of Inquiry* which is analysed above.

The intersection between 'social origin', race, colour and ethnicity also seems apparent in the application of 'social origin' discrimination principles to indigenous people in Australia,[116] the Congo,[117] Paraguay[118]

---

[114] Sylvia Chant and Carolyn Pedwell, 'Women, gender and the informal economy: An assessment of ILO research and suggested ways forward' (Discussion paper, International Labour Organization, 2008) http://www.cpahq.org/cpahq/cpadocs/wcms091228.pdf, 7.

[115] Ibid.

[116] See Observation (CEACR) - adopted 2013, published 103rd ILC session (2014), *Discrimination (Employment and Occupation) Convention, 1958 (No 111)* – Australia; Observation (CEACR) - adopted 2011, published 101st ILC session (2012), *Discrimination (Employment and Occupation) Convention, 1958 (No 111)* – Australia; Direct Request (CEACR) - adopted 2010, published 100th ILC session (2011), *Discrimination (Employment and Occupation) Convention, 1958 (No 111)* – Australia; Observation (CEACR) - adopted 2019, published 109th ILC session (2021), *Discrimination (Employment and Occupation) Convention, 1958 (No 111)* – Australia.

[117] Direct Request (CEACR) - adopted 2011, published 101st ILC session (2012), *Discrimination (Employment and Occupation) Convention, 1958 (No 111)* – Congo.

[118] Direct Request (CEACR) - adopted 2011, published 101st ILC session (2012), *Discrimination (Employment and Occupation) Convention, 1958 (No 111)* – Paraguay; Direct Request (CEACR) - adopted 2009, published 99th ILC session (2010), *Discrimination (Employment and Occupation) Convention, 1958 (No 111)* – Paraguay.

and Honduras,[119] the Roma in Europe,[120] the Creole community in Mauritius[121] and other ethnic minorities in Colombia.[122] Focus on addressing compounding inequalities faced by historically and presently disadvantaged social groups to improve their situation[123] suggests a transformational aim consistent with an intersectional approach to discrimination.

Referring to this author's analysis of the way the ILO Committee of Experts has applied 'social origin' discrimination principles, the majority of the Constitutional Court of South Africa has observed that this author's work notes 'the intersectional nature of social origin-based discrimination' and how this type of discrimination 'overlaps with discrimination against groups who are already vulnerable due to their race, ethnicity, nationality, and so on'.[124] The majority was, in particular, referring to this author's discussion of the way discrimination against First Nations Peoples in Australia 'overlaps with their race, class and social origin'.[125]

This author's discussion to which the court referred concerned an analysis of the ILO Committee of Experts' expression of concern that First Nations Peoples in Australia faced discrimination based on social origin, colour and race.[126] This concern seemed to relate to the Australian government's Northern Territory Emergency Response ('NTER') which had been

---

[119] Direct Request (CEACR) - adopted 2011, published 101st ILC session (2012), *Discrimination (Employment and Occupation) Convention, 1958 (No 111)* – Honduras; Direct Request (CEACR) - adopted 2009, published 99th ILC session (2010), *Discrimination (Employment and Occupation) Convention, 1958 (No 111)* – Honduras.

[120] Direct Request (CEACR) - adopted 2013, published 103rd ILC session (2014), *Discrimination (Employment and Occupation) Convention, 1958 (No 111)* – Latvia; Direct Request (CEACR) - adopted 2011, published 101st ILC session (2012), *Discrimination (Employment and Occupation) Convention, 1958 (No 111)* – Portugal; Direct Request (CEACR) - adopted 2010, published 100th ILC session (2011), *Discrimination (Employment and Occupation) Convention, 1958 (No 111)* – Latvia. Also see Direct Request (CEACR) - adopted 2012, published 102nd ILC session (2013), *Discrimination (Employment and Occupation) Convention, 1958 (No 111)* – Hungary; Direct Request (CEACR) - adopted 2008, published 98th ILC session (2009), *Discrimination (Employment and Occupation) Convention, 1958 (No 111)* – Latvia.

[121] Direct Request (CEACR) - adopted 2013, published 103rd ILC session (2014), *Discrimination (Employment and Occupation) Convention, 1958 (No 111)* – Mauritius.

[122] Observation (CEACR) - adopted 2012, published 102nd ILC session (2013), *Discrimination (Employment and Occupation) Convention, 1958 (No 111)* – Colombia.

[123] See, for example, Observation (CEACR) - adopted 2020, published 109th ILC session (2021), *Discrimination (Employment and Occupation) Convention, 1958 (No 111)* – Mauritius.

[124] *Centre for Child Law v Director General: Department of Home Affairs and Others* (CCT 101/ 20) [2021] ZACC 31, para [76] ('*Centre for Child Law*') citing Capuano, 'Giving Meaning to "Social Origin"' (see Chapter 1, n 72), 117–118.

[125] Centre for Child Law (n 124), fn 61 citing Capuano, 'Giving Meaning to "Social Origin"' (see Chapter 1, n 72), 117–118.

[126] Capuano, 'Giving Meaning to "Social Origin"' (see Chapter 1, n 72), 117.

introduced in 2007.[127] The NTER was implemented to address the sexual abuse of children and it involved a 'blanket imposition' of policies in prescribed areas which affected indigenous communities.[128] This includes the 'compulsory acquisition of leases over land held by Indigenous communities', imposing an 'income management regime quarantining certain welfare payments so that they could only be spent on food and other essential items', imposing 'obligations to install filters on publicly-funded computers', and 'restrictions and bans on alcohol' and 'pornography'.[129]

It may be unclear whether the NTER involved discrimination on the basis of race alone (although this opinion was held by some[130]), or class alone, or locality alone. But, once these attributes are taken together at the one intersecting axis, it seems to become more apparent that the NTER, in targeting certain indigenous communities in the Northern Territory (where indigenous people suffer from alarmingly high poverty rates and have low average incomes[131]) may have involved discrimination at the synergy of class, social origin, and race. According to this author:

> The NTER stereotyped people within Aboriginal communities by arbitrarily applying measures to those people in an attempt to address the sexual abuse of children within those communities. People living within those communities were therefore targeted on the basis of where they lived, rather than on the basis of whether they were a genuine risk to children.[132]

Whilst discrimination based on race alone may not have been readily apparent, intersectionality helps to bring into focus disadvantages and discrimination at the intersection of race, class and social origin. Race, class and social origin in these circumstances, it can be argued, could be seen to interact. To borrow Fredman's words in relation to her observation of intersectionality in Roma, Sinti and Traveller communities in Europe, this interaction may 'create multiple synergies of disadvantage' and discrimination manifests at the intersection of these three axes.[133]

---

[127] Ibid, 117–118.

[128] Ibid, 118.

[129] Ibid, 118.

[130] See, for example, Ibid, 118.

[131] Altman writes that in the Northern Territory almost 45 per cent of indigenous households are below the poverty line and the 'average Indigenous weekly income was just 26 per cent of the rate of other Territorians'. See Jon Altman, 'Deepening Indigenous poverty in the Northern Territory' (14 November 2017, Australian National University, School of Regulation and Global Governance) https://regnet.anu.edu.au/news-events/news/7002/deepening-indigenous-poverty-northern-territory.

[132] Capuano, 'Giving Meaning to "Social Origin"' (see Chapter 1, n 72), 119.

[133] Fredman (n 111), 42.

Interestingly, when the Committee of Experts mentions women in its comments on 'social origin' it has focused on economically and socially disadvantaged women[134] such as migrant workers,[135] sex workers,[136] Afro-Colombian and indigenous women[137] as well as 'rural, young and indigenous women, women of African descent, older women and women living with HIV/AIDS'.[138] The need of the Committee of Experts to focus on women, when it could have simply referred to *people* from such segments of the population, suggests that in certain contexts disadvantages based on class, social background, gender and sex intersect and overlap. It is worth noting that the Committee of Experts mention of older women and women with HIV in Honduras appears to recognize that age and disability, respectively, also intersect with sex, gender and class to create synergies of disadvantage.

The above analysis of the reports of ILO supervisory bodies not only reflects the intersectional nature of 'social origin' discrimination, and the way it overlaps with discrimination based on other attributes, but also that it is context dependent. Each of the groups mentioned above, in the respective countries in which they are mentioned, is associated with social and economic disadvantage or certain stereotypes. 'Social origin' discrimination can, therefore, be shaped by the context in which it operates.

D. Applications in the digital age

Based on the above analysis, the prohibition on 'social origin' discrimination in ILO jurisprudence includes prohibiting discrimination which is based on a person's class (as measured by economic, social and cultural capital), locality and geographic origins, and, factors reflective of social background (such as home and family dynamics, certain relatives including parents and spouses, family background and way of life cultivated from upbringing).

---

[134] Direct Request (CEACR) - adopted 2012, published 102nd ILC session (2013), *Discrimination (Employment and Occupation) Convention, 1958 (No 111)* – Bangladesh. Also see Direct Request (CEACR) - adopted 2009, published 99th ILC session (2010), *Discrimination (Employment and Occupation) Convention, 1958 (No 111)* – Saint Vincent and the Grenadines.

[135] Direct Request (CEACR) - adopted 2013, published 103rd ILC session (2014), *Discrimination (Employment and Occupation) Convention, 1958 (No 111)* – Mauritius.

[136] Direct Request (CEACR) - adopted 2012, published 102nd ILC session (2013), *Discrimination (Employment and Occupation) Convention, 1958 (No 111)* – Bangladesh.

[137] Observation (CEACR) - adopted 2012, published 102nd ILC session (2013), *Discrimination (Employment and Occupation) Convention, 1958 (No 111)* - Colombia.

[138] Direct Request (CEACR) - adopted 2009, published 99th ILC session (2010), *Discrimination (Employment and Occupation) Convention, 1958 (No 111)* – Honduras.

On this interpretation, the legal frameworks in both *ILO 111* and *ILO158* concerning 'social origin' discrimination have particular applications in the digital age for reasons which will be outlined here, and elaborated upon in Chapters 4, 5 and 6.

First, as explained in detail in Chapter 4, certain uses of social media by employers may carry particular risks of class and social background discrimination (as constituents of 'social origin' discrimination). For example:

- an employer's use of social media to screen candidates for a job ('cybervetting') carries particular risks of discrimination based on social and embodied cultural capital, and, a person's family and relatives;[139]
- an employer's use of certain targeted ad platforms (such as through Facebook and LinkedIn) may create risks of discrimination based on a person's economic capital, geographic origins and locality;[140]
- where an employer terminates an employee's employment based on certain beliefs which the employee shares on social media, this may create risks of discrimination based on embodied cultural capital and way of life cultivated from upbringing.

Second, as explained in detail in Chapter 5, an employer's use of automated candidate screening technologies may create risks of class and social background discrimination (as constituents of 'social origin'). For example, an employer's use of:

- contextual recruitment systems ('CRS') may involve, or create risks of, discrimination based on a person's locality or geographic origins, socio-economic background and/or family background;[141]
- 'hiretech' AI which utilize asynchronous video interviews ('AVIs') or 'on demand' interviews may create risks of discrimination based on embodied cultural capital;[142]
- gamification in recruitment may create risks of discrimination at the intersection of 'social origin' and disability.

Third, as explained in detail in Chapter 6, the post-pandemic shift to remote work and homeworking may disadvantage employees at the intersection of various attributes and 'social origin' (particularly home and family dynamics).

---

[139] See Chapter 4.
[140] See Chapter 4.
[141] See Chapter 5.
[142] See Chapter 5.

IV. The relevance of ILO jurisprudence to domestic contexts: 'social origin' in Australian and South African law should be interpreted consistently with the way the term is understood in *ILO 111*

'Social origin' is also a ground of discrimination in Australian and South African law. In Australia, two statutes list 'social origin' as a ground of discrimination. Section 351 of the *Fair Work Act* 2009 (Cth) (*'FW Act'*) prohibits adverse action because of 'social origin' and section 772 of that Act prohibits termination of employment based on 'social origin'. The *Australian Human Rights Commission Act* 1986 (Cth) (*'AHRC Act'*) contains a mechanism to deal with complaints of 'social origin' discrimination in employment.[143] In South Africa discrimination in employment based on 'social origin' is prohibited by the Constitution, the *Employment Equity Act* 1998 ('EEA') and the *Labour Relations Act* 1995 ('LRA').[144]

The legal frameworks and domestic case law relating to this ground of discrimination in Australian and South African law will be analysed in Chapter 3. The purpose of this part of Chapter 2 is to explain why ILO jurisprudence on 'social origin' matters to understanding the ground in the domestic law of Australia and South Africa. Based on legal rules of interpretation which will now be explained, the term 'social origin' within these domestic laws of both Australia and South Africa should be interpreted consistently with the way the term is understood in *ILO 111*.

A. The relevance of ILO jurisprudence to understanding 'social origin' in Australian law

Whilst legislation in Australia lists 'social origin' as a ground of discrimination the term is not defined in any of these pieces of legislation or clarified in extrinsic materials to these Acts. It will now be argued that it is most consistent with legislative intent that the term 'social origin' in the *FW Act* and the *AHRC Act* have the same meaning which the term bears in ILO conventions (as explained above).

First, the term 'social origin' in section 772 of the *FW Act* and within the definition of 'discrimination' in the *AHRC Act* is derived from or based on the term in ILO conventions.[145] Whilst it is not definitive that 'social origin'

---

[143] See further Chapter 3.
[144] See further Chapter 3.
[145] See Capuano, 'Giving Meaning to "Social Origin"' (see Chapter 1, n 72). The term 'social origin' in the *AHRC Act* is derived from ILO 111: See Explanatory Memorandum, Human Rights and Equal Opportunity Commission Bill 1985 (Cth), 3–4.

in s 351 of the *FW Act* derives from ILO conventions (although this seems likely),[146] it 'is a sound rule of construction to give the same meaning to the same words appearing in different parts of a statute unless there is reason to do otherwise'.[147] There appears to be no reason to do otherwise than to give 'social origin' in sections 351 and 772 of the *FW Act* a consistent meaning.[148] This is so despite the different constitutional foundations of the provisions,[149] which are explained in Chapter 3.

Second, because the term 'social origin' in the *FW Act* and *AHRC Act* derives from, or is based on, the term in ILO conventions, it is most consistent with legislative intent that the term 'social origin' should have the same meaning that the term bears in the conventions and to give it that meaning rules of treaty or convention interpretation should be used.[150] It is also explicit from the legislation that 'social origin' in the *AHRC Act* should have the same meaning which it has in *ILO 111*.[151]

Third, relying on rules of convention interpretation, given that 'social origin' in ILO conventions is ambiguous and obscure certain extrinsic materials may be used to determine its meaning.[152] Extrinsic materials include the preparatory works or *travaux preparatoires* of a treaty,[153] but the 'international case law ("la jurisprudence") and the writings of jurists ("la doctrine")' have also been viewed as admissible by the courts to help aid the interpretation of conventions.[154]

In *Commonwealth v Hamilton* ('*Hamilton*')[155] Justice Katz held that using the reports of an ILO Commission of Inquiry is 'an unexceptional illustration of the use of "la jurisprudence"'[156] and using the opinions of the Committee

---

[146] See Capuano, 'Giving Meaning to "Social Origin"' (see Chapter 1, n 72), 90–91.

[147] *Registrar of Titles (WA) v Franzon* (1975) 132 CLR 611, 618 (Mason J, with Barwick CJ and Jacobs J agreeing).

[148] See *Fair Work Ombudsman v Foot & Thai Massage Pty Ltd (in liquidation) (No 4)* [2021] FCA 1242, para [680] (Katzmann J) ('*Foot & Thai Massage*'); Capuano, 'Giving Meaning to "Social Origin"' (see Chapter 1, n 72), fn 52.

[149] See *Foot & Thai Massage* (n 148), para [680] (Katzmann J).

[150] See Capuano, 'Giving Meaning to "Social Origin"' (see Chapter 1, n 72), 91 citing *Applicant A v Minister for Immigration and Ethnic Affairs* (1997) 190 CLR 225, 230–1 (Brennan CJ), which cited *Koowarta v Bjelke-Petersen* (1982) 153 CLR 168, 265 (Brennan J); *Chan v Minister for Immigration and Ethnic Affairs* (1989) 169 CLR 379, 413 (Gaudron J). See also *Comptroller-General of Customs v Pharm-A-Care Laboratories Pty Ltd* [2020] HCA 2, para [35] (Kiefel CJ, Bell, Gageler, Keane and Gordon JJ); *FCS17 v Minister for Home Affairs* [2020] FCAFC 68; 276 FCR 644, para [59] (White and Colvin JJ).

[151] See *AHRC Act*, ss 3(1) (definition of 'convention') and 3(8).

[152] *VCLT*, Arts 31–32.

[153] *VCLT*, Art 32.

[154] See Capuano, 'Giving Meaning to "Social Origin"' (see Chapter 1, n 72), fn 61.

[155] (2000) 108 FCR 378.

[156] *Hamilton* (n 20), para [44] (Katz J).

of Experts 'is an unexceptional illustration of the use of "la doctrine"'.[157] In Australian courts, not only are these sources considered admissible but they have been held to be 'important guides to the proper construction of ILO conventions'.[158] This also includes reports of ILO supervisory bodies which came into existence after the passage of relevant legislation, and it is not just limited to material which pre-dates legislation.[159] Australian courts have consistently used the reports of the Committee of Experts[160] and Commissions of Inquiry[161] when interpreting ILO conventions or terms which are derived from, or based on, these conventions. This includes judgments which use the reports of the Committee of Experts when interpreting 'social origin' in the *FW Act*.[162]

B. *The relevance of ILO jurisprudence to understanding 'social origin' in South African law*

Much like Australia, South Africa's labour law landscape has also been shaped by the ILO.[163] It is particularly evident from the interpretative provisions of the Constitution, *EEA* and *LRA*, as well as South African case law, that, for reasons that will be explained, 'social origin' in these instruments should be interpreted consistently with the way the term is conceived in ILO jurisprudence.

First, based on a reading of the interpretative provisions within the *EEA*, *LRA* and constitution it appears that the term 'social origin' within these

---

[157] *Hamilton* (n 20), para [39] (Katz J).

[158] Capuano, 'Giving Meaning to "Social Origin"' (see Chapter 1, n 72), 93 citing *Hamilton* (n 20), 388 [39] (Katz J).

[159] See Commonwealth v Bradley (1999) 95 FCR 218 (Black CJ) and Hamilton (n 20), 388 [39] (Katz J) cited in Capuano, 'Giving Meaning to "Social Origin"' (see Chapter 1, n 72), 94.

[160] See, for example, *Qantas Airways Ltd v Christie* (1998) 193 CLR 280, 304–5 [72]–[74] (McHugh J), 316 [106] (Gummow J), 339–40 [163] (Kirby J); *Hamilton* (n 20), 387–90 [36]–[45] (Katz J); *Commonwealth v Bradley* (1999) 95 FCR 218, 237 [39] (Black CJ); *Konrad v Victoria* (1999) 91 FCR 95, 113–14 [57]–[59] (Finkelstein J); *Zhang v Royal Australian Chemical Institute Inc* (2005) 144 FCR 347, 352 [29] (Lander J), with whom Spender and Kenny JJ agreed: at 348 [1] (Spender J), 348 [2] (Kenny J); *Claveria v Pilkington Australia Ltd* (2007) 167 IR 444, 468–9 [105]–[106] (Kenny J); *Foot & Thai Massage* (n 148), para [735] (Katzmann J).

[161] See, for example, *Qantas Airways Ltd v Christie* [1998] HCA 18; 193 CLR 280, para [74] (McHugh J); *Hamilton* (n 20), para [44] (Katz J).

[162] See *Foot & Thai Massage* (n 148), [735]; *Vergara v Bunnings Group Ltd* [2022] FedCFamC2G 818, para [60]-[61] ('*Vergara*').

[163] Judge B Waglay, 'The impact of the International Labour Organization on South African labour law', in Stefan Van Eck, Pamhidzai Bamu and Chanda Chungu (eds), *Celebrating the ILO 100 Years On: Reflections on Labour Law from a Southern African Perspective* (2020, Juta and Company), 29.

instruments is intended to be interpreted in compliance with South Africa's international obligations, specifically ILO conventions. The *EEA* must be interpreted 'in compliance with the international law obligations of' South Africa, 'in particular those contained in' ILO 111.[164] The preamble to the *EEA* also states that it was enacted in order to give effect to the obligations of South Africa as a member of the ILO. The *LRA* must be interpreted 'in compliance with the public international law obligations of' South Africa.[165] Whilst the interpretative provision in the *LRA* does not explicitly refer to ILO conventions, the *LRA* 'makes clear that it is intended to give legislative effect to international treaty obligations arising from the ratification of' ILO conventions and 'South Africa's international obligations are thus of great importance to the interpretation of the Act'.[166] When interpreting the *LRA* South African courts have used *ILO 158*[167] and, interestingly, despite South Africa not having ratified it, *ILO 158* has been held to be 'an important and influential point of reference in the interpretation and application of the LRA' (it has also been observed that chapter VIII of the LRA, in which the term 'social origin' is found, draws heavily on *ILO 158*).[168] Additionally, an object of the *LRA* is to give effect to South Africa's obligations as a member of the ILO.[169]

Both the *LRA*[170] and the *EEA*[171] must also be interpreted in compliance with the Constitution. Importantly, section 233 of the Constitution states: '[w]hen interpreting any legislation, every court must prefer any reasonable interpretation of the legislation that is consistent with international law over any alternative interpretation that is inconsistent with international law'. As such, when interpreting the *LRA* and *EEA* an interpretation which is consistent with international law should be preferred, so long as that interpretation is reasonable. Further, section 39 of the South African Constitution, which concerns the interpretation of the *Bill of Rights* (which contains the prohibition against 'social origin' discrimination), relevantly provides that '[w]hen interpreting the Bill of Rights, a court, tribunal or

---

[164] *EEA*, s 3(d).

[165] *LRA*, s 3(c).

[166] *National Union of Metal Workers of South Africa and Others v Bader Bop (Pty) Ltd and Another* (CCT14/02) [2002] ZACC 30, para [26] (O'Regan J) ('*Bader Bop*').

[167] See, for example, *Mackay v ABSA Group and Another* (C 487/98) [1999] ZALC 116, paras [14]-[18] (Mlambo J); *De Klerk v Cape Union Mart International (Pty) Ltd* (C 620/2011) [2012] ZALCCT 22, paras [33]-[37] (Steenkamp J).

[168] *Avril Elizabeth Home for the Mentally Handicapped v Commission for Conciliation Mediation and Arbitration and Others* (JR782/05) [2006] ZALCJHB 19 (A Van Niekerk AJ).

[169] *LRA*, s 1(b).

[170] *LRA*, s 3(b).

[171] *EEA*, s 3(a).

forum must consider international law' and 'may consider foreign law'. ILO conventions are important sources of international law.[172]

Second, bearing in mind that 'social origin' in these South African laws should be interpreted consistently with the country's international obligations under ILO conventions, South African case law supports the position that the expressions of opinion of ILO supervisory bodies may usefully clarify the content of these obligations.[173]

In relation to interpreting Chapter VIII of the *LRA* (the chapter in which, as just noted, the term 'social origin' is found), in *Avril Elizabeth Home for the Mentally Handicapped v Commission for Conciliation Mediation And Arbitration and Others*[174] Van Niekerk AJ said:

> The observations and surveys by the ILO's Committee of Experts on Convention 158 are equally important [as the Convention] as a point of reference in the interpretation of Chapter VIII of the LRA ... since they give content to the standards that the Convention establishes. This is particularly so in the present instance because ... Chapter VIII ... draw[s] heavily on the wording of Convention 158.[175]

The Constitutional Court of South Africa has also used reports of ILO expert bodies to clarify the content of ILO conventions, and in turn other provisions of the *LRA* and constitution.

In *National Union of Metal Workers of South Africa and Others v Bader Bop (Pty) Ltd and Another*[176] the Constitutional Court heard an application for leave to appeal from a decision of the Labour Appeal Court ('LAC'). The key question was whether a union and its members were entitled to lawfully strike in order to persuade an employer to recognize the union's shop stewards. The LAC held that this strike action was unlawful, but the majority of the Constitutional Court held that the decision of the LAC failed to sufficiently take into account, amongst other matter, considerations that arose from discussing relevant ILO conventions.[177] The jurisprudence of the ILO's Committee of Experts and Freedom of Association Committee was held to be 'directly relevant to the interpretation both of the relevant

---

[172] See, for example, *South African National Defence Union v Minister of Defence (CCT27/98)* [1999] ZACC 7, para [25] (O'Regan J); *Bader Bop* (n 166), para [28] (O'Regan J).

[173] See further Waglay (n 163), 29; Tungamirai Kujinga and Stefan van Eck, 'The Right to Strike and Replacement Labour: South African Practice Viewed from an International Law Perspective' (2018) 21 PER / PELJ 2, 5.

[174] (JR782/05) [2006] ZALCJHB 19.

[175] *Avril* (n 168).

[176] (CCT14/02) [2002] ZACC 30.

[177] *Bader Bop* (n 166), para [39] (O'Regan, with Chaskalson CJ, Langa DCJ, Goldstone J, Kriegler J, Madala J, Mokgoro J, Ngcobo J, Sachs J and Yacoob J concurring).

provisions of the' LRA and 'of the Constitution'.[178] The majority relied on the reports of these committees to find that although the relevant ILO conventions did not mention the right to strike, this right was essential to collective bargaining.[179] As such, the majority held that where employers and unions have a right to engage in collective bargaining on a matter then 'the ordinary presumption would be that both parties would be entitled to exercise industrial action in respect of that matter'.[180] On this interpretation, the recognition of 'shop stewards is a legitimate subject matter for bargaining and industrial action'.[181]

In relation to the *EEA*, when discussing the *EEA*'s prohibition on discrimination based on 'social origin' the Labour Appeal Court has referred to *General Survey 1988* of the ILO Committee of Experts and this author's analysis of this report to define discrimination based on this ground.[182] This follows other uses of the reports of the ILO Committee of Experts to help interpret terms in the *EEA* which derive from *ILO 111*, such as an inherent job requirement.[183]

The above analysis has shown that the term 'social origin' in the *LRA*, *EEA* and *Bill of Rights* should be interpreted consistently with South Africa's obligations under ILO conventions, and that the courts use the reports of expert committees of the ILO to clarify the content of these obligations. It therefore follows that the ILO jurisprudence on 'social origin' discussed above in this chapter can, and should, be used to aid the interpretation of the ground 'social origin' in these South African laws.

C. The significance of ILO jurisprudence on 'social origin' in other countries

Whilst the analysis of ILO jurisprudence in this chapter is particularly useful in Australia and South Africa for the reasons just explained, its analysis has broad international significance. Other countries prohibit discrimination

---

[178] *Bader Bop* (n 166), para [33] (O'Regan J, with Chaskalson CJ, Langa DCJ, Goldstone J, Kriegler J, Madala J, Mokgoro J, Ngcobo J, Sachs J and Yacoob J concurring).

[179] *Bader Bop* (n 166), paras [27]-[32] (O'Regan J, with Chaskalson CJ, Langa DCJ, Goldstone J, Kriegler J, Madala J, Mokgoro J, Ngcobo J, Sachs J and Yacoob J concurring).

[180] *Bader Bop* (n 166), para [43] (O'Regan J, with Chaskalson CJ, Langa DCJ, Goldstone J, Kriegler J, Madala J, Mokgoro J, Ngcobo J, Sachs J and Yacoob J concurring).

[181] *Bader Bop* (n 166) (O'Regan J, with Chaskalson CJ, Langa DCJ, Goldstone J, Kriegler J, Madala J, Mokgoro J, Ngcobo J, Sachs J and Yacoob J concurring).

[182] See *Tshwane University of Technology v Maraba and Others (JA110/2019)* [2021] ZALAC 25, para [13], fn 4 (Savage AJA, Coppin JA and Molefe AJA agreeing) ('*Tshwane*').

[183] See *Allpass v Mooikloof Estates (Pty) Ltd t/a Mooikloof Equestrain Centre (JS178/09)* [2011] ZALCJHB 7, para [56]; *Independent Municipal and Allied Trade Union and Another v City of Cape Town (LC521/03)* [2005] ZALC 10, para [101].

based on 'class' (such as Taiwan), 'social class' (such as Venezuela and Vietnam), 'social origin' (such as Chile, Kenya, Morocco, Portugal, Slovakia, Uganda, and Ukraine), 'social condition' (such as Argentina and Mozambique), and other similar grounds of discrimination are contained within the laws of other jurisdictions.[184] With the exception of Taiwan, all these named jurisdictions are signatories to *ILO 111*. In a work of this size, it is not possible to analyse the law in all these jurisdictions. However, this book's discussion of ILO jurisprudence and its examination of the risks of class and social background discrimination that may arise from an employer's use of social media,[185] algorithms and AI as recruitment tools,[186] and remote working and platform work[187] will likely to also be of interest in these countries and internationally.

Conclusion

This chapter clarified the content of the ground 'social origin' in ILO conventions, in particular *ILO 111*. The reports of ILO supervisory bodies and the preparatory works to *ILO 111* were used as aids to help elucidate the convention text.

The analysis of these materials in this chapter showed that the concept of 'social origin' has a specific meaning that is distinct from a number of other protected attributes, and, that it has been expressly defined to include three constituent elements: (1) class; (2) caste; and (3) socio-occupational category. The analysis of these materials also revealed that ILO supervisory bodies appear to measure 'social origin' by reference to a number of factors that reflect social background – home and family dynamics, certain relatives (such as parents and spouses), family background, and way of life cultivated from upbringing. 'Social origin' discrimination may also, based on this analysis, include discrimination which is based on certain geographic origins of a person.

In relation to 'class', this author's analysis of the reports of the Committee of Experts[188] and preparatory works to *ILO 111* suggests that 'class', as a constituent element of 'social origin', is measured by reference to a person's economic, social and cultural capital. This view of 'class' aligns with the class theory of Pierre Bourdieu.

---

[184] See DLA Piper, 'Guide to Going Global: Employment' (Full Handbook, 2020) https://www.dlapiperintelligence.com/goingglobal/employment/handbook.pdf.

[185] See Chapter 4.

[186] See Chapter 5.

[187] See Chapter 6.

[188] See Capuano, 'Giving Meaning to "Social Origin"' (see Chapter 1, n 72).

With this meaning of 'social origin' in mind, the chapter also gave examples of 'social origin' discrimination at the single-axis, and discussed the additive and intersectional nature of this type of discrimination in ILO jurisprudence. Applications of this ILO jurisprudence in the digital age were outlined to draw attention to inequalities and risks of discrimination based on class and social background (and therefore 'social origin') that arise from an employer's use of social media,[189] algorithms and AI as recruitment tools,[190] and, the post-pandemic shift to remote work and homeworking.[191]

Finally, the chapter addressed whether the ILO jurisprudence on 'social origin' analysed within it has relevance in domestic contexts. For the reasons explained in detail in this chapter, it argued that this jurisprudence is likely to be an important aid to construing the meaning of the term 'social origin' in certain domestic laws of Australia and South Africa.

---

[189] See further Chapter 4.
[190] See further Chapter 5.
[191] See further Chapter 6.

3

Mapping the Legal Landscape in Australia, South Africa, Canada and New Zealand and its Applications in the Digital Age

Introduction

The analysis of ILO jurisprudence in Chapter 2 revealed that discrimination in employment based on class and factors that reflect social background is prohibited as part of the prohibition on 'social origin' discrimination in ILO conventions, particularly *ILO 111*. It also highlighted that the ILO jurisprudence on 'social origin' examined in Chapter 2 can, and should, be used to aid the interpretation of the ground 'social origin' in the domestic laws of Australia and South Africa.

This chapter delves further into the analysis of domestic law, to explore whether and the extent to which discrimination based on class and factors reflective of social background is prohibited in four common law countries. Parts I and II map the legal landscapes in Australia and South Africa respectively, to clarify the concept of 'social origin' discrimination in the law of each country and whether this domestic jurisprudence is consistent with the ILO jurisprudence analysed in Chapter 2. The analysis in Part I also includes discussion of other listed grounds within state and/ or territory anti-discrimination legislation in Australia. Part III maps the legal landscape in Canada, to clarify the concepts of 'social condition' and 'family status' discrimination. Finally, Part IV maps the legal landscape in New Zealand, to clarify the concept of 'family status' discrimination. The analysis in all four parts of this chapter will show that whilst 'class' and 'social background' are not listed as grounds of discrimination in legislation within these four countries, the listed grounds just mentioned reflect notions of class and/or factors that go to social background. The analysis will also direct attention to how the law in each country may have certain applications in the digital age.

I. The Australian legal landscape and its applications in the digital age

Part I of this chapter will map the legal landscape in Australia to explore the extent to which discrimination in employment based on class and/or factors reflective of social background is prohibited at the federal, state and territory level. Whilst discrimination based on 'class' and 'social background' are not expressly contained within legislation as grounds of discrimination, the below analysis will show that a number of listed grounds of discrimination either include or reflect class and/or factors reflective of social background. It will, further, outline how discrimination based on these grounds have particular applications in the digital age. The grounds of 'social origin' (in Commonwealth law), 'accommodation status' (in the law of the Australian Capital Territory) and association discrimination (in the law of various states and territories) will be examined.

A. 'Social origin' discrimination

At the federal level, two statutes address discrimination in employment based on 'social origin'. The *Fair Work Act* 2009 (Cth) (*'FW Act'*) prohibits: (1) termination of employment based on 'social origin';[1] (2) 'adverse action' because of 'social origin';[2] and (3) including terms which discriminate based on 'social origin' in modern awards[3] and enterprise agreements.[4] The *Australian Human Rights Commission Act* 1986 (Cth) ('AHRC Act') contains a mechanism to deal with complaints of 'social origin' discrimination in employment.[5]

This chapter will explain the legal frameworks that are relevant to, firstly, termination of employment and adverse action in the *FW Act*, and, secondly, discrimination in the *AHRC Act*.

1. 'Adverse action' and 'termination of employment' under the FW Act

Section 351(1) of the *FW Act* prohibits an employer taking 'adverse action' against an employee or prospective employee 'because of the person's' 'social

---

[1]   *FW Act*, s 772.
[2]   *FW Act*, s 351(1).
[3]   See *FW Act*, s 153(1).
[4]   See *FW Act*, s 194(a). Section 195(1) of the *FW Act* defines 'discriminatory term'.
[5]   See Part I(A)(2) of this chapter.

origin' and other specified grounds. 'Adverse action' includes an employer dismissing an employee, injuring an employee in his or her employment, altering an employee's position to the employee's detriment, discriminating between an employee and other employees, and/or refusing to employ a prospective employee, amongst other things.[6] This protection is found within Part 3–1 of the *FW Act*, which is titled 'general protections'.

Section 772 of the *FW Act* prohibits an employer from terminating an employee's employment for one or more specified reasons, or for reasons including one or more of these specified reasons. Under section 772(1)(f) one specified reason is 'social origin', amongst other listed grounds. These unlawful termination protections are found within Part 6–4 of the *FW Act*.

The *FW Act* contains exceptions to adverse action and termination of employment, including an inherent requirements exception. Section 351(1) of the *FW Act* does not apply to action that is 'taken because of the inherent requirements of the particular position concerned'.[7] Section 772(1) 'does not prevent a matter', such as 'social origin', 'from being a reason for terminating a person's employment if … the reason is based on the inherent requirements of the particular position concerned'.[8]

Complaints of 'adverse action' and unlawful termination on the basis of 'social origin' under the *FW Act* can be litigated, and if 'the court is satisfied that a person has contravened, or proposes to contravene, a civil remedy provision'[9] (sections 351(1) and 772(1) of the *FW Act* are 'civil remedy provisions'[10]), it may 'make any order the court considers appropriate'[11] including injunctions, compensation and reinstatement.[12] The courts may also, on application, order a person who has contravened these provisions to pay an appropriate pecuniary penalty.[13]

Whilst the *FW Act* prohibits both adverse action and termination of employment based on 'social origin', for reasons which will now be explained, workers in Australia who wish to bring claims of 'social origin' discrimination can only, at present, rely on the protection from termination of employment in s 772 of the *FW Act*.

---

[6] See *FW Act*, s 342.

[7] *FW Act*, s 351(2)(b).

[8] *FW Act*, s 772(2)(a). See, for example, *Keys v Department of Disability, Housing & Community Services* [2011] FCA 1424, para [60] (Bennett J); *Sue Jacobs v Adelaide Theosophical Society Inc. (New Dimensions Bookshop)* [2022] FWCFB 79, para [88].

[9] *FW Act*, s 545.

[10] *FW Act*, s 539.

[11] *FW Act*, s 545.

[12] *FW Act*, s 545(2).

[13] *FW Act*, s 546. See further Beth Gaze and Belinda Smith, *Equality and Discrimination Law in Australia: An Introduction* (2017, Cambridge University Press), 246.

The general protections in the *FW Act* (which include the prohibition on adverse action in s 351(1)) rely mainly on the corporations[14] and territories head of power in the Australian constitution,[15] and on the Commonwealth's 'power to make laws with respect to Commonwealth places'.[16] Given these constitutional underpinnings, the coverage of the general protections is limited in two important ways which will now be explained.

First, the general protections apply to persons including national system employers and employees[17] (concerning action by foreign corporations, or trading or financial corporations formed within the Commonwealth,[18] the Commonwealth,[19] Territory employers,[20] amongst other specified actions in s 338). Whilst many employees in Australia work for a national system employer, some do not.[21]

Second, an exception to adverse action in s 351(2)(a) of the *FW Act* provides that section 351(1) does not apply to action that is 'not unlawful under any anti-discrimination law in force in the place where the action is taken'.[22] Under s 351(3) 'anti-discrimination law' includes four Commonwealth anti-discrimination statues,[23] and the anti-discrimination statutes of each Australian state[24] and territory.[25] The *AHRC Act* is not mentioned in this subsection, and is therefore not to be regarded as an anti-discrimination law for the purposes of section 351(2)(a) of the *FW Act*.

An action is 'not unlawful' under an anti-discrimination law listed in section 351(3) if the law does not prohibit that action (that is, it is not expressed to be unlawful), and the term 'not unlawful' 'is not confined to "express defences, carve outs, exemptions and authorisations"' in these laws.[26] Given that anti-discrimination law (as defined in s 351(3) of the *FW*

---

[14] See Australian Constitution, s 51(xx) which allows the Commonwealth Parliament to make laws with respect to 'foreign corporations, and trading or financial corporations formed within the limits of the Commonwealth'.

[15] See Explanatory Memorandum, Fair Work Bill 2008 (Cth), para [1348].

[16] Ibid, para [1348].

[17] See *FW Act*, ss 14, 337–339; Fair Work Bill 2008, Explanatory Memorandum, paras [1334], [1348].

[18] See *FW Act*, ss 12, 338(2); Australian Constitution, s 51(xx).

[19] *FW Act,* s 338(2)(b).

[20] *FW Act*, s 338(1)(e)(ii).

[21] See Fair Work Commission, 'What is a national system employer?' https://www.fwc.gov.au/what-national-system-employer.

[22] *FW Act*, s 351(2)(a).

[23] Section 351(3) of the *FW Act* lists the *Age Discrimination Act* 2004 (Cth), the *Disability Discrimination Act* 1992 (Cth), the *Racial Discrimination Act* 1975 (Cth), and the *Sex Discrimination Act* 1984 (Cth).

[24] Section 351(3) of the *FW Act* lists the *Anti-Discrimination Act* 1977 (NSW), *Equal Opportunity Act* 2010 (Vic), *Anti-Discrimination Act* 1991 (Qld), *Equal Opportunity Act* 1984 (WA), *Equal Opportunity Act* 1984 (SA), and the *Anti-Discrimination Act* 1998 (Tas).

[25] Section 351(3) of the *FW Act* lists the *Discrimination Act* 1991 (ACT) and the *Anti-Discrimination Act* (NT).

[26] See *Foot & Thai Massage* (see Chapter 2, n 148), para [762].

Act) does not presently make 'social origin' discrimination unlawful then the exception in s 351(2)(a) applies to defeat claims of adverse action because of 'social origin'.[27] This reflects that s 351 of the *FW Act* 'was not intended to expand the scope of federal, State or Territory anti-discrimination laws but to work harmoniously with them'.[28]

The absence of 'social origin' as a ground of discrimination in state and territory anti-discrimination legislation has led the courts to conclude that litigants could not rely on section 351 of the *FW Act* in claims of adverse action because of 'social origin'.[29] As this type of discrimination was 'not unlawful' under 'anti-discrimination law' in the place where the action was taken, the exception in section 351(2)(a) applied to defeat the claims.[30]

Unlike the general protections in section 351(1) of the *FW Act* which are limited by their constitutional underpinnings (as just discussed), the unlawful termination provisions in the *FW Act* 'apply to all employees in Australia'.[31] This extended coverage arises because these provisions rely on the Commonwealth's external affairs power in the Australian constitution[32] and give effect to Australia's obligations under ILO conventions.[33] When enacting section 772 of the *FW Act* the Parliament evinced an intention that employees who could not rely on section 351(1) of the *FW Act* could fall back on the unlawful termination protections.[34] This coverage includes employees who are excluded from the general protections due to the operation of the exceptions (such as section 351(2)(a)[35] which is discussed above).

---

[27] See, for example, *Foot & Thai Massage* (see Chapter 2, n 148), para [765]; *Vergara* (see also Chapter 2, n 162) para [32]–[39].

[28] *Foot & Thai Massage* (see Chapter 2, n 148), para [764]. It is also worth noting here that, for Katzmann J, the "anomaly" (that the operation of s 351(2)(a) of the *FW Act* means employees can bring action for unlawful termination of employment based on 'social origin' but not adverse action based on this same ground) 'can be explained by the different history and constitutional foundations of the unlawful termination provisions in Pt 6–4 on the one hand and the general protection provisions in Pt 3–1 on the other': para [760].

[29] See *Foot & Thai Massage* (see Chapter 2, n 148), [752], [762]; See also *Vergara* (see Chapter 2, n 162), [32]–[35], [39]. This seems consistent with the legislative intent behind the exception in s 351(2)(a) of the *FW Act*. See Supplementary Explanatory Memorandum, *Fair Work Bill* 2008 (Cth), [220] 40.

[30] See, for example, *Foot & Thai Massage* (see Chapter 2, n 148), para [765].

[31] Explanatory Memorandum, *Fair Work Bill* 2008, para [1342]. See also *Foot & Thai Massage* (see Chapter 2, n 148), para [680].

[32] See Explanatory Memorandum, *Fair Work Bill* 2008 (Cth), 213 [1342], 341 [2239], 407 [2702], 419 [2770].

[33] Explanatory Memorandum, Fair Work Bill 2008, para [2702]. See also Capuano, 'Giving Meaning to "Social Origin"' (see Chapter 1, n 72).

[34] See, for example, *FW Act*, s 723; Explanatory Memorandum, Fair Work Bill 2008, paras [1342], [2702].

[35] See, for example, *In Mr Scott McIntyre v Special Broadcasting Services Corporation T/A SBS Corporation* [2015] FWC 6768, para [37]–[38], [43]–[44] (Commissioner Cambridge).

This means that employees nationally can presently bring claims of termination of employment based on 'social origin', but not adverse action based on 'social origin' (because of the operation of the exception to adverse action in s 351(2)(a), as explained above).[36] As such, the *FW Act* only currently provides national coverage and protection from termination of employment based on 'social origin'. This will continue to be the case until anti-discrimination law, as defined in the *FW Act*, is reformed to include a prohibition on 'social origin' discrimination (for example, if a state or territory amends its anti-discrimination legislation to include 'social origin' as a prohibited ground of discrimination, people in that state or territory will be able to rely on section 351(1) of the *FW Act* as well as the state or territory's anti-discrimination legislation to bring claims of 'social origin' discrimination).

2. 'Discrimination' under the AHRC Act

Workers may also seek to rely on the *AHRC Act* to lodge complaints of 'discrimination' in employment to the Australian Human Rights Commission ('AHRC'). In the *AHRC Act* 'discrimination' is relevantly defined to include 'any distinction, exclusion or preference made on the basis of race, colour, sex, religion, political opinion, national extraction or social origin that has the effect of nullifying or impairing equality of opportunity or treatment in employment or occupation'.[37]

Under the *AHRC Act* 'discrimination' is distinct from 'unlawful discrimination', which means 'any acts, omissions or practices that are unlawful under' any of the four federal anti-discrimination statutes (for example, Part 4 of the *Age Discrimination Act* 2004 (Cth), Part 2 of the *Disability Discrimination Act* 1992 (Cth), Part II or IIA of the *Racial Discrimination Act* 1975 (Cth), and Part II of the *Sex Discrimination Act* 1984 (Cth)). Claims of 'unlawful discrimination' can be the subject of complaints to the AHRC and are reviewable by the courts.[38]

In contrast to claims of 'unlawful discrimination', complaints of 'discrimination' (such as 'social origin' discrimination) are only subject to the inquiry of the AHRC and are not reviewable by the courts. In response to a complaint of 'social origin' discrimination under the *AHRC Act*, the AHRC may 'inquire into any act or practice (including any systemic practice) that may constitute discrimination'.[39] The AHRC may also, where it considers it

---

[36] See *Foot & Thai Massage* (see Chapter 2, n 148), para [760] referring to *Rumble v The Partnership trading as HWL Ebsworth* [2019] FCA 1409, para [146].

[37] *AHRC Act*, s 3(1).

[38] See *AHRC Act*, Part IIB.

[39] *AHRC Act*, s 31(b)(i) and s 32(1)(b).

appropriate, 'endeavour, by conciliation, to effect a settlement of the matters that gave rise to the inquiry'.[40] If, after the inquiry, the AHRC 'is of the opinion that the act or practice constitutes discrimination' it 'may report to the Minister in relation to the inquiry'.[41] Where it makes a finding that an 'act or practice constitutes discrimination', the AHRC may also give written reasons for those findings and make 'recommendations', such as the 'payment of compensation'.[42] However, these 'recommendations are not … enforceable'.[43]

The *AHRC Act* includes defences to 'discrimination' which employers may seek to rely upon in response to complaints, such as an inherent requirements defence. Under the *AHRC Act* 'discrimination' 'does not include any distinction, exclusion or preference … in respect of a particular job based on the inherent requirements of the job'.[44]

(a) The scope of 'discrimination' in the AHRC Act

Given the definition of 'discrimination' in the *AHRC Act* derives from *ILO 111* it is most consistent with legislative intent that the term should have the same meaning as the term bears in the convention as determined by using rules of convention interpretation.[45] The reports of ILO supervisory bodies are (and most certainly should be[46]) used by the courts to elucidate the proper meaning of terms, such as 'discrimination', in *ILO 111* and therefore the *AHRC Act*.[47]

In *Hamilton* Justice Katz used the reports of ILO supervisory bodies to clarify that 'discrimination' in *ILO 111* and therefore the *AHRC Act* extends to indirect discrimination.[48] 'Indirect discrimination', for the purposes of the definition of 'discrimination' in the *AHRC Act*, was interpreted consistently with the way the concept is understood by the ILO Committee of Experts[49] (that is, it occurs when: (1) a neutral practice or condition; (2) results with unequal treatment or is disproportionately harsh on some people on the basis of protected characteristics (such as 'social origin'); and (3) they are not closely related to the inherent requirements of a job.[50]

---

[40] *AHRC Act*, s 31(b)(ii).
[41] *AHRC Act*, s 32A.
[42] *AHRC Act*, s 35(2).
[43] Australian Human Rights Commission, *Federal Discrimination Law* (Online Handbook, 2016). 5 [1.3.2].
[44] *AHRC Act*, s 3.
[45] See Chapter 2; *Hamilton* (see Chapter 2, n 20), paras [30]–[31] (Katz J).
[46] See Chapter 2.
[47] See *Hamilton* (see Chapter 2, n 20), para [45] (Katz J).
[48] See *Hamilton* (see Chapter 2, n 20), para [45] (Katz J).
[49] See *Hamilton* (see Chapter 2, n 20), paras [35]–[45].
[50] See further Chapter 2. See also *Hamilton* (see Chapter 2, n 20), para [58].

In other legislation in Australia the definition of indirect discrimination includes a 'reasonableness' test which requires that a requirement, practice or condition be unreasonable,[51] but such a test (which operates as a defence or exception) does not appear to be a feature of the definition in ILO jurisprudence.[52] It would be a 'forensic error' to use definitions in other pieces of legislation to inform the meaning of 'discrimination' in the *AHRC Act*,[53] particularly because Acts which give effect to international conventions (the *AHRC Act* is the 'vehicle under which Australia's obligations under' *ILO 111* are to 'be implemented'[54]) are 'consequently bound to apply the definitions which the convention contains'.[55] As such, it appears that the concept of 'indirect discrimination' for the purposes of 'discrimination' in *ILO 111* (and therefore section 3 of the *AHRC Act*) is defined broadly to capture practices or conditions which are not closely related to the inherent requirements of a job and disproportionately impact people on the basis of 'social origin'.

Additionally, with the above in mind, it can be argued that 'discrimination' in the *AHRC Act* should also, consistently with the way the term is understood in ILO jurisprudence, cover all stages of the recruitment process (that is, job advertisements, screening, selecting for interview and hiring).[56] The AHRC has also treated 'discrimination' as covering access to employment, consistent with the way the term is understood in *ILO 111*.[57]

3. Judicial interpretations of the ground 'social origin' in Australian labour law

A number of judgments have considered complaints of 'social origin' discrimination under the *FW Act*[58] or complaints of termination of employment

---

[51]   See, for example, Capuano, 'Post-Pandemic Workplace Design' (see Chapter 1, n 154), 893. The reasonableness test in the definition of indirect discrimination in anti-discrimination legislation within Australia, as argued elsewhere by this author, has numerous problems of application in the post-pandemic world and requires reform: at 900–4.

[52]   See *Hamilton* (see Chapter 2, n 20), para [54]–[59] (Katz J).

[53]   See *Hamilton* (see Chapter 2, n 20), para [72] (Katz J).

[54]   Explanatory Memorandum, *Human Rights and Equal Opportunity Commission Bill 1985* (Cth), 1 [2]. The *Human Rights and Equal Opportunity Commission Act 1986* was subsequently renamed the *AHRC Act*. See *Leach v Burston* [2022] FCA 87, para [98], [110]. The Human Rights and Equal Opportunity Commission ('HREOC') changed its name to the AHRC in 2009. See *Disability Discrimination and Other Human Rights Legislation Amendment Act 2009* (Cth), sch 3.

[55]   See *Yager v R* [1977] HCA 10 (Mason J).

[56]   See Chapter 2.

[57]   See, for example, *Ms Jessica Smith v Redflex Traffic Systems Pty Ltd* [2018] AusHRC 125, paras [22]-[23]; *AV v Dial-an-Angel Pty Ltd* [2015] AusHRC 97, paras [29]–[30].

[58]   See *Vergara* (see Chapter 2, n 162); *Ms Karen Lee Cook v St Vincent De Paul Society Victoria* [2022] FWC 1440, para [14] ('*Cook*') (which concerned an application for an unfair

based on 'social origin' under predecessor instruments to this Act.[59] Only four of these judgments, which will be analysed below, illuminate the meaning of 'social origin' in Australian labour law. It should be recalled here that, as explained above, claims of 'social origin' discrimination under the *AHRC Act* are only subject to the inquiry of the AHRC and they are not reviewable by the courts. As at the time of writing, there do not appear to be any inquiries or reports of the AHRC available to the public that deal with 'social origin' discrimination.[60]

For reasons explained in detail in Chapter 2, it seems most consistent with legislative intent that the term 'social origin' in both the *FW Act* and the *AHRC Act* should have the same meaning that the term bears in ILO conventions. The ILO jurisprudence discussed in Chapter 2 of this book can, and should, for reasons explained in that chapter, be used to aid the interpretation of 'social origin' in ILO conventions, and therefore the *FW Act* and the *AHRC Act*. As such, it is proposed that 'social origin' in the *FW Act* and *AHRC Act*, consistently with the way the term is understood in the ILO jurisprudence discussed in Chapter 2, includes 'class' (as measured by economic, social and cultural capital), certain geographic origins, and, factors reflective of 'social background' (such as family and home dynamics, relatives such as parents and spouses, family background, and way of life cultivated from upbringing).[61]

(a) 'Social origin' includes class as measured by economic, social and cultural capital

Interestingly, there is a growing body of case law in Australia which supports the position that 'social origin' includes class and that class should be measured

---

    dismissal remedy under the *FW Act*); *Foot & Thai Massage* (see Chapter 2, n 148); *Roos v Winnaa Pty Ltd* [2017] FWC 3737; *Campbell v Aero & Military Products Pty Ltd* [2015] FCCA 2310; *McDonald v Civic Disabilities Services Ltd* [2014] FCCA 1464, para [31].

[59] See *Bahonko v Sterjov* [2007] FCA 1244 ('*Bahonko*'); *O'Hara v Victoria (Department of Education and Training)* [2006] FCA 420 (in which the applicant made a claim under s 170CK of the *Workplace Relations Act* 1996 (Cth) alleging that he was dismissed for reasons including his 'social origin', but apart from summarizing the claims of the applicant the judgment did not discuss the concept of 'social origin'). Additionally, *Nikolich v Goldman Sachs J B Were Services Pty Ltd* [2006] FCA 784 involved, amongst other things, a claim under s 170CK of the *Workplace Relations Act* 1996 (Cth) alleging unlawful termination of employment because of a mental disability or the applicant's temporary absence from work due to illness. Justice Wilcox said at paragraph [194] that 'social origin' is an 'immutable' rather than 'temporary' attribute (such as pregnancy, some disabilities etc). No further guidance was however provided on the meaning of 'social origin' by Justice Wilcox, thus the judge does not add anything of substance about 'social origin' apart from reasoning that it is immutable. See also *Janice Shackley v Australian Croatian Club Ltd* (1995) 61 IR 430.

[60] See Australian Human Rights Commission, 'Reports to the Minister under the AHRC Act' https://humanrights.gov.au/our-work/legal/projects/human-rights-reports.

[61] See further Chapter 2.

by reference to Bourdieu's species of capital – economic, social and cultural capital. This is evident in two recent decisions which will now be analysed in detail, *Fair Work Ombudsman v Foot & Thai Massage Pty Ltd (in liquidation) (No 4) ('Foot & Thai Massage')*[62] and *Ms Karen Lee Cook v St Vincent De Paul Society Victoria ('Cook')*.[63]

Before analyzing these two decisions it is important to note here that the position that 'social origin' in the *FW Act* includes class also finds support in another recent judgment, *Vergara v Bunnings Group Ltd*[64] (*'Vergara'*). In *Vergara* to determine the meaning of 'social origin' in the *FW Act* the court had regard to interpretations of the term in reports of the ILO Committee of Experts[65] which define 'social origin' by reference to factors including class.[66] The court then concluded that there was 'much force' to the submission that 'social origin' relates to social stratification,[67] but beyond this the concept of 'social origin' was not usefully explored.[68]

(i) Foot & Thai Massage

In *Foot & Thai Massage* the Fair Work Ombudsman ('FWO') brought proceedings on behalf of seven workers who were recruited from the Philippines to work for Foot & Thai Massage Pty Ltd (in liquidation) ('FTM') as massage therapists.[69] The workers were sponsored by FTM under a temporary work visa (then a subclass 457 visa) which entitled the workers to enter Australia for a limited period and work for an approved business.[70] FTM owned and operated a massage shop located in the ACT.[71]

The FWO alleged, amongst other things, that FTM had taken adverse action against the workers (that is, injuring the employees in their employment[72]) because of their race, national extraction, and/or 'social origin'.[73] The workers were alleged to have been injured in their employment

---

[62] [2021] FCA 1242.
[63] [2022] FWC 1440.
[64] [2022] FedCFamC2G 818.
[65] *Vergara* (see Chapter 2, n 162), para [59].
[66] See *Vergara* (see Chapter 2, n 162), paras [60]–[61].
[67] *Vergara* (see Chapter 2, n 162), para [62].
[68] No decisions which interpret 'social origin' in the *FW Act*, including *Foot & Thai Massage* (see Chapter 2, n 148) and *Cook* (n 58), were brought to the attention of the court. See *Vergara* (see Chapter 2, n 162), para [49]. The reasoning in *Vergara* concerning 'social origin' is vague: see paras [30], [51]–[54].
[69] *Foot & Thai Massage* (see Chapter 2, n 148), paras [1]–[4].
[70] See *Foot & Thai Massage* (see Chapter 2, n 148), para [240].
[71] *Foot & Thai Massage* (see Chapter 2, n 148), paras [34], [235].
[72] *Foot & Thai Massage* (see Chapter 2, n 148), para [674].
[73] *Foot & Thai Massage* (see Chapter 2, n 148), para [52].

by certain acts of the employer. This included the employer failing to pay them minimum hourly, public holiday and overtime rates, failing to pay them annual leave entitlements on termination of employment, requiring them to make fortnightly cash repayments, failing to pay them in full due to unauthorized deductions,[74] requiring or requesting that they 'work unreasonable additional hours' and threatening to send them back to the Philippines or kill their families if they complained to anyone about their working conditions.[75] Justice Katzmann held that these actions satisfied the definition of 'adverse action' in that it was beyond doubt that they were injuries in the workers' employment or 'threats to injure them in their employment'.[76]

A question for the court was whether this adverse action was taken for reasons which included the 'social origin' of the workers.[77] The FWO pleaded that the workers had a number of characteristics, including that they:[78]

(a) were born and lived in a country with low socio-economic circumstances relative to Australia;
(b) were each sponsored on a 457 visa and therefore dependent on [FTM] … to stay in Australia;
(c) had English as their second language;
(d) were not educated in Australia and were unaware of their legal rights;
(e) were socially isolated from the broader Australian community by virtue of them residing in [a house] … where the gates were locked overnight and being directed not to talk to anyone about their working conditions; and
(f) had financially dependent family members back in the Philippines and regularly remitted funds back to the Philippines to support them.

On the question of 'social origin' the FWO pleaded that by reason of these characteristics the workers:

had the 'social origin' of a 'vulnerable worker on a temporary subclass 457 visa recruited to work in Australia from a lower

---

[74] On the facts, it was alleged that certain deductions were made from the wages of the workers and described as 'staff loans' on their pay slips, when FTM could not prove that any the exceptions in section 324(1) of the *FW Act*, which allow workers to be paid less than in full, applied. See *Foot & Thai Massage* (see Chapter 2, n 148), paras [507]–[518]. Section 323(1)(a) of the *FW Act* provides that '(1) [a]n employer must pay an employee amounts payable to the employee in relation to the performance of work: (a) in full (except as provided by section 324)'. Section 324 of the *FW Act* then sets out permitted deductions.

[75] *Foot & Thai Massage* (see Chapter 2, n 148), para [674].

[76] *Foot & Thai Massage* (see Chapter 2, n 148), para [684].

[77] *Foot & Thai Massage* (see Chapter 2, n 148), para [697].

[78] See *Foot & Thai Massage* (see Chapter 2, n 148), para [697], [741].

socio economic South East Asian country' for the purposes of section 351(1) of the FW Act.

Particulars

A. The term 'social origin' refers to somebody's socio-occupational or 'sociooccupational category' and is measured by the lack of a person's economic, social, cultural or human capital.[79]

Justice Katzmann accepted that the 'social origin' of each of the workers 'can fairly be described in the way the Ombudsman pleaded the matter, namely that of a vulnerable worker on a temporary subclass 457 visa recruited to work in Australia from a lower socio-economic South East Asian country'.[80]

Justice Katzmann noted that '"[s]ocial origin" discrimination was defined by the ILO Committee of Experts on the Application of Conventions and Recommendations to include discrimination because of class, caste or socio-occupational category'.[81] Her Honour noted that it can reasonably be inferred that 'social origin' is intended to have its ordinary meaning given that the term is not defined in the legislation.[82] Justice Katzmann's reasoning, which will now be analysed in detail, suggests that 'social origin' was measured by reference to economic, social and cultural capital.

First, Justice Katzmann accepted that 'the place and circumstances of their birth'[83] and 'the circumstances in which they came to Australia'[84] were 'aspects of the social origins of the' workers.[85] In relation to the *place and circumstances* of their birth, the workers were born in the Philippines[86] which is, relative to Australia, a poor country.[87] In relation to the *circumstances in which the workers came to Australia*, the workers appear to have left the Philippines for Australia primarily for economic reasons. Whilst in the Philippines the

---

[79] *Foot & Thai Massage* (see Chapter 2, n 148), para [697]. It is worth noting that the particulars use, word for word, this author's proposed definition of 'social origin' which is based on an analysis of the reports of the ILO Committee of Experts. See Capuano, 'Giving Meaning to "Social Origin"' (see Chapter 1, n 72), 85, 128. In the interests of full disclosure, in October 2019 Lead Counsel for the FWO in *Foot & Thai Massage*, Michael Seck, via email requested and was provided with this author's research on 'social origin' discrimination for the purposes of this matter.

[80] *Foot & Thai Massage* (see Chapter 2, n 148), para [748].

[81] *Foot & Thai Massage* (see Chapter 2, n 148), para [735], citing General Survey 1988 (see Chapter 2, n 28), para [54].

[82] *Foot & Thai Massage* (see Chapter 2, n 148), para [676].

[83] *Foot & Thai Massage* (see Chapter 2, n 148), [747] (Katzmann J).

[84] *Foot & Thai Massage* (see Chapter 2, n 148), para [747].

[85] *Foot & Thai Massage* (see Chapter 2, n 148), para [747].

[86] *Foot & Thai Massage* (see Chapter 2, n 148), para [58].

[87] See the pleadings of the FWO on this point: *Foot & Thai Massage* (see Chapter 2, n 148), para [697].

workers each earned sums between $140 and $300 per month,[88] they were told by the director of FTM that he was advertising for full-time massage therapists in Australia at a salary of $52,000 per year (with paid holidays, free accommodation, amongst other benefits).[89] Some of the workers were interested in the position because it would significantly increase their income.[90] It appears that the workers therefore came to Australia to escape their circumstance of poverty and lack of economic capital. Therefore, it seems that the economic capital (or lack thereof) and vulnerability of the workers was, in their particular circumstances, indicia of their 'social origin'.

Second, Justice Katzmann accepted that the fact 'that they are not native English speakers and were educated in the Philippines' was 'also relevant to' the 'social origins' of the workers.[91] In the context of the pleadings of the FWO, education was relevant to the capacity of the workers to understand their legal rights. Lack of such education reflects the limited cultural capital of the workers, which made them vulnerable to exploitation by the employer.

Third, Justice Katzmann reasoned that the family circumstances of the workers could be relevant to their social origins where they indicate that the workers 'did not come from wealth and their families were dependent on them for financial support'.[92] This relates not just to the lack of economic capital of the workers themselves (as mentioned above), but, also, that of their family. It therefore suggests that the economic circumstances of a person's family (for example, being financially dependent on the person) and upbringing (for example , not coming from wealth) may reflect 'social origin'. This demonstrates how social capital (or lack thereof), in the form of the level of resources which are available through family, appears to have been viewed as relevant to 'social origin'.

Fourth, Justice Katzmann held that the employer knew of the social origins of the workers, particularly their 'socio-economic background' and 'precarious residential status'.[93] This clearly shows that, for Her Honour, these two factors – socio-economic background and precarious residential status – were direct evidence of the social origin of the workers.

It is particularly interesting to note that Her Honour chose to measure 'social origin' by reference to socio-economic *background*, rather than status or position. This suggests that 'social origin' may be concerned with socio-economic circumstances that relate to, or result from, a person's 'background',

88 See *Foot & Thai Massage* (see Chapter 2, n 148), paras [59], [63], [71], [72], [73].
89 *Foot & Thai Massage* (see Chapter 2, n 148), para [64], [75].
90 *Foot & Thai Massage* (see Chapter 2, n 148), para [75].
91 *Foot & Thai Massage* (see Chapter 2, n 148), para [747].
92 *Foot & Thai Massage* (see Chapter 2, n 148), para [747].
93 *Foot & Thai Massage* (see Chapter 2, n 148), para [749].

such as family,[94] upbringing[95] or origin.[96] On the facts, the workers in *Foot & Thai Massage* were born in a poor Asian country, they came from poor families which relied upon them for financial support, and they lacked an Australian education. The 'socio-economic backgrounds' of the workers, of which the employer had knowledge, therefore appears to have related to economic and educational disadvantages from their circumstance of birth and upbringing. It therefore seemed to reflect the (lack of) economic, educational and social resources which the workers had available to them through family and the people around them during upbringing (social capital).

A person's precarious residential status is a reflection of his or her lack of economic capital (that is, inability to afford stable housing and thus not being self-reliant and independent). Relevantly, on the facts the workers had lived with their supervisor[97] in houses which were owned by the sole director of their employer, FTM.[98] This appears to be an example of the 'precarious residential status' to which Her Honour was referring.

Justice Katzmann also referred to the blurred lines between race, colour, national extraction, religion and social origin.[99] This observation is consistent with the way the ground 'social origin' is understood in ILO jurisprudence, particularly reflecting on the reasoning of the *Romanian Commission of Inquiry* examined in Chapter 2. Reflecting on this and the above analysis, in *Foot & Thai Massage* 'social origin' appears to have been interpreted in a manner consistent with way the ground is understood in ILO jurisprudence.[100]

Finally, whilst Her Honour reasoned that the 'social origin' of the workers could be reflected by a number of circumstances of the past and present as explained above, she noted that 'the circumstances in which' the workers 'were placed in Australia by FTM ... do not speak to their social "origins"'.[101] This position was not explained in the judgment, but it could refer to the workers being sponsored and therefore entering Australia under a temporary work visa.

In relation to the claim of adverse action based on 'social origin', Her Honour held that:

FTM has failed to discharge its burden of proving that the social origin of the Massage Therapists was not a substantial and operative reason for

---

94   See, for example, Cambridge Dictionary, 'socioeconomic background' https://diction ary.cambridge.org/example/english/socioeconomic-background.
95   See, for example, Ibid.
96   Macquarie Dictionary, 'Background' (Online) https://www.macquariedictionary.com. au/features/word/search/?search_word_type=Dictionary&word=background.
97   *Foot & Thai Massage* (see Chapter 2, n 148), para [80].
98   *Foot & Thai Massage* (see Chapter 2, n 148), para [70], [241].
99   *Foot & Thai Massage* (see Chapter 2, n 148), para [704].
100   For an analysis of ILO jurisprudence, see Chapter 2.
101   *Foot & Thai Massage* (see Chapter 2, n 148), para [747].

the actions it took to injure the Massage Therapists in their employment. Through ... [the sole director of FTM], FTM knew of their social origins, in particular their socio–economic backgrounds and precarious residential status, and exploited these matters to its advantage.[102]

Applying the reverse onus of proof placed on employers by operation of s 361 of the *FW Act*, it was presumed that the action was taken for these reasons as FTM could not prove otherwise. It therefore appears that the workers were treated as they were, and thus suffered adverse action, because the employer knew of their lack of economic, social and cultural capital. Whilst FTM was held to have taken action against the workers because of their 'social origin', the exception to adverse action in s 351(2)(a) of the *FW Act* (which is explained above in this chapter) applied to defeat the claim. This was because 'social origin' discrimination was not unlawful in the ACT at the time of the contraventions, so, by operation of the exception, section 351(1) did not apply to the action.[103]

Whilst this exception presently operates to defeat claims of adverse action based on 'social origin' brought under section 351 of the *FW Act*, the reasoning in *Foot & Thai Massage* on the meaning of 'social origin' is useful to understanding the ground in section 772 of this Act (which, as explained above, prohibits termination of employment based on numerous grounds including 'social origin'). This is because 'social origin' in sections 351 and 772 of the *FW Act* should have the same meaning.[104]

Whilst *Foot & Thai Massage* provides some clarity on the concept of 'social origin' in the *FW Act*, this guidance has limitations. The interpretation of 'social origin' in *Foot & Thai Massage* is restricted to the specific facts of the case, so it did not tease out or explore all indicia of 'social origin', just those characteristics of the workers in the case which were relevant to the ground. Given that 'social origin' 'is to be interpreted broadly, consistently with the legislative purpose of protecting people from workplace discrimination',[105] the courts have scope to build on this reasoning.

(ii) Cook

In *Cook* an employer sought to implement government directives that employees be vaccinated against COVID-19 in order to attend the workplace. The employer was required, from 15 October 2021, to not allow

---

[102] *Foot & Thai Massage* (see Chapter 2, n 148), para [749].

[103] *Foot & Thai Massage* (see Chapter 2, n 148), [765].

[104] See *Foot & Thai Massage* (see Chapter 2, n 148), para [680]. See also Capuano (see Chapter 1, n 72), 91.

[105] *Foot & Thai Massage* (see Chapter 2, n 148), para [738]. See also *Commonwealth of Australia v Anti Discrimination Tribunal (Tasmania)* (Corrigendum 19 June 2008) [2008] FCAFC 104

employees who did not provide COVID-19 vaccination evidence to attend the workplace.[106] The applicant, who was employed by the employer since January 2020, did not provide the employer with this vaccination evidence and was therefore dismissed on 12 November 2021.[107] The matter concerned an application by the applicant for an unfair dismissal remedy under s 394 of the *FW Act*. A dismissal is unfair where it is 'harsh, unjust or unreasonable',[108] and in considering whether the applicant's dismissal was harsh, unjust or unreasonable the Fair Work Commission must take into account, amongst other things, whether there was a 'valid reason for the dismissal related to the person's capacity or conduct'.[109]

The applicant alleged that the employer did not have a valid reason for the dismissal and 'that she was dismissed on the discriminatory ground of being an 'anti-vaxxer', which [she contended] … is a social origin group'.[110] If there was unlawful discrimination 'then the dismissal would be prejudiced and the reason would not be a valid reason'.[111]

In considering the applicant's claim of 'social origin' discrimination, Commission Johns recalled both sections 351 and 772 of the *FW Act* prohibit this type of discrimination.[112] Given that the Parliament relied on *ILO 111* in 1993 when enacting the protection against termination of employment based on 'social origin', the Commissioner found that the term 'social origin' in the *FW Act* should have the same meaning that it does in *ILO 111*.[113] Importantly, the Commissioner relied on this author's analysis of the reports of the ILO Committee of Experts and proposed definition of 'class' (as a constituent element of 'social origin' in *ILO 111*) to find that '[s]ocial origin includes notions of class'.[114] The Commission then said:

> Working-class stereotypes such as 'bogan' or 'cashed up bogan' or other terms that are held up to middle-class ridicule is a way of defining

---

(13 June 2008), paras [180] – [181] citing *IW v City of Perth* [1997] HCA 30; *Konrad v Victoria Police (includes corrigendum dated 9 August 1999)* [1999] FCA 988, para [94] – [104]; *Qantas v Christie* [1998] HCA 18, para [152] (Kirby J); *Fair Work Ombudsman v Theravanish Investments Pty Ltd & Ors* [2014] FCCA 1170, para [37]; *Pavolvich v Atlantic Contractors Pty Ltd* [2012] FMCA 1080, para [26]; *Evans v Trilab Pty Ltd* [2014] FCCA 2464.

[106] *Cook* (n 58), para [2], [5].

[107] *Cook* (n 58), para [5].

[108] *Cook* (n 58), para [8], referring to s 385(b) of the *FW Act*.

[109] *FW Act*, s 387(a).

[110] *Cook* (n 58), para [3].

[111] *Cook* (n 58), para [14].

[112] *Cook* (n 58), para [15].

[113] *Cook* (n 58), para [15].

[114] *Cook* (n 58), para [16] citing Capuano, 'Giving Meaning to "Social Origin"' (see Chapter 1, n 72).

the notion of class. [citation omitted] Such stereotypes would likely fall into the notion of social origin. Access to economic, social and cultural capital can define a person's class position. Cultural capital is a complex idea. It includes 'dispositions of the mind and body' and ways of thinking. Embodied cultural capital might 'capture the properties of one's self which a person requires [sic] or cultivates during one's life'. I consider it plausible that being an 'anti-vaxxer' is a disposition of the mind and a form of cultural capital resulting in a class of people that can be considered to fall within the concept of social origin.[115]

In considering it arguable that the applicant was discriminated against on the basis of her 'social origin', Commissioner Johns concluded that the discrimination was not direct (she was 'not dismissed because she is an anti-vaxxer')[116] and so the possibility of indirect discrimination was considered.[117] Indirect discrimination was defined as an 'unreasonable rule or policy that is the same for everyone that has an unfair effect on people who share a particular attribute'.[118] On the question of whether there was indirect 'social origin' discrimination, whilst the actions of the employer 'had an adverse effect on the Applicant because of her social origin status as an anti-vaxxer', the government's directions and the employer's compliance with those directions 'was not unreasonable'.[119] As a result, the Commissioner found that the applicant was not subject to unlawful discrimination.[120]

The Fair Work Commission's reasoning in *Cook* is important because it directly adopts the meaning of 'class' (as a constituent element of 'social origin') which this author has proposed, namely that class is understood (consistently with Bourdieu's class theory) by reference to a person's economic, social and cultural capital.[121] Significantly, the Commission also accepted that cultural capital includes embodied cultural capital, such as dispositions of the mind and body as well as ways of thinking. Further, the Commission accepted that certain working-class stereotypes in Australia, such as 'bogan' or 'cashed up bogan',[122] 'would likely fall into the notion of social origin'.[123] The 'bogan', as explained in Chapter 1, can be identified by reference to their embodied cultural capital so this reasoning seems to reinforce the significance

---

[115] *Cook* (n 58), para [16].
[116] *Cook* (n 58), para [17].
[117] *Cook* (n 58), para [18].
[118] *Cook* (n 58), para [18].
[119] *Cook* (n 58), para [18].
[120] *Cook* (n 58), para [18].
[121] Capuano, 'Giving Meaning to "Social Origin"' (see Chapter 1, n 72).
[122] See further Ibid.
[123] *Cook* (n 58), para [16].

of such capital in not only forming class identity in Australia, but also being an indicium of 'social origin'.

It is interesting to note that, though this is not mentioned in the *Cook* decision, a connection has been drawn between 'anti-vaccinationism' or vaccine hesitancy and the 'working class' in Victorian England[124] and more recently the COVID-19 pandemic which commenced in 2020. Analyzing results of a survey of 2,097 adults conducted by the Kaiser Family Foundation in April 2021, the New York Times reported that 'working class' members of every surveyed racial group (white, black and Hispanic) and political affiliation (democrat and republican) were less likely to be vaccinated and more likely to be skeptical.[125] Another poll has similar findings.[126] This is reinforced by what health experts call 'social determinants of health',[127] the idea that social and contextual factors such as class and where a person grew up reflects personal health.[128] For Anita Sreedhar ('a primary-care physician in the Bronx') and Anand Gopal ('a professor at Arizona State University'), who 'research vaccine hesitancy and access around the world', during COVID-19 'the real vaccination divide is class'.[129] In light of this, in some circumstances the connection between class, social background and being an anti-vaxxer may be able to be drawn on a case-by-case basis depending on the evidence in a matter.

(b) 'Social origin' includes factors that reflect social background

As explained in Chapters 1 and 2, Bourdieu's species of capital can often overlap with and result from a person's social and family background. The above analysis of Justice Katzmann's reasoning in *Foot & Thai Massage* also demonstrates how certain indicia of 'social origin' may include both capital formulative of class, and, factors that reflect a person's social and family background. For example, these factors included the place and circumstances of birth of the workers,[130]

---

[124] See Nadja Durbach, '"They Might As Well Brand Us": Working-Class Resistance to Compulsory Vaccination in Victorian England' (2000) 13(1) *Social History of Medicine* 45.

[125] David Leonhardt, 'The Vaccine Class Gap' (24 May 2021, New York Times) https://www.nytimes.com/2021/05/24/briefing/vaccination-class-gap-us.html.

[126] See Heather Tirado Gilligan, 'Economic Factors Are Shaping Individual Vaccine Decisions, Polling Suggests' (Blog, 7 June 2021, California Health Care Foundation) https://www.chcf.org/blog/polling-suggests-economic-factors-shaping-individual-vaccine-decisions/.

[127] See, for example, World Health Organization, 'Social determinants of health' (accessed 13 August 2022) https://www.who.int/health-topics/social-determinants-of-health#tab=tab_1.

[128] Anita Sreedhar and Anand Gopal, 'Behind Low Vaccination Rates Lurks a More Profound Social Weakness' (3 December 2021, Opinion, Guest Essay, New York Times) https://www.nytimes.com/2021/12/03/opinion/vaccine-hesitancy-covid.html.

[129] Sreedhar and Anand Gopal, ibid.

[130] *Foot & Thai Massage* (see Chapter 2, n 148), [747] (Katzmann J).

the workers not coming from wealth and having family which depended on them financially,[131] as well as the 'socio-economic background' and 'precarious residential status' of the workers.[132]

The position that 'social origin' is measured by reference to factors that reflect social background also finds support in older authorities which will now be analysed.

In *Bahonko v Sterjov*[133] the applicant claimed that, amongst other things, her employment had been terminated because of a number of grounds including her 'social and ethnic origin'.[134] At the relevant time, section 170CK(2)(f) of the *Workplace Relations Act* 1996 (Cth) ('*WR Act*') prohibited termination of employment based on grounds including 'social origin'. The application relating to unlawful termination was dismissed, and a subsequent appeal to the Full Court of the Federal Court of Australia was also dismissed.[135] Special leave to the High Court of Australia was refused.[136]

Importantly, Justice Jessup dismissed the application because there was no evidence of the applicant's 'social origin' before the court:

> There was no evidence of [the applicant's] 'social origin'. The applicant gave evidence of her educational qualifications, but said nothing of her background or upbringing within society or any particular part of the community. The court knows nothing of where she grew up, of her family circumstances, of the groups with whom she associated or to whom she related, of any class-identity she may have claimed within society. For those reasons I propose to dismiss so much of the applicant's case under s 170CK(2)(f) of the WR Act as relates to political opinion and social origin.[137]

This reasoning shows that Justice Jessup seems to have regarded the following eight factors as evidence of a person's 'social origin':

- 'Background';
- 'Upbringing within society';
- Upbringing within a 'particular part of the community';
- Where a person grows up;
- A person's 'family circumstances';

---

[131] *Foot & Thai Massage* (see Chapter 2, n 148), para [747].
[132] *Foot & Thai Massage* (see Chapter 2, n 148), para [749].
[133] [2007] FCA 1244.
[134] *Bahonko* (n 59), para [94].
[135] See *Bahonko v Sterjov* [2008] FCAFC 30 (Gyles, Stone and Buchanan JJ). On appeal, the Full Court made no mention of 'social origin'.
[136] See *Bahonko v Sterjov* [2008] HCASL 403.
[137] *Bahonko* (n 59), para [102].

- The groups with whom a person associated;
- People with whom a person related; and
- '[A]ny class identity' a person claimed within society.

Most of the above factors (which Justice Jessup suggests are evidence of a person's 'social origin') are reflective of a person's 'historical social context'. Whilst His Honour also refers to a person's 'family circumstances' as evidence of 'social origin', this should now be read together with the reasoning of Justice Katzmann in *Foot & Thai Massage* (analysed above) that family circumstances may be relevant to 'social origin' where they are related to certain economic considerations.

The *Bahonko* judgment also clarifies what is *not* evidence of a person's 'social origin'. Given the view of Justice Jessup that there was no evidence of the applicant's 'social origin' before him, it follows that evidence which was before His Honour could *not* have been evidence of 'social origin'. Justice Jessup observed that the applicant was white skinned and had a European appearance.[138] His Honour also noted that '[i]t is established on the evidence that the applicant is a Christian of the Roman Catholic faith, and that she is of Polish extraction'.[139] The applicant in *Bahonko* also 'gave evidence of her educational qualifications',[140] but her qualifications related to postgraduate qualifications[141] rather than early life education (such as primary school and high school). Therefore, evidence existed of the applicant's Polish extraction, Catholic faith, racial appearance, and postgraduate qualifications. It therefore seems that, for Justice Jessup, national extraction, religion, racial appearance and postgraduate qualifications are not, on their own, evidence of 'social origin'.

It is worth noting here that in *Bahonko* Justice Jessup acknowledged that 'the exact meaning of ... [social origin] was not explored' in argument and the 'question of the applicant's 'social origin' was barely referred to in the evidence'.[142] As such, *Bahonko* only has limited consideration of the concept of 'social origin' and the ground was not explored in any detail.

Another judgment from 1994, *Merlin Gerin (Australia) Pty Ltd v Marion Wojcik* ('*Merlin Gerin*'),[143] measured 'social origin' by reference to a person's ethnic and religious acculturation. In *Merlin Gerin* the complainants, who had non-English speaking backgrounds,[144] were employed under the *Metal*

---

[138] *Bahonko* (n 59), para [161]. Interestingly, despite this observance, His Honour noted that '[t]here is no evidence about the applicant's "race"'.

[139] *Bahonko* (n 59). para [104]. See also para [161].

[140] *Bahonko* (n 59), para [102].

[141] See *Bahonko* (n 59), paras [14], [24], [35].

[142] *Bahonko* (n 59), para [102].

[143] [1994] VicSC 209 (Unreported, 29 April 1994) ('*Merlin Gerin*').

[144] *Merlin Gerin* (n 143), page 1.

Industries Award 1984 ('the Award'). Clause 6(vi) of the Award provided that termination of employment on grounds including 'national extraction and social origin' would be harsh, unjust and unreasonable.[145] The complainants alleged that they were made redundant because they were not native English speakers or because of their national extractions, social or ethnic origins.[146]

Justice Nathan considered the meaning of 'social origin' in the Award. His Honour reasoned that a person may be seen to have a particular 'social origin' where that person: (1) maintains certain social customs such as religious dress,[147] use of language or 'mother tongue', dress and diet;[148] (2) that reflect acculturation;[149] and (3) are distinct from those which prevail in the community[150] amongst the majority group.[151] A person may have a distinct 'social origin' even where the person is born in Australia[152] and it is not only self-defined but may also depend on the way a person is perceived by the majority group.[153]

Whilst this reasoning provides very little assistance in understanding what is distinct about 'social origin' (as compared with religion, race, national extraction and ethnicity), it does seem consistent with the position that 'social origin' may reflect the embodiment or manifestation of culture and traditions cultivated through socialization and upbringing (such as dress, language and diet, for example). Justice Nathan observed that '"[s]ocial origin" is wider than "national origin",[154] nationality and "national extraction"'[155] and that 'ethnic origin is encompassed by social origin',[156] but precisely how 'social origin' overlaps and differs from these other grounds was not clearly explained in the judgment.

Whilst *Merlin Gerin* has been cited in recent decisions[157] the judgment has also been held to be 'of little, if any, assistance in determining what is meant by the term "social origin" in' the *FW Act* because the judgment interprets the term as it appeared in an Award.[158] Therefore, *Merlin Gerin* should be used with great caution or not at all when interpreting 'social origin' in the *FW Act*. This is particularly so now, because recent decisions

---

145 *Merlin Gerin* (n 143), page 3.
146 *Merlin Gerin* (n 143), page 1–2.
147 *Merlin Gerin* (n 143), pages 12–13.
148 *Merlin Gerin* (n 143), page 11.
149 *Merlin Gerin* (n 143), page 11.
150 Ibid.
151 See *Merlin Gerin* (n 143), page 12–13.
152 See *Merlin Gerin* (n 143), page 12–13.
153 *Merlin Gerin* (n 143), page 11.
154 *Merlin Gerin* (n 143), page 4.
155 *Merlin Gerin* (n 143), page 12.
156 *Merlin Gerin* (n 143), page 15.
157 See, for example, *Foot & Thai Massage* (see Chapter 2, n 148), para [732].
158 *Vergara* (see Chapter 2, n 162), para [47] (Deputy Chief Judge Mercuri).

which directly interpret 'social origin' in the *FW Act* are available (*Foot & Thai Massage, Cook* and *Vergara*).

4. Applications in the digital age

Based on the above analysis, consistent with the ILO jurisprudence analysed in Chapter 2, there is a growing body of case law in Australia which supports the position that 'social origin' in the *FW Act* includes class (as measured by economic, social and cultural capital)[159] and certain factors that reflect social background. It appears that a number of factors reflective of social background are, based on this case law, indicative of 'social origin'. This includes place and circumstances of birth, family wealth (for example, not coming from wealth and having financially dependent family), socio-economic background, precarious residential status,[160] historical social context (upbringing within certain parts of the community and where a person grows up) and associations (group and personal associations).[161]

Whilst the term 'social origin' in the *AHRC Act* has not been the subject of express judicial interpretation, it can be argued that the term in both the *FW Act* and the *AHRC Act* should be interpreted consistently because, in both Acts, the term should have the same meaning as it bears in ILO conventions.[162] The developing body of case law on the meaning of 'social origin' in the *FW Act* analysed above does not rely on any unique aspects of this Act to construe the meaning of the term. Rather, it relies on, or seems consistent with, the way 'social origin' appears to be understood in ILO jurisprudence.

The developing body of case law in Australia also appears to be most consistent with legislative intent, which is that, for reasons explained in detail in Chapter 2, 'social origin' in both the *FW Act* and the *AHRC Act* should have the same meaning which the term bears in ILO jurisprudence. Therefore, consistent with ILO jurisprudence, 'social origin' may also refer to locality and geographic origins, home dynamics, family background, and certain relatives.

It is also worth noting here that 'social origin' should be defined symmetrically, and thus protect all people from this type of discrimination (not just the disadvantaged), to permit consistency with the way other neutrally drafted terms are treated by the courts.[163]

---

[159] See *Cook* (n 58) and *Foot & Thai Massage* (see Chapter 2, n 148), analysed above.

[160] See *Foot & Thai Massage* (see Chapter 2, n 148), analysed above.

[161] See *Bahonko* (n 59), analysed above.

[162] See Chapter 2. See also *Vergara* (see Chapter 2, n 162), [55]-[59].

[163] See *AB v Registrar of Births, Deaths and Marriages* [2007] FCAFC 140, para [19]-[20] (Black CJ) ('*AB*') (concerning the ground of 'marital status'); *Howe v Qantas Airways Ltd* [2004] FMCA 242, para [255] (Driver FM) (concerning the ground of 'family responsibilities').

Based on the above analysis, the legal frameworks in both the *FW Act* and the *AHRC Act* concerning 'social origin' discrimination have particular applications in the digital age. However, for reasons that will be outlined here and elaborated upon in Chapters 4, 5 and 6, these applications vary considerably given the different frameworks of each Act.

First, as explained in detail in Chapter 4, certain uses of social media by employers may carry particular risks of class and social background discrimination (as constituent elements of 'social origin' discrimination) under the *AHRC Act*. For example:

- an employer's use of social media to screen candidates for a job ('cybervetting') carries particular risks of discrimination based on social and embodied cultural capital and a person's group or personal associations, particularly family and relatives;[164]
- an employer's use of certain targeted job advertisement platforms (such as through Facebook and LinkedIn) may create risks of discrimination based on factors including a person's family wealth, circumstances of birth and historical social context (such as where a person grew up), locality and geographic origins.[165]

Second, as explained in detail in Chapter 5, an employer's use of automated candidate screening technologies may also create risks of class and social background discrimination (as constituent elements of 'social origin') under the *AHRC Act*. For example, an employer's use of:

- contextual recruitment systems ('CRS') may involve, or create risks of, discrimination based on factors including historical social context (such as where a person grew up and went to school), socio-economic background, locality, economic capital and/or social capital;[166]
- 'hiretech' AI which utilize asynchronous video interviews (AVIs) or 'on demand' interviews may create risks of discrimination based on embodied cultural capital.[167]

Third, as explained in Chapter 6, the post-pandemic shift to remote working may also disadvantage certain workers at the convergence of home dynamics

---

Neutrally drafted terms tend to be defined symmetrically unless the text, context and purpose of the relevant legislation suggests otherwise. See *AB* (n 163), paras [71], [109]–[115] (Kenny J).

[164] See Chapter 4.

[165] See Chapter 4.

[166] See Chapter 5.

[167] See Chapter 5.

and/or precarious residential status and other attributes, creating risks of 'social origin' discrimination.

Whilst, at present, the *AHRC Act* is not used frequently by workers to make complaints of 'social origin' discrimination to the AHRC,[168] there may be numerous reasons why workers do not rely on the legislation. The ground 'social origin', as explained above in this chapter, has not been well understood in Australian case law and Australian workers are even less likely to understand the ground. The detailed analysis in this book explains how 'social origin' (including 'class') discrimination is a serious problem in Australian workplaces and how it will likely be an increasing problem in the future.[169] This book may therefore assist potential complainants and employers to understand what 'social origin' means. Also, as 'class' tends to be a taboo topic in Australia which is not usually discussed openly,[170] this book would assist in destigmatizing it so it becomes a topic of discussion in discrimination law and workplaces.

Whilst the above practices may create risks of 'social origin' discrimination under the *AHRC Act*, for reasons which are explained above complaints of 'social origin' discrimination to the AHRC made under this Act can only result with non-binding recommendations and are not reviewable by a court (for the Act to truly be the 'vehicle' which implements Australia's obligations under *ILO 111* as Parliament intended, its compliance mechanisms require considerable strengthening). Complainants may therefore prefer to rely on the *FW Act* to bring claims of 'social origin' discrimination (either under section 351 for adverse action or, if they are not covered by section 351, then section 772 for termination of employment) because of, amongst other things, the availability of possible remedies (as explained above). Problematically, however, the *FW Act* has limited application to addressing 'social origin' discrimination in the digital age, for reasons which will now be explained.

(a) Limitations of the *FW Act* and proposed law reform

This book examines a number of practices in the digital age to show how they each create risks of 'social origin' discrimination under the *AHRC Act* and *ILO 111*. This includes examining the use of cybervetting and

---

[168] See, for example, Australian Human Rights Commission, '2021–22 Complaint statistics' https://humanrights.gov.au/sites/default/files/ahrc_ar_2021-2022_complaint_stats_0.pdf.

[169] See Chapters 1, 4, 5 and 6.

[170] See, for example, Jessica Gerrard and Steven Threadgold, 'The concept of class is often avoided in public debate, but it's essential for understanding inequality' (21 November 2022, The Conversation) https://theconversation.com/the-concept-of-class-is-often-avoided-in-public-debate-but-its-essential-for-understanding-inequality-187777; Deborah Warr, Keith Jacobs and Henry Paternoster, 'Bogan Talk' in *Class in Australia* (see Chapter 1, n 119), ch 8.

targeted job advertisement tools (Chapter 4), algorithms and AI as candidate screening tools (Chapter 5), and, the post-pandemic shift to remote work as well as certain aspects of technologically driven platform work (Chapter 6). Whilst the *FW Act* also prohibits adverse action based on 'social origin', the below text will explain why this Act is not equipped to address this type of discrimination as it arises in the digital age.

Even if the exception in section 351(2)(a) of the *FW Act*, explained above, did not apply to automatically defeat claims of adverse action based on 'social origin', the *Act's* design means that it cannot be relied upon to challenge these practices, for two main reasons.

First, the definition of 'adverse action' in section 342 of the *FW Act* restricts its coverage to hiring decisions and the employment relationship, thus it does not apply to various instances of discrimination that may occur in recruitment processes (which occur before hiring decisions are made) from the use of AI, algorithms and social media as recruitment tools.

Second, when determining whether adverse action is taken for a prohibited reason (such as 'social origin') the courts must make a factual finding that it was taken for a prohibited reason or motivated by that reason.[171] The 'reason must be an "operative or immediate reason" for the action',[172] and this 'requires considering the decision-maker's mental processes'[173] and a 'finding of fact as to his or her "true reason" for the action',[174] 'true intentions'[175] or 'reasons or motivations for a decision'.[176]

Whilst in *Klein v Metropolitan Fire and Emergency Services Board*[177] ('*Klein*') Justice Gordon held that a particular form of 'adverse action' (where an employer 'discriminates') includes indirect discrimination, Her Honour was describing indirect discrimination *of a certain kind* such as where an employer chose a 'facially neutral' criterion *for a prohibited reason*.[178] Given the requirement

---

[171] See Capuano, 'Post-Pandemic Workplace Design' (see Chapter 1, n 154) citing *FW Act*, s 360; *Board of Bendigo Regional Institute of Technical and Further Education v Barclay* (2012) 248 CLR 500, 534–5 [101] (Gummow and Hayne JJ) ('*Barclay*'); Salama v Sydney Trains [2021] FCA 251, para [86] (Burley J).

[172] Capuano, Ibid, citing Explanatory Memorandum, Fair Work Bill 2008, para [1458]. See also Barclay (n 171), 535 [104] (Gummow and Hayne JJ).

[173] Capuano, 'Post-Pandemic Workplace Design' (see Chapter 1, n 154) citing Barclay (n 171), 544 [140] (Heydon J).

[174] Capuano, 'Post-Pandemic Workplace Design' (see Chapter 1, n 154) citing Construction, Forestry, Mining and Energy Union v BHP Coal Pty Ltd (2014) 253 CLR 243, 249 [9] (French CJ and Kiefel J) ('*BHP Coal*').

[175] Capuano, Ibid, citing *BHP Coal* (n 174), 249 [9] (French CJ and Kiefel J), 267 [85] (Gageler J).

[176] Capuano, Ibid, citing Barclay (n 171), 534–5 [101] (Gummow and Hayne JJ).

[177] (2012) 208 FCR 178 ('*Klein*').

[178] *Klein* (n 177), 206 [102].

in the *FW Act* that adverse action must be 'because of' a prohibited reason and the intent or mental processes of the decision-maker is relevant to that inquiry, a more general conception of 'indirect discrimination' (whereby the intention to discriminate is irrelevant) would conflict with this requirement.

The *FW Act* would therefore not be equipped to address inequalities based on 'social origin' which may arise from the use of detailed targeting in job advertisements,[179] the workings of certain recruitment algorithms and AI,[180] or homeworking.[181] Although these practices have significant opportunities for 'social origin' discrimination for reasons explained in Chapters 4, 5 and 6, it will likely be very difficult to establish that an employer adopted these seemingly neutral practices for a prohibited reason (that is, to discriminate on the basis of 'social origin'). Whilst these practices may involve the making of distinctions or disadvantage people on the basis of class and social background,[182] it would be difficult to conclusively prove that an employer adopts them for a prohibited reason or to have an adverse impact on a particular group or groups. Additionally, an employer is very unlikely to admit that this is the reason why it uses the practices. Relatedly, given that an employer can point to a multitude of 'reasons' for adopting the practices (cost and time savings, reducing human bias and error, etc), employers may often be able to rebut the reverse onus of proof which is placed upon them by section 361 of the *FW Act*.

Given that computers tend not to explain their decisions or predictions[183] the adverse action protections in the *FW Act* also risk becoming gradually irrelevant in the digital age as employer actions are increasingly made with the use of AI. For instance, where a machine learning model permits AI to make decisions or predictions from what it has 'learned' from previous tasks or historical data,[184] how is it possible to determine the reason for which the AI made that decision? If AI is used to hire or select candidates for interviews, for example, it may not be possible to determine the reason for the hiring or selection, or, whether it is based on any attribute. The reasons for adverse action may therefore be concealed in AI decision-making processes.

The design of the *FW Act*, for the reasons just explained, therefore means that the legislation is unable to address the increasing problem of 'social origin' discrimination which may arise from an employer's use of social media, algorithms and AI as recruitment tools, and, the post-pandemic shift to remote working. Workers will therefore only be able to rely on

---

[179] See Chapter 4.
[180] See Chapter 5.
[181] See Chapter 6.
[182] See Chapters 4 and 5.
[183] Christoph Molnar, *Interpretable Machine Learning* (2020, Leanpub), 315.
[184] See, for example, , Ibid, 13.

the protection from termination of employment based on 'social origin' in section 772 of the *FW Act* to challenge employment decisions which may involve this type of discrimination. Whilst this means that the *FW Act* has limited applications in the digital age, one of these applications may be to challenge an employer's decision to terminate an employee's employment for certain social media posts.[185]

Additionally, the design of the *FW Act* is a missed opportunity to strengthen Australia's response to modern slavery and address class discrimination against vulnerable migrant workers.[186] The reasoning in *Foot & Thai Massage* (analysed above) suggests that prohibiting 'social origin' discrimination may help address key structural factors that make workers vulnerable to exploitation, namely the economic dependence of these workers on sponsoring employers (for both work and the right to remain in Australia).[187] Due to the operation of the exception in section 351(2)(a) of the *FW Act*, however, workers or the FWO are presently unable to rely on the legislation in relation to claims of adverse action based on 'social origin'.

The deficiencies of the *FW Act* just mentioned, which make the legislation incapable of addressing numerous inequalities based on 'social origin' which arise in the digital age, could be addressed through law reform. First, legislators could turn their minds to expanding the definition of 'adverse action' so that it covers recruitment and selection stages before hiring. Second, legislators could also consider reforming the *FW Act* so that it prohibits 'indirect discrimination' (as it is defined in certain anti-discrimination laws) in addition to adverse action, as has already been proposed by this author[188] and Dominique Allen.[189] Finally, given that 'social origin' discrimination is a serious problem in workplaces and will likely be an increasing problem in the future,[190] states and territories in Australia could include 'social origin' as a ground of discrimination in their anti-discrimination laws (to circumvent the operation of section 351(2)(a) of the *FW Act* and issues that may arise from the complex constitutional underpinnings of the legislation, as explained above). Simply removing section 351(2)(a) from the *FW Act* may disturb these constitutional foundations of the Act.

---

[185] See further Chapter 4.

[186] See Chapter 6.

[187] See, for example, *Foot & Thai Massage* (see Chapter 2, n 148), para [740].

[188] Capuano, 'Post-Pandemic Workplace Design' (see Chapter 1, n 154), 890. It should be noted here that, as argued by this author in the article cited in this footnote, the definition of indirect discrimination should be modelled on the approach in Victorian anti-discrimination legislation and there are problems with the definition which need to be overcome.

[189] Dominique Allen, 'Adverse Effects: Can the Fair Work Act Address Workplace Discrimination for Employees with a Disability?' (2018) 41(3) *UNSW Law Journal* 846, 868.

[190] See Chapters 1, 4, 5 and 6.

B. Association discrimination

A number of states and territories prohibit 'association discrimination' which is, broadly speaking, discrimination against a person which is based on his or her association with a person who has or is perceived to have one or more specified attributes.[191] The attributes upon which association discrimination is prohibited varies between jurisdictions and include, though are not limited to, 'political belief or activity'[192] and 'religious belief or activity',[193] 'political belief or affiliation' or 'activity'[194] and 'religious belief or affiliation' or 'activity',[195] 'political conviction and 'religious conviction',[196] and 'political opinion, affiliation or activity'.[197] Under these state and territory laws employers must not discriminate when deciding who should be offered work or employment.[198]

The concept of 'association discrimination' captures part of the concept of 'social origin' discrimination, as it was interpreted by the ILO *Romanian Commission of Inquiry*[199] and Justice Jessup in *Bahonko*, because it could include discrimination which is based on the political or religious beliefs or activities of a person's associations (for example, parents). The state and territory laws which prohibit 'association discrimination', however, each list specific grounds upon which the discrimination should occur so if a person faces discrimination because of the identity of a parent, but the discrimination was based on an unlisted ground, then the association discrimination would not be unlawful in these states or territories.

'Association discrimination', particularly based on religion or political opinion, may, for reasons that are explained in Chapter 4, be an increasing issue in the digital age with the increased uptake of social media for cybervetting.

---

[191] See, for example, *Equal Opportunity Act* 2010 (Vic), s 6(q); *Anti-Discrimination Act* 1991 (Qld), s 7(p); *Discrimination Act* 1991 (ACT), s 7(c); Anti-Discrimination Act 1998 (Tas), s 16(s); *Anti-Discrimination Act* 1992 (NT), s 19(r).

[192] *Equal Opportunity Act* 2010 (Vic), ss 6(k), 6(q); *Anti-Discrimination Act* 1991 (Qld), ss 7(j), 7(p).

[193] *Equal Opportunity Act* 2010 (Vic), ss 6(n), 6(q); *Anti-Discrimination Act* 1991 (Qld), ss 7(i), 7(p) (in which the ground is 'religious belief or religious activity'); *Anti-Discrimination Act* 1992 (NT), s 19(r).

[194] *Anti-Discrimination Act* 1998 (Tas), ss 16(n)-(m) and 16(s).

[195] *Anti-Discrimination Act* 1998 (Tas), ss 16(o)-(p) and 16(s).

[196] *Discrimination Act* 1991 (ACT), s 7(c).

[197] *Anti-Discrimination Act* 1992 (NT), s 19(r).

[198] See Anti-Discrimination Act (Qld), s 14; *Equal Opportunity Act* 2010 (Vic), s 16; *Discrimination Act* 1991 (ACT), s 10(1). In Tasmania an area of activity covered by the legislation is 'employment': *Anti-Discrimination Act* 1998 (Tas), s 22(1)(a).

[199] See Chapter 2.

C. 'Accommodation status' discrimination

The Australian Capital Territory ('ACT') prohibits direct and indirect discrimination based on accommodation status[200] (which has a non-exhaustive definition[201] and it includes, amongst other things, being a tenant, homelessness, or, receiving or waiting for certain housing assistance[202]), employment status[203] (for example, being unemployed or employed part-time, as a casual, temporarily, or as a shift or contract worker, receiving a pension or social security[204]), and profession, trade, occupation or calling.[205]

Whilst all these grounds have some connection to the concept of class[206] risks of discrimination based on 'accommodation status' may, in particular, arise from the post-pandemic shift to remote work and homeworking for reasons that are explained in Chapter 6.

II. The South African legal landscape and its applications in the digital age

This chapter will now turn to map the legal landscape in South Africa to explore the extent to which discrimination in employment based on class and/or factors reflective of social background is prohibited. Whilst 'class' and 'social background' are not expressly contained within legislation as grounds of discrimination, the below analysis will show that South African law prohibits discrimination in employment based on 'social origin' and this ground has been interpreted by the courts to refer to class and social position. The courts, as the below analysis will show, have also used an intersectional lens to bring this type of discrimination into focus.[207] Further, the below text will then outline risks of this intersectional-based 'social origin' discrimination in the digital age.

A. The South African legal framework: 'social origin' discrimination

The legal framework in South Africa contains both constitutional and legislative protections against 'social origin' discrimination in employment.

---

[200] *Discrimination Act* 1991 (ACT), ss 7(a), 8.

[201] Explanatory Statement, Discrimination Amendment Bill 2016, 15.

[202] *Discrimination Act* 1991 (ACT), Dictionary.

[203] *Discrimination Act* 1991 (ACT), ss 7(f), 8.

[204] *Discrimination Act* 1991 (ACT), Dictionary.

[205] *Discrimination Act* 1991 (ACT), ss 7(p), 8. The attribute 'profession, trade, occupation or calling' has a long history in the ACT's anti-discrimination legislation and it was inserted by section 4 of the *Discrimination (Amendment) Act (No. 2)* 1994 (ACT), which commenced on 14 May 1994. This attribute is not defined in the Act.

[206] See Chapter 1.

[207] For an explanation of intersectionality and its use as an analytical tool, see Chapter 1.

This chapter will now set out the legal framework relating to these protections, to highlight the scope and coverage of the protections provided by these laws. This analysis will also reveal important contextual considerations which influence the way the concept of 'social origin' discrimination is interpreted by South African courts.

1. The prohibition on 'social origin' discrimination in the South African constitution

South Africa's past is tainted by decades of racial segregation[208], a practice extended by the National Party government which ruled from 1948 to 1994 and which named its racial segregation policies 'apartheid'.[209] As a result of internal and international pressure as well as a deteriorating economy apartheid fell, and in April 1994 South Africa had its first democratic elections under an interim constitution.[210] On 10 December 1996 the South African constitution was signed into law[211] and, as South Africa's supreme law, it sought to, amongst other things, heal the divisions of the past.[212] Apartheid left South Africa with 'many scars' and the 'cardinal fault line' of its past oppression has been described to run 'along race, class and gender'.[213]

South Africa's constitution 'ardently demands' addressing this 'social unevenness'.[214] The constitution's attempt to address such social inequalities is evidenced by, amongst other provisions, the equality provision in section 9 which prohibits unfair discrimination (including on the basis of 'social origin') and also permits measures designed to achieve substantive equality.[215] Section 9 is found within Chapter 2 of the Constitution ('*Bill of Rights*').

---

[208] See South African Government, 'History' https://www.gov.za/about-sa/history.

[209] Britannica, 'apartheid' (online) https://www.britannica.com/topic/apartheid.

[210] South African Government, 'History' https://www.gov.za/about-sa/history.

[211] Constitution of the Republic of South Africa, 1996 - Explanatory Memorandum https://www.gov.za/documents/constitution-republic-south-africa-1996-explanatory-memorandum.

[212] *Constitution of South Africa*, Preamble.

[213] *Head of Department, Mpumalanga Department of Education & another v Hoërskool Ermelo & another* 2010 (2) SA 415 (CC) cited in *Head of Department Western Cape Education Department and Others v S* (1209/2016) [2017] ZASCA 187, para [51] (Navsa ADP).

[214] *Head of Department, Mpumalanga Department of Education & another v Hoërskool Ermelo & another* 2010 (2) SA 415 (CC), para [47] cited in *Head of Department Western Cape Education Department and Others v S* (1209/2016) [2017] ZASCA 187, para [51] (Navsa ADP).

[215] See *Head of Department, Mpumalanga Department of Education & another v Hoërskool Ermelo & another* 2010 (2) SA 415 (CC), para [47] cited in *Head of Department Western Cape Education Department and Others v S* (1209/2016) [2017] ZASCA 187, para [51] (Navsa ADP).

Section 9 of South Africa's constitution, as a whole, reads:

1. Everyone is equal before the law and has the right to equal protection and benefit of the law.
2. Equality includes the full and equal enjoyment of all rights and freedoms. To promote the achievement of equality, legislative and other measures designed to protect or advance persons, or categories of persons, disadvantaged by unfair discrimination may be taken.
3. The state may not unfairly discriminate directly or indirectly against anyone on one or more grounds, including race, gender, sex, pregnancy, marital status, ethnic or social origin, colour, sexual orientation, age, disability, religion, conscience, belief, culture, language and birth.
4. No person may unfairly discriminate directly or indirectly against anyone on one or more grounds in terms of subsection (3). National legislation must be enacted to prevent or prohibit unfair discrimination.
5. Discrimination on one or more of the grounds listed in subsection (3) is unfair unless it is established that the discrimination is fair.

Section 9(2) permits 'remedial measures to address inequality and advance persons who were disadvantaged by unfair discrimination'.[216] For such remedial measures to not constitute unfair discrimination contrary to section 9(3), they must satisfy the three tests set out by Justice Moseneke in *Minister of Finance v Van Heerden*[217] ('*Van Heerden*'). These three tests are that the measures must: (1) target the historically disadvantaged from unfair discrimination; (2) be designed for the protection and advancement of these people; and (3) promote 'the achievement of equality'.[218] To ensure internal consistency, it has been recognized that remedial measures based on the protected attributes in section 9(3) should not be presumed to be unfair.[219]

Section 9 of the constitution therefore 'read as a whole, embraces … a substantive conception of equality inclusive of measures to redress existing inequality'.[220] Generally speaking, this reflects that '[a]t the heart of the constitutional project is an aspiration to achieve substantive equality and undo

---

[216] *Minister of Constitutional Development and Another v South African Restructuring and Insolvency Practitioners Association and Others* (CCT13/17) [2018] ZACC 20, para [2] (Jafta J, writing for the majority).

[217] [2004] ZACC 3.

[218] *Minister of Constitutional Development and Another v South African Restructuring and Insolvency Practitioners Association and Others* (CCT13/17) [2018] ZACC 20, para [2] (Jafta J, writing for the majority) citing *Minister of Finance v Van Heerden* [2004] ZACC 3, para [37].

[219] *Minister of Finance and Other v Van Heerden* (CCT 63/03) [2004] ZACC 3, para [33] (Moseneke J).

[220] *Van Heerden*, para [31].

the burdens of' South Africa's 'past'.[221] For reasons that will become clear below in this chapter's analysis of South African case law, this 'transformative constitutionalism' has influenced the development of an intersectional approach to 'social origin' discrimination.

2. The prohibition on 'social origin' discrimination in South African labour law

Two pieces of legislation, the *Labour Relations Act 1995 ('LRA')* and the *Employment Equity Act 1998 ('EEA')* also prohibit discriminatory treatment based on 'social origin'.

Chapter VIII of the *LRA* prohibits unfair dismissals and, pursuant to section 187 of the *LRA*, a dismissal is automatically unfair if the reason for the dismissal is 'that the employer unfairly discriminated against an employee, directly or indirectly, on any arbitrary ground, including, but not limited to' 'social origin' amongst other grounds.[222] The provisions of the *LRA* must be interpreted 'in compliance with the Constitution'.[223]

Section 6(1) of the *EEA* provides that '[n]o person may unfairly discriminate, directly or indirectly, against an employee, in any employment policy or practice, on one or more grounds, including' 'social origin', amongst other grounds. The *EEA* is linked to section 9 of the constitution, in that the preamble to the *EEA* states that the Act promotes the constitutional right to equality. The *EEA* must also be interpreted in compliance with South Africa's constitution and international law obligations, particularly those in *ILO 111*.[224]

Whilst the constitution of South Africa prohibits 'social origin' discrimination, most claims of this type of discrimination in employment will likely be brought under the *LRA* or the *EEA*. Kate O'Regan, a former judge of the Constitutional Court, has observed that 'not many challenges are brought directly under Section 9 of the Constitution' because South Africa has a comprehensive equality law framework[225] so litigants can instead rely on protections within that framework. Additionally, O'Regan writes that the 'main circumstance in which a litigant may bring a challenge based on' section 9 of the constitution, instead of equality law, is where he or she considers a law to be in conflict with the right to equality in section 9.[226] The right to equality in section 9 of the constitution therefore tends to be used

---

[221] *Mahlangu* (see Chapter 1, n 171), para [97].

[222] *LRA*, s 187(1)(f).

[223] *LRA*, s 3(b).

[224] *EEA*, s 3.

[225] Kate O'Regan, 'The Right to Equality in the South African Constitution', (2013) 25 *Columbia Journal of Gender and Law* 110, 113.

[226] Ibid, 112–113.

to challenge the validity of laws created by the state rather than to resolve disputes about discrimination or dismissals in employment. As such, claims of unfair dismissals based on 'social origin' would likely be brought under the *LRA* whilst clams of discrimination in employment based on 'social origin' would likely be brought under the *EEA*.

For the sake of completeness, it is worth noting that the *Promotion of Equality and Prevention of Unfair Discrimination Act* 2000 ('PEPUDA') also includes 'social origin' as a prohibited ground of discrimination. However, the PEPUDA 'under the doctrine of constitutional subsidiarity, is the primary legal basis for *non-employment related claims* [emphasis added] relating to discrimination by government officials, or by private actors, such as landlords or educational institutions'.[227] The PEPUDA 'does not apply to any person to whom and to the extent to which the' *EEA* applies.[228]

(a) The scope of the protection from discrimination in employment based on 'social origin'

Given that, as just explained, the *EEA* is likely to be relied upon by employees to bring claims of 'social origin' discrimination, a number of questions concerning the Act's operation and coverage must be addressed in order to assess its application in the digital age. First, what is the meaning of 'discrimination' in the *EEA*? Second, what is the *EEA*'s coverage, and does it apply to early recruitment stages before hiring?

Section 6 of the *EEA* prohibits 'unfair discrimination' against an 'employee' which is based on a number of grounds including 'social origin' (an 'employee' is defined in section 9 of the *EEA* to include 'an applicant for employment'). Both direct and indirect discrimination is prohibited by the *EEA*.[229] Indirect discrimination occurs where: (1) a differentiation or distinction may be 'neutral' or 'innocent' on its face; but (2) it has a 'disproportionate' impact or adverse affect on people with a protected attribute (for example, black people).[230] Proof of intention is not required to establish such indirect discrimination.[231]

---

227 Ibid, 113.
228 *PEPUDA*, s 5(3).
229 *EEA*, s 6(1).
230 *Mahlangu* (see Chapter 1, n 171), para [92] (Victor AJ, delivering reasons for the majority) citing *Pretoria City Council v Walker* [1998] ZACC 1, paras [31]–[32]; *Department of Correctional Services and Another v Police and Prison Civil Rights Union (POPCRU) and Others* (CA 6/2010) [2011] ZALAC 21, para [28]; *Ntai and Others v South African Breweries Limited* (J4476/99) [2000] ZALC 134, para [79] (Basson J).
231 *City Council of Pretoria v Walker* (CCT8/97) [1998] ZACC 1, para [43] (Langa DP, with Chaskalson P, Ackermann, Goldstone, Kriegler, Madala, Mokgoro and O'Regan JJ concurring) ('*Walker*').

The courts use the three-stage test set out in *Harksen v Lane NO*[232] ('*Harksen*') to determine whether there has been 'unfair discrimination' in discrimination claims under the constitution[233] and labour law.[234] The three-stage test requires asking: (1) whether a practice or policy differentiates between people; (2) whether the differentiation amounts to 'discrimination'; and (3) if it does, whether this is 'unfair discrimination'.[235]

In relation to the first stage of the test, a differentiation appears to include circumstances where a claimant is treated differently as a result of a practice or policy.[236] The second stage of the test requires an objective assessment as to whether the differentiation is attributable to a protected attribute, such as 'social origin'.[237] The discrimination resulting from the differentiation can be either direct or indirect.[238] Finally, in relation to the third stage of the test, once direct or indirect discrimination based on any listed attributes in section 9 of the constitution (such as 'social origin') is established then the 'conduct in question is presumed to be unfair'.[239] It then falls on the employer to rebut this presumption to show that it is fair.[240]

The *EEA* clearly prohibits unfair discrimination in recruitment processes, not just in hiring or in the employment relationship. First, as noted above, the protection from discrimination conferred by section 6(1) of the *EEA* extends to applicants for employment[241] (it does not just cover employees). Second, section 5 of the *EEA* provides that '[e]very employer must take steps to promote equal opportunity in the workplace by eliminating unfair discrimination in any employment policy or practice'.[242] The term 'employment policy or practice' is defined in the *EEA* to include, amongst other things, 'recruitment procedures, advertising and selection criteria'.[243] As such, it appears that employers must promote equal opportunity in employment by eliminating unfair discrimination based on 'social origin' in policies and practices including recruitment procedures, job advertisements and selection criteria. Employers who have discriminatory recruitment procedures, but do not eliminate that discrimination, may therefore be in breach of the *EEA*.

---

[232] [1997] ZACC 12.

[233] *Centre for Child Law* (see Chapter 2, n 124), para [40].

[234] *Tshwane* (see Chapter 2, n 182), para [14] (Savage AJA).

[235] *Walker* (n 231), para [29]. See also *Tshwane* (see Chapter 2, n 182), para [14] (Savage AJA).

[236] *Walker* (n 231), paras [23]-[24]; *Tshwane* (see Chapter 2, n 182), paras [16]-[18].

[237] See *Tshwane* (see Chapter 2, n 182), paras [17]-[18].

[238] See *Mahlangu* (see Chapter 1, n 171), para [92] (Victor AJ, writing for the majority).

[239] *Mahlangu* (see Chapter 1, n 171), para [92]. See also *Tshwane* (see Chapter 2, n 182), para [14] (Savage AJA).

[240] See, for example, *University of South Africa v Reynhardt* (JA36/08) [2010] ZALAC 9, para [21].

[241] See *EEA*, s 9.

[242] *EEA*, s 5.

[243] *EEA*, s 1.

The *EEA* contains defences to discrimination, including an inherent requirements defence and an affirmative action defence.

In South Africa, under the *EEA* it is not unfair discrimination to 'distinguish, exclude or prefer any person on the basis of an inherent requirement of a job'.[244] The 'inherent requirements of a job' 'refer to elements of a job that are essential to its outcome and part of its core activities'.[245] An assessment will need to be made on a case-by-case basis as to whether a person's 'social origin' means they cannot perform the 'inherent requirements' of a 'job'.

The affirmative action defence allows employers to 'take affirmative action measures' that are consistent with the purposes of the Act.[246] A relevant purpose of the Act is the implementation of 'affirmative action' measures to redress disadvantages which 'designated groups' experience in employment with the aim of ensuring 'their equitable representation in all occupational levels in the workforce'.[247] 'Designated groups' 'means black people, women and people with disabilities' who meet South African citizenship or naturalization requirements.[248] As such, affirmative action measures which aim to improve the employment outcomes or workforce participation of people from 'disadvantaged' backgrounds generally (as opposed to black people, women and people with disability) will not likely fall within the meaning of the affirmative action defence in the *EEA*. The Parliament therefore appears to have evinced an intention that only people from these *designated groups* be the recipients of measures designed to achieve substantive equality in employment. Such affirmative action measures are an exception to the general rule against 'unfair discrimination' in section 6(1) of the *EEA*.[249]

It therefore appears that, unless the affirmative action exception applies, the protection against 'unfair discrimination' in section 6(1) of the *EEA* is generally symmetrical.[250] It follows that in the *EEA* the prohibition against unfair discrimination based on 'social origin' applies symmetrically to protect everyone from this type of discrimination (not just the disadvantaged).

---

[244] *EEA*, s 6(2)(b).

[245] *Damons v City of Cape Town* (CCT 278/20) [2022] ZACC 13, para [136] (Majiedt J, with Madlanga J, Madondo AJ, Mhlantla J, Rogers AJ, Theron J, Tlaletsi AJ and Tshiqi J concurring).

[246] *EEA*, s 6(2)(a).

[247] *EEA*, s 2(b).

[248] *EEA*, s 1.

[249] See *EEA*, s 6(2)(a).

[250] See, for example, *Reynhardt v University of South Africa* (JS 1061/02) [2007] ZALC 96 in which a white university professor successfully claimed that his former employer's decision to appoint a person of colour, instead of him, to a Dean position based on its employment equity policy amounted to unfair discrimination based on race contrary to the *EEA*: see paras [1], [5], [6], [133], [138], [146]. The employer's appeal to the Labour Appeal Court was dismissed: See *University of South Africa v Reynhardt* (JA36/08) [2010] ZALAC 9, para [37].

A final point to make is that if an employer is alleged to have engaged in unfair discrimination based on a ground listed in section 6(1) of the *EEA* (such as 'social origin') then that employer bears the burden of proving that the discrimination did not occur or was rational, fair or justifiable.[251] As such, if an employer's recruitment or workplace policies are alleged to involve unfair discrimination based on protected grounds in the *EEA* (other than arbitrary grounds), it would fall on the employer to disprove the discrimination.

B. The meaning of 'social origin' in the Constitution, EEA and LRA

The Constitution, *EEA* and *LRA* do not contain a definition of the term 'social origin'. To elucidate the proper meaning of the ground 'social origin' in the *Bill of Rights*, *EEA* and *LRA*, Chapter 2 of this book relied on the interpretative provisions in each of these instruments to argue that the ILO jurisprudence discussed in that chapter can, and should, be used to clarify the content of 'social origin' in these South African laws. The term 'social origin' in each of these instruments, consistently with ILO jurisprudence, may therefore include class (as measured by economic, social and cultural capital) and certain factors that reflect social background.[252]

This chapter will now analyse South African case law to examine whether it has developed a meaning of 'social origin' which is in harmony with the way the term is understood in ILO jurisprudence. South African courts have considered claims of, or whether certain facts give rise to, 'social origin' discrimination under the *Bill of Rights*[253] and the

---

[251] *EEA*, s 11.

[252] See Chapter 2.

[253] See *Centre for Child Law* (see Chapter 2, n 124); *Rafoneke v Minister of Justice and Correctional Services and Others* (3609/2020) [2021] ZAFSHC 229 ('*Rafoneke*'); *Mahlangu* (see Chapter 1, n 171); *Magidiwana and Another v President of the Republic of South Africa and Others* (37904/2013) [2013] ZAGPPHC 292; *Mvumvu and Others v Minister of Transport and Another* (7490/2008) [2010] ZAWCHC 105; 2010 (12) BCLR 1324 (WCC); [2011] 1 All SA 90 (WCC); *Ramuhovhi and Others v President of the Republic of South Africa and Others* (CCT194/16) [2017] ZACC 41; *Mabaso v Law Society of the Northern Provinces* (CCT 76/03) [2004] ZACC 8; *Letta BHE and Others v Magistrate, Khayelitsha and Others* (9489/02) [2003] ZAWCHC 49; *One South Africa Movement and Another v President of the Republic of South Africa and Others* (24259/2020) [2020] ZAGPPHC 249; *South African Transport Allied Workers Union obo Finca v Old Mutual Life Assurance Company (SA) Limited and Another* (C198/2004) [2006] ZALC 51. See also *Ramuhovhi and Another v President of the Republic of South Africa and Others* (412/2015) [2016] ZALMPTHC 21; *Ramuhovhi and Another v President of the Republic of South Africa and Others* (412/2015) [2016] ZALMPTHC 18; *J and Another v Director General, Department of Home Affairs and Others* (CCT46/02) [2003] ZACC 3, para [9]; *Centre for Child Law and Others v Minister of Basic Education and Others* (2840/2017) [2019] ZAECGHC 126; *Benyon v Rhodes University and Another*

EEA[254] as well as claims of unfair dismissal on the basis of 'social origin' under the *LRA*.[255] The courts have also considered claims of 'social origin' discrimination under the *PEPUDA*.[256] Whilst a number of claims of discrimination or unfair dismissal on the basis of 'social origin' have been brought before South African courts, only a handful of these judgments, which will now be analysed, consider the meaning of 'social origin' in any useful detail.

1. Judicial interpretations of 'social origin' in the Bill of Rights

Claims of 'social origin' discrimination under section 9 of the constitution have been predominately relied upon by litigants to challenge South African laws rather than allege discrimination in employment. Nonetheless, given that, as noted above, South Africa's labour laws such as the *LRA* and the *EEA* must be interpreted in compliance with the constitution, decisions on the meaning of 'social origin' in the *Bill of Rights* may assist in understanding the proper meaning of the term in these labour laws. Additionally, section 39(2) of the Constitution 'creates an obligation to interpret all legislation in a manner that promotes "the spirit, purport and objects of the Bill of Rights"' and '[t]his means that all statutes … must be interpreted through the prism of the Bill of Rights'.[257]

(a) 'Social origin' refers to class and social position

South African courts have measured 'social origin' by reference to class and social position,[258] and the ground appears to have been understood mainly

---

(5351/2016) [2016] ZAECGHC 161; *S v Khanyisile and Another* (CA 12/2012) [2012] ZANWHC 35, para [23]; *Mabuza v Mbatha* (1939/01) [2002] ZAWCHC 11, para [29].

[254] See *Tshwane* (see Chapter 2, n 182); Mbana v Shepstone & Wylie (CCT85/14) [2015] ZACC 11; *Maraba and Others v Tshwane University of Technology* (JS1032/12) [2019] ZALCJHB 209; Anyanwu and Another v 15-On-Orange Hotel (Pty) Ltd (C39/2012) [2013] ZALCCT 20; Khumalo v University of Johannesburg (JS533/16) [2018] ZALCJHB 31; Dayimani v National Department of Health and Another (JS753/18) [2019] ZALCJHB 44.

[255] See Anyanwu and Another v 15-On-Orange Hotel (Pty) Ltd (C39/2012) [2013] ZALCCT 20; Mias v Minister of Justice and others (CA15/00) [2001] ZALAC 6; De Bruyn v Metorex Proprietary Limited (JA 40/2020) [2021] ZALAC 18; Kanku and Others v Grindrod Fuelogic (C602/2014) [2017] ZALCCT 26; Tharage v Digital healthcare Solutions (Pty) Ltd (JS386/2008) [2010] ZALC 158. See also Ndlovu v Mondi Kraft a division of Mondi Ltd (D1060/2000) [2001] ZALC 224.

[256] *Osman v Minister of Safety and Security and Others* (EC09/2008) [2010] ZAEQC 1 (which concerned a complaint against police officers); *Social Justice Coalition and Others v Minister of Police and Others* (EC03/2016) [2018] ZAWCHC 181 (which concerned, amongst other things, whether poverty was a ground of discrimination under the PEPUDA).

[257] *Centre for Child Law* (see Chapter 2, n 124), para 27 (Victor AJ, with Jafta J, Khampepe J, Madlanga J, Majiedt J, Mhlantla J, Theron J and Tshiqi J concurring).

[258] See Centre for Child Law (see Chapter 2, n 124), para [76] (Victor AJ, with Jafta J, Khampepe J, Madlanga J, Majiedt J, Mhlantla J, Theron J and Tshiqi J concurring).

in terms of economic capital[259] (for example, poverty[260]) and the 'working class'.[261] However, as will now be discussed, in recent years the courts have increasingly used an intersectional lens when considering claims of 'social origin' discrimination. This is unsurprising given that an intersectional approach has been viewed as the kind of approach which will achieve a 'progressive realisation' of South Africa's 'transformative constitutionalism'.[262]

(i) The intersectional approach to 'social origin' discrimination

In *Centre for Child Law v Director General: Department of Home Affairs and Others* ('*Centre for Child Law*')[263] a judgment for the majority of the Constitutional Court of South Africa found that a law had unfairly discriminated on the basis of 'social origin', and it used an intersectional prism to assist in revealing this discrimination.

The law in question was section 10 of the *Births and Deaths Registration Act* 51 of 1992 ('BDRA'), which provided that notices of the birth of children born out of wedlock must be given under the mother's surname or, where the mother and father jointly request it, the father's surname.[264] Under the BDRA's regulations, parents who were not citizens of South Africa needed to produce a certified copy of a valid passport or visa to give notice of a birth.[265] There was no provision made for situations where one parent was a South African citizen and the other a foreign national who did not have a valid passport or visa.[266]

---

[259] See *Rafoneke* (n 253).

[260] In *Magidiwana and Another v President of the Republic of South Africa and Others* (37904/2013) [2013] ZAGPPHC 292 Makgoka J considered a claim of 'social origin' discrimination under the constitution and found that whilst the applicants had a common 'social origin' in that they were 'poor', it was not the basis upon which they had been differentiated: at [91].

[261] See *Mvumvu and Others v Minister of Transport and Another* (7490/2008) [2010] ZAWCHC 105, in which the applicants submitted that a law which limited, in the event of a road accident, the compensation which was payable to passengers of 'offending' vehicles discriminated based on 'social origin' because it discriminated against 'working class people' who travel in their employer's vehicle in the course of their employment: see [1], [8]-[13], [14], [17], [22]-[23]. Bozalek J concluded that discrimination based on 'social origin' was established: at [24].

[262] See Mahlangu (see Chapter 1, n 171), para [79] (Victor AJ, with Mogoeng CJ, Khampepe J, Madlanga J, Majiedt J, Theron J, Tshiqi J concurring).

[263] (CCT 101/20) [2021] ZACC 31.

[264] Centre for Child Law (see Chapter 2, n 124), para [4]-[5].

[265] Regulations on the Registration of Births and Deaths, GN R128 GG 37373, Regs 3(3) (f), 4(3)(f), 5(3)(f) and 8(3)(c) cited in *Centre for Child Law* (see Chapter 2, n 124), paras [5], [9].

[266] Centre for Child Law (see Chapter 2, n 124), para [5].

The background facts concerned a South African citizen and member of the South African Defence force, Mr Naki, who was stationed in the Democratic Republic of Congo ('DRC') for a peace keeping mission.[267] Whilst there, in 2008 he met Ms Ndovya (a citizen of the DRC) and they married in accordance with her culture and customs, but the customary marriage could not be registered in the DRC because these marriages were not recognized in the country.[268] They subsequently had two children, including a daughter who was born in Grahamstown in South Africa on 1 February 2016.[269] Shortly before the birth Ms Ndovya's visa had expired and, as she was in the advanced stages of pregnancy, she could not apply for a new visa or travel back to the DRC.[270] Following their daughter's birth the Department of Home Affairs ('DHA') refused to register the birth because it refused to recognize the customary law marriage in the DRC. As such, the daughter was treated as a child born out of wedlock. Ms Ndovya did not have a valid visa, thus she could not comply with the regulations to register the birth.[271]

The majority found, amongst other things, that section 10 of the BDRA unfairly discriminated against unmarried fathers on the basis of sex, gender and marital status[272] and infringed 'a child's constitutional right not to be discriminated against on the grounds of social origin and birth (out of wedlock)' as set out in section 9(3) of the constitution.[273]

In relation to finding that section 10 of the BDRA unfairly discriminated on the basis of 'social origin' Victor AJ, writing for the majority, said:

> In my view, section 10 of the Act unfairly discriminates on the ground of social origin. In this context, social origin refers to an amalgam of intersecting factors related to a person's class or social position in society. Some commentators have noted the intersectional nature of social origin-based discrimination and how it often overlaps with discrimination against groups who are already vulnerable due to their race, ethnicity, nationality, and so on.[274]

The commentary on the intersectional nature of social origin-based discrimination to which Victor AJ was referring was this author's analysis of

---

[267] Centre for Child Law (see Chapter 2, n 124), para [8].
[268] Centre for Child Law (see Chapter 2, n 124), para [8].
[269] Centre for Child Law (see Chapter 2, n 124), para [8].
[270] Centre for Child Law (see Chapter 2, n 124), para [8].
[271] Centre for Child Law (see Chapter 2, n 124), para [9].
[272] Centre for Child Law (see Chapter 2, n 124), para [53]-[56].
[273] Centre for Child Law (see Chapter 2, n 124), para [75].
[274] Centre for Child Law (see Chapter 2, n 124), para [76] (Victor AJ, with Jafta J, Khampepe J, Madlanga J, Majiedt J, Mhlantla J, Theron J and Tshiqi J concurring).

discrimination faced by indigenous people in Australia on the basis of their class, race and social origin.[275] Her Honour then continued:

> This observation is pertinent on these facts as the applicant has demonstrated that section 10 has a disproportionate impact on children from homes who cannot litigate in the DRC in order to obtain the necessary marriage certificate in order to comply with the Act. In addition, it is no coincidence in my view, that on these facts, section 10 had an impact on a child whose mother was a foreign national and who was unable to register their birth on her own for this reason. Thus, the intersectional nature of social origin-based discrimination is evident in this matter.[276]

Section 10 of the BDRA, therefore, appeared to disproportionately impact children based on a mixture of factors that related to their family and home background (for example family observance of customary marriage in the DRC), family resources (for example, inability to litigate in the DRC), and the circumstances of their parents (for example, a parent's status as a foreign national and temporary disability due to pregnancy). These factors appeared to all intersect to compound the disadvantages experienced by children from families such as those of Mr Naki and Ms Ndovya, to bring into focus how section 10 of the BDRA resulted with intersectional social origin-based discrimination against children from these families.

The majority judgment in *Centre for Child Law* is significant because it makes an explicit finding of intersectional social origin-based discrimination. Previous judgments find discrimination based on 'social origin' and certain other attributes, but these judgments neither explain the meaning of 'social origin' and nor do they provide clarity as to why a law or action was discriminatory on this basis.[277]

---

[275] Centre for Child Law (see Chapter 2, n 124), fn 61 citing Capuano, 'Giving Meaning to "Social Origin"' (see Chapter 1, n 72), 117–8.

[276] Centre for Child Law (see Chapter 2, n 124), para [76] (Victor AJ, with Jafta J, Khampepe J, Madlanga J, Majiedt J, Mhlantla J, Theron J and Tshiqi J concurring).

[277] See, for example, *Ramuhovhi and Others v President of the Republic of South Africa and Others* (CCT194/16) [2017] ZACC 41, in which the Constitutional Court confirmed a declaration of constitutional invalidity of section 7(1) of the *Recognition of Customary Marriages Act* 120 of 1998 which was made by the High Court, which had found that the provision was discriminatory on the basis of gender, race and ethnic or social origin (see para [9]). However, neither the Constitutional Court nor the High Court explained the concept of 'social origin' or clarify why the provision was discriminatory on this ground. The High Court in *Ramuhovhi and Another v President of the Republic of South Africa and Others* (412/ 2015) [2016] ZALMPTHC 18 only explained that the 'provision in section 7(1) is also discriminatory on the basis of race and or ethnic or social origin insofar as women in "old"

In *Rafoneke v Minister of Justice and Correctional Services and Others*[278] ('*Rafoneke*') the applicants alleged that a law unfairly discriminated based on 'social origin' and nationality[279] but the court did not give a definitive view on whether the applicants had properly proven 'social origin' discrimination because they had sufficiently proven discrimination based on nationality.[280] Musi CJ, with whom Molitsoane J and Wright AJ concurred, nonetheless considered the meaning of 'social origin'[281] (this reasoning concerning 'social origin' was not disturbed by the Constitutional Court on appeal) and accepted 'that there may be intersectionality between different forms of discrimination, e.g. poverty and race and race and gender',[282] and '[p]robably between nationality and social origin'.[283] Musi CJ also noted that this author's published work provides 'a thorough discussion of the concept' 'social origin'.[284] This work cited by Musi CJ argues that 'social origin' in the *International Covenant on Economic, Social and Cultural Rights* refers to inherited social status and that such status

---

polygamous customary marriages are excluded from the protection afforded to women in monogamous marriages. It further differentiates between women in "old" polygamous marriages and women in "new" polygamous customary marriages, by providing protection only for the latter': at [46]. See also Centre for Child Law and Others v Minister of Basic Education and Others (2840/2017) [2019] ZAECGHC 126, fn 65; South African Transport Allied Workers Union obo Finca v Old Mutual Life Assurance Company (SA) Limited and Another (C198/2004) [2006] ZALC 51 (in this case, Revelas J found that a racist remark which conveyed 'malcontentedness' to share an 'immediate office space with Africans' constituted 'direct unfair discrimination against persons based on their race, ethnic and social origin as foreseen by Section 9(3) of the Constitution': at [8]. The court did not clarify why the remark constituted unfair discrimination on these grounds. However, the two versions of the remark put to the court were 'why did you put me next to the kaffirs?' and 'Why must I be surrounded by the whole of Khayelitsha?': at [7].

278 (3609/2020) [2021] ZAFSHC 229.

279 Rafoneke (n 253), para [25].

280 Rafoneke (n 253), para [97]. On appeal the Constitutional Court found no violation of sections 9(3) and 9(4) of the constitution because differentiation based on citizenship was held to not be unfair. On the question of 'social origin' the court was not persuaded that 'citizenship' falls under the ground, and otherwise it did not clearly explain 'social origin' except to suggest that it might refer to concepts including class, clan or family membership (the court did not, however, explain these concepts or make more definitive statements in its reasoning, thus it offers very little useful or practical guidance on the meaning of 'social origin'): See Rafoneke and Others v Minister of Justice and Correctional Services and Others (Makombe Intervening) (CCT 315/21, CCT 321/21, CCT 06/22) [2022] ZACC 29, [93]-[102].

281 See Rafoneke (n 253), para [94]–[97].

282 Rafoneke (n 253), para [97].

283 Rafoneke (n 253), para [97].

284 Rafoneke (n 253), fn 32 (Musi CJ, with Molitsoane J and Wright AJ concurring). The court cited Angelo Capuano, 'The Meaning of "Social Origin" in International Human Rights Treaties: A Critique of the CESCR's Approach to "Social Origin" Discrimination in the ICESCR and its (Ir)relevance to National Contexts such as Australia' (2017) 41(3) *New Zealand Journal of Employment Relations* 91–110.

appears to be measured by the extent of a person's property or land tenure, economic and social situation such as poverty and homelessness, or descent.[285]

2. Judicial interpretations of 'social origin' in labour law legislation

Until recently, few judgments considered the meaning of 'social origin' in South African labour law legislation. Recent case law, which will now be analysed, now supports the position that 'social origin' in this legislation – consistently with the way the term has been interpreted in *Centre for Child Law* and ILO jurisprudence – refers to class.

(a) 'Social origin' refers to class

In *Tshwane University of Technology v Maraba and Others* ('*Tshwane*')[286] the Labour Appeal Court of South Africa considered an appeal from a decision of the Labour Court which had found that Tshwane University of Technology unfairly discriminated against three employees on the basis of their 'social origin'.[287] Tshwane University of Technology was established following a merger of three institutions which came into effect on 19 November 2008.[288] As a result of the merger all employees who had their positions downgraded had their salaries capped,[289] but this cap was lifted on 1 April 2011.[290] The complainants were employed as professional nurses and, from the date of the merger, they were employed at grade 9 level.[291] After salaries were uncapped on 1 April 2011 the salary of a professional nurse at what was previously the Pretoria Technikon was, along with other staff, increased to more than what was received by the respondents even though they were all at grade 9 level.[292]

The respondents argued that this salary differentiation was 'social origin' discrimination because nursing staff at 'the previously well-resourced and advantaged Pretoria Technikon remained higher on salaries scale and benefits than the nurses from historically disadvantaged institutions'.[293] The Labour Court agreed, finding that because the University paid staff at historically disadvantaged institutions (the complainants) less than staff at Pretoria Technikon

---

[285] See Capuano (n 284), 96–98.

[286] (JA110/2019) [2021] ZALAC 25.

[287] Tshwane (see Chapter 2, n 182), para [1]. See also *Maraba and Others v Tshwane University of Technology* (JS1032/12) [2019] ZALCJHB 209.

[288] Tshwane (see Chapter 2, n 182), para [3].

[289] Tshwane (see Chapter 2, n 182), para [3].

[290] Tshwane (see Chapter 2, n 182), paras [3], [7].

[291] Tshwane (see Chapter 2, n 182), para [4].

[292] Tshwane (see Chapter 2, n 182), para [7].

[293] Tshwane (see Chapter 2, n 182), para [5].

and failed to present a justifiable ground for its conduct, it had unfairly discriminated against the complainants on the basis of their 'social origin'.[294]

When evaluating the appeal, Savage AJA (with Coppin JA and Molefe AJA agreeing) noted that section 6(1) of the *EEA* prohibits unfair discrimination based on 'social origin'[295] and then went on to refer to the meaning of the term 'social origin' in international human rights treaties and ILO jurisprudence. Savage AJA noted that in international human rights treaties 'social origin' 'refers to a person's **inherited social status, descent-based discrimination by birth and economic and social status** (emphasis added)'.[296] Savage AJA also noted that discrimination based on 'social origin' 'has been defined by the Committee of Experts of the International Labour Organisation ('ILO') to include discrimination on the basis of **class, caste or socio-occupational category** (emphasis added)'.[297] Having articulated this meaning of 'social origin', the Labour Appeal Court found that the Labour Court erred and the evidence showed that 'the differential treatment that arose from the decision to uncap salaries was not attributable to the respondents' social origin'.[298]

This 2021 decision of the Labour Appeal Court shows that 'social origin' under the *EEA* was interpreted consistently with the way 'social origin' is understood in international human rights law and ILO jurisprudence, as analysed by this author.[299] The decision, however, does not clearly elaborate on the meaning of important concepts, such as class. Nonetheless, it does reinforce that international law was used to aid the interpretation of 'social origin' in the *EEA*.

The ground 'social origin' in the *LRA* has received little judicial attention, but in *Kanku and Others v Grindrod Fuelogic*[300] ('*Kanku*') the Labour Court reasoned that nationality 'is, at the very least, analogous to the listed ground of 'ethnic or social origin', if not encompassed by that concept'.[301] It can however be argued that, with respect, this interpretation in *Kanku* is likely

---

[294] Tshwane (see Chapter 2, n 182), para [7], [9]-[10].

[295] Tshwane (see Chapter 2, n 182), para [13].

[296] Tshwane (see Chapter 2, n 182), para [13] citing Committee on Economic, Social and Cultural Rights CESCR General Comment 20: Non-Discrimination in Economic, Social and Cultural Rights (art 2, para 2) E/C.12/GC/20 (4–22 May 2009), [24] and Capuano, 'A Critique of the CESCR's Approach to "Social Origin"' (n 284), 97.

[297] Tshwane (see Chapter 2, n 182), para [13] (Savage AJA, with Coppin JA and Molefe AJA agreeing) citing *General Survey 1988* (see Chapter 2, n 28) 53 [54] as quoted in Capuano, 'Giving Meaning to "Social Origin"' (see Chapter 1, n 72), 85.

[298] Tshwane (see Chapter 2, n 182), para [17].

[299] Savage AJ cited this author's published work when considering the meaning of 'social origin' in international human rights treaties and ILO jurisprudence. See Tshwane (see Chapter 2, n 182), fn 3 and 4.

[300] (C602/2014) [2017] ZALCCT 26.

[301] Kanku, para [54].

erroneous in light of the reasoning in *Rafoneke* and in particular the reasoning of the Constitutional Court on appeal from that decision (discussed above). Since *Kanku* was decided, other judgments such as *Centre for Child Law* and *Tshwane* have offered much clearer and comprehensive guidance on the meaning of 'social origin' which clarifies that the ground refers to class and related concepts. There does not appear to be any reason why the reasoning in *Centre for Child Law, Tshwane* and *Rafoneke* should not inform how 'social origin' should be interpreted in the *LRA*.

C. Applications in the digital age

The above analysis shows that there is a growing body of case law in South Africa which interprets 'social origin' in the constitution and labour law as referring to class and social position. Whilst these judgments do not define the concept of class, some judges have treated 'social origin' to be synonymous with poverty and working-class status.

Importantly, however, as explained above, an intersectional lens has recently been used by judges in cases which have concerned claims of 'social origin' discrimination. This intersectional approach to 'social origin' discrimination has particular applications in the digital age. For example, for reasons that will be explained in later chapters, there are risks of intersectional social origin-based discrimination from:

- an employer's use of automated candidate screening technologies such as gamification, which may create risks of discrimination at the intersection of lack of economic capital (for example, poverty) and disability;[302]
- the post-pandemic shift to remote working and homeworking, which may create risks of discrimination at the intersection of various axes including lack of economic capital (for example, poverty), family background, gender, sex, and family responsibility.[303]

Section 6(1) of the *EEA* expressly prohibits unfair discrimination based on all these grounds (including 'gender', 'sex', 'family responsibility', 'social origin', and 'disability'.

As argued in Chapter 2, the term 'social origin' in the constitution, *EEA* and *LRA* should be interpreted consistently with the way the term is understood in ILO jurisprudence. Applications of ILO jurisprudence on 'social origin' discrimination in the digital age (as set out in Chapter 2) may therefore be useful to understanding possible other applications of

---

[302] See Chapter 5.
[303] See Chapter 6.

South African law which prohibits this type of discrimination. This is provided the *Harksen* test, which is explained above, can be satisfied in the particular circumstances.

Therefore, consistent with the way the term is understood in ILO jurisprudence (as explained in chapter 2), 'social origin' in both the *EEA* and *LRA* may refer to class (as it is measured by economic, social and cultural capital), locality and geographic origins, and certain factors that go to social background (such as home dynamics, family and certain relatives). It is important to emphasize here that whilst South African courts have not yet expressly interpreted 'social origin' in the *LRA* and *EEA* in this particular way, chapter 2 argues that the term in these Acts *should* have this meaning (for the reasons which are set out in that chapter). There may, as a result and for reasons which are explained in detail in chapters 4 and 5, also be possible risks that an employer's use of social media[304] as well as algorithms and AI as recruitment tools[305] could amount to 'social origin' discrimination under South African law.

III. The Canadian legal landscape and its applications in the digital age

This chapter will now turn to map the legal landscape in Canada to explore the extent to which discrimination in employment based on class and/or factors reflective of social background is prohibited at the federal and provincial levels. Whilst discrimination based on 'class' and 'social background' are not expressly contained within legislation as grounds of discrimination, the below analysis will show that other specified grounds reflect class and/or certain factors that go to social background. In particular, the grounds of 'social condition' (in the law of Quebec, the Northwest Territories and New Brunswick), 'family status' (in federal law, and certain provincial laws) and 'association discrimination' (in certain provincial law) will be examined. It will, further, outline how discrimination based on these grounds has particular applications in the digital age.

Whilst provincial laws in Canada prohibit discrimination based on various other attributes such as 'source of income',[306] 'receipt of public

---

[304] See Chapter 4.

[305] See Chapter 5.

[306] See, for example, *Alberta Human Rights Act*, RSA 2000, c A-25.5, s 7(1); The Human Rights Code, CCSM c H175, s 9(2)(j); *Human Rights Act*, RSPEI 1988, c H-12, s 1(d); *Human Rights Act*, 2010, SNL 2010, c H-13.1, s 9(1); *Human Rights Act*, RSY 2002, c 116, s 7(l). See also *Human Rights Act*, SNu 2003, c 12, s 7(1), which prohibits discrimination based on 'lawful source of income'.

assistance',[307] 'social disadvantage'[308] and 'ancestry',[309] this book will focus on discrimination based on 'social condition', 'family status' and association. This is because these three grounds, for reasons that are explained in Chapters 4 and 6, have most application in the digital age.

A. Discrimination based on 'social condition'

Discrimination in employment (and other specified areas) on the basis of 'social condition' is prohibited in Québec,[310] the Northwest Territories[311] and New Brunswick.[312] New Brunswick and the Northwest Territories contain legislative definitions of 'social condition' whilst Québec relies on judicial interpretations of the concept. The meaning of 'social condition' within these jurisdictions has been explained by this author elsewhere,[313] and an analysis of case law shows that the courts have not fundamentally developed or changed this meaning.[314] This chapter will build on this work

---

[307] *The Saskatchewan Human Rights Code*, 2018, c S-24.2, ss 2(1)(n), 16.

[308] *Human Rights Code*, CCSM 2015, c H175, ss 9(1), 9(2)(m), 9(2.1), 14(1). 'Social disadvantage' is defined as 'diminished social standing or social regard due to (a) homelessness or inadequate housing; (b) low levels of education; (c) chronic low income; or (d) chronic unemployment or underemployment': *Human Rights Code*, CCSM c H175, s 1. The ground is therefore defined narrowly and seems to capture severe forms of social disadvantage.

[309] See *Human Rights Code*, RSO 1990, c H.19, s 5(1); *The Saskatchewan Human Rights Code*, 2018, c S-24.2, ss 2(1)(j), 16; *Human Rights Code*, RSBC 1996, c 210, s 13(1); *Alberta Human Rights Act*, RSA 2000, c A-25.5, s 7(1); *Human Rights Act*, RSY 2002, c 116, s 7(a); *Human Rights Act*, SNu 2003, c 12, s 7(1); *The Human Rights Code*, CCSM c H175, s 9(2)(a); *Human Rights Act*, RSNB 2011, c 171, s 2.1(d); *Human Rights Act*, SNWT 2002, c 18, s 5(1).

[310] *Charter of Human Rights and Freedoms*, CQLR 1975, c C-12, ss 10, 16–19.

[311] *Human Rights Act*, SNWT 2002, c 18, ss 5, 7–10.

[312] *Human Rights Act*, RSNB 2011, c 171, ss 2.1, 4.

[313] Capuano, 'Giving Meaning to "Social Origin"' (see Chapter 1, n 72), 110–115.

[314] In relation to recent complaints of 'social condition' discrimination in Quebec, see Aluminerie de Bécancour inc. c. Commission des droits de la personne et des droits de la jeunesse (Beaudry et autres), 2021 QCCA 989 ('*Bécancour*'); R.L (see Chapter 1, n 130); R.O. c. Ministre de l'Emploi et de la Solidarité sociale, 2021 QCCA 1185; *Kin c. McNicoll*, 2021 QCTDP 34; Commission des droits de la personne et des droits de la jeunesse (Beaudry et autres) v Aluminerie de Bécancour inc., [2018] Q.H.R.T.J. No. 12; P.T. c. Mohammad Naqeeb, 2021 QCCS 1378, para [68]; P.T. c. Mohammad Naqeeb, 2021 QCCS 1378; Commission des droits de la personne et des droits de la jeunesse (Miller et autres) c. Ville de Montréal (Service de police de la Ville de Montréal) (SPVM), 2019 QCTDP 31; Commission des droits de la personne et des droits de la jeunesse (Asmar) c. Ville de Montréal (Service de police de la Ville de Montréal) (SPVM), 2019 QCTDP 17; Commission des droits de la personne et des droits de la jeunesse (Beaudry et autres) c. Aluminerie de Bécancour inc., 2018

by analyzing legislation and case law to show that whilst in these provinces 'social condition' refers to class, it tends to be measured in a Weberian sense which reflects market capacities.

1. 'Social condition' refers to class (as measured by Weberian market capacities)

In New Brunswick, the Northwest Territories and Québec, 'social condition' is, at its foundation, defined consistently and it refers to a person's inclusion within a socially identifiable group that suffers from social or economic disadvantage.[315] The definitions then branch out from this base. The below analysis will show that: (1) this social and economic disadvantage is measured by factors that reflect Weberian market capacities; and (2) defining 'social condition' by reference to Weberian market capacities limits the law's ability to address class discrimination which may arise in the digital age.

(a) The approach in New Brunswick

In New Brunswick this social or economic disadvantage must be on the basis of a person's *source of income, occupation or level of education* [emphasis

---

QCTDP 12; Syndicate of nurses, respiratory therapists, nursing assistants of Cœur-du-Québec (SIIIACQ) (CSQ) v SIUSSS-MCQ, 2017 CanLII 13636 (QC SAT). See also Beaulieu c. Facebook inc., 2021 QCCS 3206. In relation to recent complaints of 'social condition' discrimination in the Northwest Territories, see *Moore v Northwest Territories Housing Corporation*, 2022 CanLII 13384 (NT HRAP); Lessard v Northwest Territories (Department of Education, Culture & Employment), 2018 CanLII 109795 (NT HRAP); Bates v Northwest Territories (Education, Culture and Employment) (No. 1), 2017 CanLII 98893 (NT HRAP); Portman v Yellowknife (City) (No. 1), 2016 CanLII 154167 (NT HRAP); Portman v Yellowknife (City), 2017 CanLII 338 (NT HRAP); Portman v Yellowknife (City), 2016 CanLII 62610 (NT HRAP); Lodovici v Wam Development Corporation, 2015 CanLII 78454 (NT HRAP). See also Bates v Northwest Territories, 2018 CanLII 61920 (NT HRAP), in which the Northwest Territories Human Rights Commission sought '[a] declaration that providing income assistance without conducting any individualized assessment is discrimination on the ground of social condition, contrary to the Human Rights Act'. In relation to a recent complaint of 'social condition' discrimination in New Brunswick, see Gorham v Delorey, [2017] N.B.J. No. 274 (in which the court dismissed the application and did not explain the concept of 'social condition').

[315] *Human Rights Act*, RSNB 2011, c 171, s 2 (definition of 'social condition'); *Human Rights Act*, SNWT 2002, c 18, s 1 (definition of 'social condition'); *Commission des droits de la personne (Québec) v Gauthier* (1993) 19 CHRR D/312 ('*Gauthier*'); *Syndicate of nurses, respiratory therapists, nursing assistants of Cœur-du-Québec (SIIIACQ) (CSQ) v SIUSSS-MCQ*, 2017 CanLII 13636 (QC SAT), paras [48], [53], [70]; *Order of Certified General Accountants of Quebec c. Quebec (Attorney General)*, 2004 CanLII 20542 (QC CA), para [69].

added]'.[316] However, there has been limited consideration of the ground 'social condition' by the courts in New Brunswick,[317] thus there is no clear authoritative guidance on the meaning of the ground beyond what is contained in the legislative definition.[318]

(b) The approach in the Northwest Territories

In the Northwest Territories, this 'social or economic disadvantage' must result from one or more of five factors, such as 'poverty, source of income, illiteracy, level of education or any other similar circumstance'.[319] A person's membership to a group suffering such disadvantage must also be other than on a temporary basis to be a 'social condition'.[320]

'Social condition' has been interpreted broadly to also refer 'to the position that someone holds in society'.[321] It is therefore not restricted to those who may struggle to obtain life's necessities due to the five factors listed in the legislation.[322] As such, it has been held to cover a seasonal worker who, though not destitute, suffered both social and economic disadvantage due to their source of income and low education levels.[323] 'Social condition', in the seasonal worker's circumstances, was viewed to consist of several factors that impacted seasonal workers, such as living in 'high areas of unemployment, being 'required to work away from home', earning 'less than national and provincial average salaries', having 'lower education levels and fewer job opportunities', and reliance on employment insurance 'to supplement their income'.[324] This demonstrates that economic and educational factors such as education level, income level and reliance on welfare, consistent with Weberian market capacities, are used by the courts in the Northwest Territories to measure or identify 'social condition'.[325]

---

[316] *Human Rights Act*, RSNB 2011, c 171, s 2.

[317] See, for example, *Gorham v Delorey*, [2017] N.B.J. No. 274.

[318] For guidelines on 'social condition' in New Brunswick, see New Brunswick Human Rights Commission 'Guideline on Social Condition' (February 2019), 5–6 https://www2.gnb.ca/content/dam/gnb/Departments/hrc-cdp/PDF/GuidelineonSocialCondition.pdf.

[319] *Human Rights Act*, SNWT 2002, c 18, s 1 (definition of 'social condition').

[320] Ibid. See also *Mercer v Northwest Territories and Nunavut (Workers' Compensation Board)*, 2007 NWTHRAP 4 (CanLII), para [13]; *Bates v Northwest Territories (Education, Culture and Employment) (No. 1)*, 2017 CanLII 98893 (NT HRAP), para [40].

[321] *WCB v Mercer*, 2012 NWTSC 57, para [48].

[322] WCB v Mercer [2012] NWTSC 57, [46]–[50].

[323] WCB v Mercer, 2012 NWTSC 57 (CanLII), para [45], [50].

[324] WCB v Mercer, 2012 NWTSC 57 (CanLII), para [78]-[79].

[325] See also Giroux v Yellowknife Housing Authority, 2014 NWTSC 42 (CanLII), para [46]; *Lessard v Northwest Territories (Department of Education, Culture & Employment)*, 2018 CanLII 109795 (NT HRAP), para [27]; *Portman v Yellowknife (City) (No. 1)*, 2016 CanLII

(c) The approach in Québec

When the *Charter of Human Rights and Freedoms*[326] ('*Quebec Charter*') was adopted in 1975 the legislature preferred 'social condition' over 'social origin' as a ground of discrimination.[327] 'Social condition' discrimination has therefore been unlawful in Québec for almost five decades. The term 'social condition' is not defined in the *Quebec Charter* and the courts were left to develop a definition of the ground.

The courts have consistently used the definition of 'social condition' adopted in 1979 by Justice Tôth of the Quebec Superior Court in *Commission des droits de la personne (Québec) v Centre hospitalier St Vincent de Paul de Sherbrooke CS (St-François)* ('*Sherbrooke*'),[328] who wrote:

'social condition' refers either to the rank, the place, the position that an individual occupies in society, or even to the class to which he belongs, by birth, by his income, by his level of education, by his occupation; or to all the circumstances and events that cause a person or a group to occupy a particular situation or position in society.[329]

15416/ (NT HRAP), para [12]. Whilst a decision of the Northwest Territories Human Rights Adjudication Panel suggests that 'social condition' discrimination may include differential treatment which creates a distinction between income assistance recipients from a certain hamlet and those in the rest of the Northwest Territories, this is not made clear in the decision and it can only be implied from the conclusion in that decision. See *Bates v Northwest Territories (Education, Culture and Employment) (No. 1)* 2017 CanLII 98893 (NT HRAP), para [62].

[326] CQLR c C-12.

[327] See *Commission des droits de la personne (Larente) c. Gauthier, 1993 CanLII 8751 (QC TDP)*.

[328] (Unreported, Tribunal du Québec, Tôth J, 7 September 1979).

[329] *Commission des droits de la personne (Québec) v Centre hospitalier St Vincent de Paul de Sherbrooke CS (St-François)* (Unreported, Tribunal du Québec, Tôth J, 7 September 1979), cited with approval in *R.O. c. Ministre de l'Emploi et de la Solidarité sociale*, 2021 QCCA 1185 (CanLII), para [58]; Bécancour (n 314), para [50] (Thibault JCA, Levesque JCA, Hogue JCA); *Champagne vs. Quebec (Administrative Tribunal)*, 2001 CanLII 24787 (QC CS), para [27] (Mayrand JCS); Commission des droits de la personne et des droits de la jeunesse (Bia-Domingo) c. Sinatra, 1999 CanLII 52 (QC TDP), para [40] (P Rivet); Couet c. Quebec (Attorney General), 1997 CanLII 8766 (QC CS), para [55] (Piché JCS); *Johnson & Johnson Products Inc. and Union of Energy and Chemical Workers, Local 115*, 1995 CanLII 15888 (QC SAT); *Commission des droits de la personne (Leroux) c. J.M. Brouillette inc.*, 1994 CanLII 191 (QC TDP); *Commission des droits de la personne (Larente) c. Gauthier*, 1993 CanLII 8751 (QC TDP); *D'Aoust c. Vallières*, 1993 CanLII 422 (QC TDP); Regina Hospital Center Limited c. Human Rights Commission, 1985 CanLII 5254 (QC CS), paras [70]–[71]; *Levesque v Quebec (Attorney General)*, 1987 CanLII 964 (QC CA); *Johnson v Social Affairs Commission*, 1984 CA 61. See also Kin c. McNicoll, 2021 QCTDP 34 (CanLII), para [90] (Lewis J); Commission des droits de la personne et des droits de la jeunesse (Mercier et une autre)c. Dion, 2008 QCTDP 9 (CanLII), para [54] (Audet J); *Québec Poultry Ltée c. Quebec (Commission des droits de la personne) et Devost (No. 2)*, 1978 CanLII 3385 (QC CS), para [12] (Phelan J).

The definition of 'social condition' adopted by Justice Tôth refers to objective measures of class or rank (such as birth, income, education level, and occupation). In *Commission des droits de la personne (Larente) c. Gauthier*[330] Judge Rouleau elaborated upon this definition, clarifying that 'social condition' also includes a subjective measure which refers to a person's value based on perceptions and stereotypes generated from these objective elements.[331] The existence of the subjective component is a useful indicator of discrimination but it is not essential and the 'focus should be on the effects of the distinction rather than the cause'.[332]

Apart from this minor development, the courts in Quebec have not significantly developed the meaning of 'social condition'. Recent cases measure it by reference to economic disadvantage[333] such as poverty and the receipt of social assistance.[334] This lack of development, it can be argued, may be due to judicial hesitancy to further develop, or broadly and liberally interpret, the concept of 'social condition', particularly in view of the ambiguity of the term which has no legislative definition.[335]

In one of the few employment cases on 'social condition' the Quebec Court of Appeal has recently held that 'social condition' includes student status.[336] In *Aluminerie de Bécancour inc. c. Commission des droits de la personne*

[translation of original French text: 'condition sociale réfère soit au rang, à la place, à la position qu'occupe un individu dans la société, ou encore à la classe à laquelle il appartient, de par sa naissance, de par son revenu, de par son niveau d'éducation, de par son occupation; soit à l'ensemble des circonstances et des événements qui font qu'une personne ou qu'un groupe occupe telle situation ou telle position dans la société. Le Tribunal est d'accord avec cette proposition.']

[330] 1993 CanLII 8751 (QC TDP).

[331] [translation from French] *Commission des droits de la personne (Larente) c. Gauthier*, 1993 CanLII 8751 (QC TDP). See also *Syndicate of nurses, respiratory therapists, nursing assistants of Cœur-du-Québec (SIIIACQ) (CSQ) v SIUSSS-MCQ*, 2017 CanLII 13636 (QC SAT), para [53]; *Commission des droits de la personne et des droits de la jeunesse (Bia-Domingo) c. Sinatra*, 1999 CanLII 52 (QC TDP), paras [41]–[44]; *R.O. c. Ministre de l'Emploi et de la Solidarité sociale*, 2021 QCCA 1185 (CanLII), paras [59]-[60]; *Commission des droits de la personne et des droits de la jeunesse (Miller et autres) c. Ville de Montréal (Service de police de la Ville de Montréal) (SPVM)*, 2019 QCTDP 31 (CanLII), para [177].

[332] Bécancour (n 314), para [79].

[333] See, for example, *Falkiner v Ontario (Minister of Community and Social Services)*, 2002 CanLII 44902 (ON CA), para [88] in which the court observed that a present situation of being in receipt of social assistance, whilst defined by economic disadvantage, often results from other forms of disadvantage and vulnerabilities.

[334] *R.L.* (see Chapter 1, n 130), para [147] (Pless JSC) citing *Whittom c. Québec (Commission des droits de la personne)*, 1997 CanLII 10666 (QC CA).

[335] This point was made by Mayrand JCS in *Champagne vs. Quebec (Administrative Tribunal)*, 2001 CanLII 24787 (QC CS), para [27].

[336] See *Commission des droits de la personne et des droits de la jeunesse (Beaudry and others) c. Bécancour Smelter Inc.*, 2018 QCTDP 12. On appeal the Quebec Court of Appeal held

et des droits de la jeunesse (Beaudry et autres)[337] ('*Bécancour*') the Quebec Court of Appeal affirmed that student status is part of 'social condition' as set out in section 10 of the *Quebec Charter* because of the economic vulnerability of students as a group.[338] The court held that paying certain workers lower wages based on such 'social condition' (that is, student status) was in breach of section 19 of the *Quebec Charter*[339] (which requires employers to pay equal salaries to workers who perform equivalent work at the same place without discrimination, subject to certain exceptions). Importantly, student status was held to be a 'social condition' despite the relative privilege of the students (as compared to those on minimum wage).[340] The idea that student status cannot support a claim of 'social condition' discrimination because it is 'the result of a personal choice' was also rejected.[341] The Court of Appeal noted that whilst a person's decision to pursue post mandatory education is to some extent a choice, it is 'not a real decision' but, rather, imposed 'to develop to one's fullest and earn a living'.[342]

Bécancour therefore seems to support the position that 'social condition' may capture economically vulnerable groups which lack market capacities. This includes students who tend to experience economic vulnerability during studies[343] in order to acquire the educational qualifications needed to enter a profession or work of their choice. It may also extend to capture other similarly economically vulnerable groups who face or endure such vulnerabilities in order to earn a living or develop to one's fullest. The Court of Appeal said:

> according to case law, social condition results from characteristics that are generally attributed to a person on the basis of socio-economic criteria and the underlying idea that this person occupies an inferior place due, in particular, to , [sic] income, such as social assistance, students, refugees, etc. Overall, it can be noted that Quebec case law has favored the protection of different categories of people who generally (but not always) have a low income or a precarious economic situation as a common denominator.[344]

---

that the Quebec Human Rights Tribunal did not err in finding that 'student status is part of the notion of social condition contained in section 10 of the Quebec Charter'. See *Bécancour* (n 314), para [82].

[337] 2021 QCCA 989.

[338] See Bécancour (n 314), para [47], [62]-[64], [82].

[339] Bécancour (n 314), para [70], [82].

[340] See Bécancour (n 314), para [69]-[73].

[341] Bécancour (n 314), para [62].

[342] Bécancour (n 314), para [63].

[343] See, for example, *Bécancour* (n 314), para [64].

[344] Bécancour (n 314), para [47].

The Quebec Court of Appeal's decision may therefore leave scope for further judicial development of the concept of 'social condition'. A future court may, by analogy, find that it covers similarly economically vulnerable groups. This could include, for example, migrant workers. Unlike the law in the Northwest Territories which requires 'social condition' to be a permanent state, in Quebec 'social condition' under the *Quebec Charter* may be a temporary state.[345] This may broaden the reach of 'social condition' to cover groups which face social and economic disadvantages temporarily, similarly to students.

Outside of the case law, the Human Rights Tribunal of Québec's guidelines on 'social condition' recognize that 'social condition' refers to social status and class.[346] The guidelines state that the classes are distinguished by differences in 'culture' identifiable by 'material' and 'symbolic consumption' (objectified cultural capital) and 'cultural baggage and habits' (embodied cultural capital) and formed by differences in education levels which are usually associated with certain incomes.[347] The guidelines therefore approach class in a very similar way to Bourdieu by defining class in terms of certain forms of cultural capital which are cultivated during a person's upbringing from access to education and other opportunities that arise from income (economic capital) or family income (social capital).[348] This view of 'social condition' and therefore class has not yet been used or endorsed by the courts in Quebec.

(d) Applications in the digital age

The above analysis has shown that in New Brunswick, the Northwest Territories and Quebec 'social condition', which, at its foundation, refers to a person's inclusion within a socially identifiable group that suffers from social or economic disadvantage,[349] is measured by reference to resources which reflect Weberian 'market capacities'.

---

[345] Bécancour (n 314), para [51] citing *Commission des droits de la personne c. Gauthier*, [1994] R.J.Q. 253.

[346] Alberte Ledoyen, 'Lignes directrices sur la condition sociale' (Paper No 2.120.8.4, Commission des droits de la personne et de la jeunesse (Québec), 31 March 1994) 6.

[347] Ibid 12 [author's trans]. See Capuano, 'Giving Meaning to "Social Origin"' (see Chapter 1, n 72), 113–114. The original French text reads:

> Ce qui distingue ces classes en termes de statut, ce sont essentiellement des 'cultures de classe' différentes et identifiables par le mode de consommation matérielle et surtout symbolique (bagage et habitudes culturels). Ces cultures de classe opposables découlent principalement de niveaux d'éducation différents, lesquels sont souvent associés à des niveaux de revenu particuliers etidentifiables.

[348] Capuano, 'Giving Meaning to "Social Origin"' (see Chapter 1, n 72), 114.

[349] *Human Rights Act*, RSNB 2011, c 171, s 2 (definition of 'social condition'); *Human Rights Act*, SNWT 2002, c 18, s 1 (definition of 'social condition'); *Commission des droits de*

In New Brunswick, which has the most restrictive legislative definition of 'social condition', only three factors are relevant to social and economic disadvantage ('source of income', 'occupation', or 'level of education'[350]). In the Northwest Territories, the legislative definition of 'social condition' is more expansive than this and factors that are relevant to social and economic disadvantage include not only 'source of income' and 'level of education', but also 'poverty', 'illiteracy' and 'any other similar circumstance'.[351] Quebec, as explained above, relies on judicial development of the concept 'social condition' in the absence of a legislative definition of the term in the *Quebec Charter*. Since 1979, as explained above, the courts have consistently held that 'social condition' refers to social class and rank as measured by income, poverty or wealth, occupation, and education level.

'Social condition' is therefore largely defined by reference to lack of economic and educational resources which have income producing capacities and open up life chances – for example, income, wealth, occupation, and education. These resources reflect Weberian 'market capacities'. The conception of 'class' as a constituent element of 'social condition' in Canadian legislation and jurisprudence therefore excludes other resources which Bourdieu viewed as formulative of class identity – social capital (such as networks) and embodied cultural capital (such as tastes, likes, interests, accents, speech and other 'dispositions of the mind and body'). It also excludes various factors that reflect social background.

The failure of Canadian legislation and case law to define 'social condition' broadly in terms of Bourdieu's species of capital (particularly social and cultural capital that is broader than formal education or literacy) limits the law's ability to address class discrimination as it arises in the digital age. Subsequent chapters of this book argue that an employer's use of certain social media and automated candidate screening technology creates inequalities and risks of class discrimination based on factors that do not fall within the meaning of 'social condition' (such as embodied cultural capital and social capital). Laws in Canada which prohibit 'social condition' discrimination in employment, therefore, are unable to address these risks of class discrimination.

In Quebec, the Northwest Territories and New Brunswick it is unclear whether intersectionality can be used in the courts to bring into focus

---

la personne *(Québec) v Gauthier* (1993) 19 CHRR D/312 ('*Québec v Gauthier*'); *Syndicate of nurses, respiratory therapists, nursing assistants of Cœur-du-Québec (SIIIACQ) (CSQ) v SIUSSS-MCQ*, 2017 CanLII 13636 (QC SAT), paras [48], [53], [70]; *Order of Certified General Accountants of Quebec c. Quebec (Attorney General)*, 2004 CanLII 20542 (QC CA), para [69].

[350] Human Rights Act, RSNB 2011, c 171, s 2.

[351] *Human Rights Act*, SNWT 2002, c 18, s 1 (definition of 'social condition').

discrimination (such as 'social condition' discrimination). In *Commission des droits de la personne et des droits de la jeunesse (Sam) c. 9377–1905 Québec inc*[352] the Human Rights Tribunal of Quebec considered a claim based on intersectionality. The tribunal noted that whilst 'the *Charter* obviously does not exclude "a robust intersectional analysis"'[353] it 'is still required to clearly identify in its resolution the personal characteristics under s. 10 that are involved',[354] and it then proceeded to consider the claim based on single grounds.[355] This seems to reinforce Atrey's observation of the 'continuing struggles of intersectionality' in the anti-discrimination law regime in Canada.[356] As such, this book will proceed on the basis that intersectionality is not yet used by the courts to bring into focus 'social condition' discrimination (to the same extent that it has been used in South Africa to illuminate 'social origin' discrimination, as explained earlier in this chapter).

Despite these shortcomings of the definition of 'social condition' which limit its application, as a ground of discrimination, in the digital age, there may be scope for the *Quebec Charter* to have greater application in 'wage theft', underpayment and modern slavery cases in light of the recent decision of the Quebec Court of Appeal in *Bécancour*.[357]

B. Discrimination based on 'family status', 'association' and 'family affiliation'

Various laws in Canada prohibit discrimination which is based on a person's association with certain other people. For the purposes of this book the most relevant prohibited ground of discrimination relating to association with other people is 'family status', which will now be explained.

Discrimination in employment based on 'family status' is prohibited at the federal level,[358] and at the provincial level in British Columbia,[359] Alberta,[360] Saskatchewan,[361] Manitoba,[362] Ontario,[363] New Brunswick,[364]

---

[352] 2022 QCTDP 3 (CanLII).

[353] 2022 QCTDP 3 (CanLII), para [44].

[354] 2022 QCTDP 3 (CanLII), para [45].

[355] 2022 QCTDP 3 (CanLII), paras [54]-[87].

[356] Atrey (see Chapter 1, n 157), 14.

[357] See further Chapter 6.

[358] *Canadian Human Rights Act*, RSC 1985, c H-6, ss 3(1), 7.

[359] *Human Rights Code*, RSBC 1996, c 210, s 13(1).

[360] Alberta Human Rights Act, RSA 2000, c A-25.5, s 7(1).

[361] The Saskatchewan Human Rights Code, 2018, s 2(1).

[362] The Human Rights Code, CCSM c H175, ss 9(2)(i), 14(1), 14(2).

[363] Human Rights Code, RSO 1990, c H.19, s 5(1).

[364] Human Rights Act, RSNB 2011, c 171, ss 2.1(k), 4(1).

Newfoundland and Labrador,[365] the Northwest Territories,[366] Nunavut[367] and Prince Edward Island.[368] Ontario, Saskatchewan, Newfoundland and Labrador, and Prince Edward Island have legislative definitions of 'family status' which define the term to mean 'the status of being in a parent and child relationship'.[369]

In *B v Ontario (Human Rights Commission)*[370] ('*B v Ontario*') the Supreme Court of Canada interpreted 'family status' in the Ontario *Human Rights Code*, R.S.O. 1990, c. H-19 ('*OHRC*') to be 'broad enough to encompass circumstances where the discrimination results from the particular identity of the complainant's spouse or family member'.[371] 'Family status' was held to protect against discrimination based not only on 'absolute status' (for example, being in a certain type of family) but also 'relative status' (for example, the identities of a person's family members).[372] For the court, restricting the meaning of 'family status' to absolute status 'would ignore the very condition that brings the status into being in the first place',[373] thus the relationships which permit the existence of a 'family status' are included within its meaning. The ground in the *OHRC* therefore also covers discrimination which is based on a person's family members.

For the Supreme Court, embracing a more inclusive interpretation of 'family status' to include relative status furthered the broad goal of anti-discrimination law,[374] in particular 'preventing the drawing of negative distinctions based on irrelevant personal characteristics'.[375] Such an interpretation was also supported by 'the words of the statute, the applicable principles of interpretation, and the weight of existing discrimination jurisprudence'.[376] This inclusive interpretation of 'family status' from *B v Ontario* has also been followed by courts and tribunals when interpreting the term in the *Canadian Human Rights Act*, RSC 1985, c H-6[377] and the human

---

[365] Human Rights Act, 2010, SNL 2010, c H-13.1, ss 9(1), 14(1).

[366] Human Rights Act, SNWT 2002, c 18, ss 5(1), 7(1).

[367] Human Rights Act, SNu 2003, c 12, ss 7(1), 9(1).

[368] Human Rights Act, RSPEI 1988, c H-12, ss 1(1)(d), 6(1).

[369] See Human Rights Act, 2010, SNL 2010, c H-13.1, s 2; The Saskatchewan Human Rights Code, 2018, SS 2018, c S-24.2, s 2(1); Human Rights Code, RSO 1990, c H.19, s 10(1); *Human Rights Act*, RSPEI 1988, c H-12, s 1(1)(h.11).

[370] [2002] 3 SCR 403 ('*B v Ontario*').

[371] B v Ontario (n 370), para [46].

[372] See B v Ontario (n 370), paras [36], [37], [39].

[373] B v Ontario (n 370), para [39].

[374] B v Ontario (n 370), para [4].

[375] B v Ontario (n 370), para [4].

[376] *B v Ontario* (n 370), para [4].

[377] See *Canada (Attorney General) v Hicks*, 2015 FC 599 (CanLII), paras [22], [67].

rights legislation of British Columbia,[378] Alberta[379] and Saskatchewan.[380] This broad view of 'family status' is also reflected in legislative definitions of the term in Nanavut[381] and Alberta[382] which define 'family status' to mean 'the status of being related to another person by blood, marriage or adoption'.

Therefore, based on the above analysis, at the federal level in Canada and in Ontario, British Columbia, Alberta, Nanavut and Saskatchewan 'family status' appears to cover discrimination which is based on a person's family members. The legislative definition of 'family status' in Prince Edward Island and in Newfoundland and Labrador may also be similarly read, but it has not been the subject of clear interpretation.[383]

A discriminatory practice in a number of these jurisdictions includes, amongst other things, refusing to employ a person on the basis of a prohibited attribute (such as 'family status').[384] In Ontario, where an employer elicits information relating to a prohibited attribute of a job candidate, by asking them questions or making written or oral inquiries, this may infringe the province's human rights legislation.[385]

This prohibition on 'family status' discrimination in employment has particular applications in the digital age because, as chapter 4 will explain, an employer's use of social media to vet job candidates ('cybervetting') may involve or create risks of discrimination based on the identity of the candidate's family members or relatives.

It is important to note here that some of these jurisdictions may have relevant defences which employers could rely on to justify this type of discrimination. This includes defences which permit employers to engage in 'nepotism'[386] or 'anti-nepotism'[387] in certain circumstances and make

---

[378] See Christensen and another v Save-A-Lot-Holdings, 2020 BCHRT 67, paras [15]-[21]; Martin v Grapevine Optical and another, 2021 BCHRT 68, para [33].

[379] See *Fisher (Marshall) v Devolbren Property Services Inc.*, 2022 AHRC 67 (CanLII), para [109], [125], [126].

[380] Byers v Royal Enterprises Corp., 2003 CanLII 74507, paras [36]–[37].

[381] Human Rights Act, SNu 2003, c 12, s 1.

[382] Alberta Human Rights Act, RSA 2000, c A-25.5, s 44(1).

[383] See, for example, *S.M. v St. John's (City)*, 2020 CanLII 49887 (NL HRC).

[384] See Canadian Human Rights Act, RSC 1985, c H-6, s 7(a); Human Rights Code, RSBC 1996, c 210, s 13(1)(a); Alberta Human Rights Act, RSA 2000, c A-25.5, s 7(1)(a); Human Rights Act, RSNB 2011, c 171, s 4(1)(a); Human Rights Act, 2010, SNL 2010, c H-13.1, s 14(1); Human Rights Act, SNWT 2002, c 18, s 7(1); Human Rights Act, SNu 2003, c 12, s 9(1)(a). See also The Human Rights Code, CCSM c H175, s 14(2).

[385] Human Rights Code, RSO 1990, c H.19, s 23(2). See also *Yildiz v M.A.G. Lighting*, 2012 HRTO 2232, para [16]–[24].

[386] See, eg Human Rights Code, RSO 1990, c H.19, s 24(1)(d); The Saskatchewan Human Rights Code, 2018, s 16(11).

[387] See, for example, Human Rights Code, RSO 1990, c H.19, s 24(1)(d); The Saskatchewan Human Rights Code, 2018, s 16(11).

decisions which are based on a *bona fide* occupational requirement.[388] Whether the defences apply will depend on the circumstances of a particular case.

A ground related to 'family status' is 'association discrimination', which is prohibited in Nova Scotia, Yukon and Manitoba. Nova Scotia[389] and Yukon[390] prohibit association discrimination based on a number of grounds, including religion, creed, mental disability, political belief, political affiliation ('association' in Yukon) or political activity. Manitoba's *Human Rights Code*[391] contains a number of definitions of discrimination, one of which is 'differential treatment of an individual on the basis of the individual's actual or presumed membership in or association with some class or group of persons, rather than on the basis of personal merit'[392]. Similarly, the Northwest Territories prohibits discrimination in employment based on 'family affiliation'.[393] There may, for reasons to be explained in chapter 4, also be scope for an employer's use of cybervetting to create risks of discrimination on the basis of these grounds.

C. Discrimination based on 'social origin'

Discrimination on the basis of 'social origin' is prohibited in Newfoundland and Labrador[394] but the ground in this jurisdiction has been defined narrowly as being synonymous with national extraction[395] or originating from a place such as Newfoundland and Labrador.[396] A search of Newfoundland and Labrador case law reveals that the courts have not used or referred to ILO materials, so ILO jurisprudence on the concept of 'social origin' does not appear to be used in this jurisdiction to inform the meaning of the provincial legislation.

---

[388] See, for example, Canadian Human Rights Act, RSC 1985, c H-6, s 15(1)(a); Alberta Human Rights Act, RSA 2000, c A-25.5, s 7(3).

[389] See *Human Rights Act*, RSNS 1989, c 214 s 5(1)(v).

[390] See *Human Rights Act*, RSY 2002, c 116, s 7(m).

[391] CCSM c H175.

[392] *The Human Rights Code*, CCSM c H175, s 9(1)(a).

[393] See *Human Rights Act*, SNWT 2002, c 18, s 5(1).

[394] *Human Rights Act*, SNL 2010, c H-13.1, s 9.

[395] See Human Rights Commission of Newfoundland and Labrador, Annual Report for 2004/05, 7 (concerning Keith et al v Newfoundland Dental Board (October 18, 2004) (unreported)); Newfoundland Dental Board v Human Rights Commission, et al 2005 NLTD 125 (CanLII), para [1], [35].

[396] See Resource Development Trades Council of Newfoundland and Labrador v Long Harbour Employers Association Inc, 2013 CanLII 62193 (NL LA).

IV. The legal landscape in New Zealand and its applications in the digital age

This chapter will now turn to map the legal landscape in New Zealand to explore the extent to which discrimination in employment based on class and/or factors reflective of social background is prohibited. In New Zealand the *Human Rights Act* 1993 (NZ) ('*NZ HRA*') prohibits discrimination in employment based on a number of specified grounds, the most relevant of which to the analysis in this book is 'family status'.[397] 'Family status' is defined in the *NZ HRA* to include, amongst other things, 'being a relative of a particular person'.[398]

Section 22 of the *NZ HRA* makes it unlawful for employers to, amongst other things, refuse to employ a qualified applicant for employment by reason of their family status.[399] It is also unlawful for a person to make an inquiry about a job applicant which could reasonably be understood to indicate an intention to breach section 22.

This prohibition on 'family status' discrimination in the *NZ HRA* has particular applications in the digital age. For reasons that will be explained in chapter 4, an employer's use of social media to screen or vet job applicants may create risks of discrimination based on an applicant's relative.

It is worth noting that employers can rely on exceptions in the *NZ HRA* which permit discrimination based on 'family status' (as defined above) in certain circumstances. This includes an exception to work involving New Zealand's national security,[400] certain initiatives established or arranged by the Crown,[401] or where hiring an employee's relative would mean that there is a 'reporting relationship' between them or it would create a risk of collusion between them to the detriment of the employer.[402]

The *Employment Relations Act* 2000 (NZ) ('*NZ ERA*') permits a person to pursue a grievance against an employer or former employer for a number of reasons including discrimination in the employee's employment.[403] However, as this only appears to cover conduct in employment it does not seem relevant to the issue of cybervetting.

---

[397] See Human Rights Act 1993 (NZ) ('*NZ HRA*'), ss 21(1)(l), 22–23.
[398] *NZ HRA*, s 21(1)(l)(iv).
[399] *NZ HRA*, s 22(1)(a).
[400] *NZ HRA*, s 25(1)(a)(iv).
[401] *NZ HRA*, s 73.
[402] *NZ HRA*, s 32(a).
[403] See *NZ ERA*, ss 102, 103(1)(c), 104.

Conclusion

This chapter set out to map the legal landscapes in Australia, South Africa, Canada and New Zealand, to unravel whether discrimination in employment based on class and social background is prohibited in employment, and, highlight key differences in the law in each country. It found that whilst 'class' and 'social background' are not explicitly listed as grounds of discrimination in legislation within each country, the legislation lists other grounds which reflect, or include, class and various factors reflective of social background.

Part I of this chapter mapped the legal landscape in Australia. It found that the *FW Act* prohibits adverse action and termination of employment based on 'social origin', but at present workers can only rely on the protection from termination of employment. It also found that the *AHRC Act* contains a mechanism to address complaints of 'social origin' discrimination in employment, including access to employment. The analysis revealed that there is a developing body of case law in Australia which supports the position that 'social origin' includes class (as measured by economic, social and cultural capital, which reflects Bourdieusian class theory) and factors that go to social background (such as socio-economic background, family wealth, historical social context including where a person went to school and grew up, and associations). This developing body of case law adopts a view of 'social origin' which is consistent with the way the term is understood in the ILO jurisprudence examined in Chapter 2. For reasons which are also explained in Chapter 2, it is most consistent with legislative intent that the term 'social origin' in both the *FW Act* and *AHRC Act* should have the same meaning as it bears in ILO jurisprudence. Therefore, in addition to these factors, 'social origin' in these Acts may also, consistently with ILO jurisprudence, also refer to home dynamics, family background, certain relatives and geographic origins.[404]

The mapping of the Australian legal landscape also revealed that discrimination based on other grounds reflective of class and/or social background is prohibited, including association with people who have particular protected attributes (under certain state and territory legislation) and 'accommodation status' (under ACT legislation).

Part II of this chapter mapped the legal landscape in South Africa. It found that the Constitution, *EEA*, *LRA* and *PEPUDA* each prohibit discrimination based on 'social origin', but employment disputes are brought under the *EEA* (which covers recruitment processes and the employment relationship) and *LRA* (which covers dismissals). The analysis revealed that in recent South African case law 'social origin' refers to a mixture of

---

[404] See Chapter 2.

factors relating to class and social position. Whilst South African judges do not articulate the meaning of class as a constituent element of 'social origin', for reasons that are explained in Chapter 2 the ground in the *EEA* and *LRA* should have a meaning which is consistent with the way the term is understood in ILO jurisprudence. It may, it can therefore be argued, be measured by reference to economic, social and cultural capital. It also follows that, consistent with ILO jurisprudence, 'social origin' may include home dynamics, family background, certain relatives, locality and geographic origins. This argument is further supported by recent judicial decisions in South Africa which each use international law to interpret 'social origin', as explained above.

Importantly, the analysis of case law in South Africa shows that the courts have recently started to use an intersectional prism in cases which have concerned 'social origin' discrimination. The use of intersectionality has helped to reveal discrimination at the convergence of 'social origin' and certain other attributes (which may not be clear if a single grounds approach is used). This use of intersectionality appears to be unique to South African jurisprudence (among the jurisdictions studied in this book), and it seems to be used to further the country's project of transformative constitutionalism.

Whilst the term 'social origin' in relevant laws within Australia (the *FW Act* and *AHRC Act*) and South Africa (the *EEA* and *LRA*) should have a meaning which is consistent with the way the term is understood in ILO jurisprudence, this chapter set out the legal frameworks relating to each of these instruments to explain how they apply differently.

Part III of this chapter mapped the legal landscape in Canada. It found that three jurisdictions – Quebec, New Brunswick and the Northwest Territories – each prohibit 'social condition' discrimination in employment. Based on the above analysis of the law in each of these jurisdictions, 'social condition' refers to, or reflects, class but it is measured by reference to factors that reflect Weberian market capacities. It therefore does not take into account how Bourdieu's class theory built upon those of Marx and Weber, to introduce a cultural shift in class analysis.

The mapping of the Canadian legal landscape also revealed that certain laws within Canada prohibit discrimination based on other grounds which reflect social background. This includes 'family status' at the federal level and in certain provinces which adopt a broad view of the ground so that it captures relative, and not just absolute, status. As a result, discrimination which is based on family members may fall within the meaning of 'family status' discrimination in these jurisdictions within Canada. As explained above, discrimination based on association with people who have particular protected attributes and on 'family affiliation' is also prohibited in certain provinces. Whilst other grounds of discrimination which reflect class and social background are also contained within legislation in Canada, 'social condition', 'family status', association and 'family affiliation' are likely to be the most relevant in the digital age for reasons which are explained in subsequent chapters.

Finally, Part IV of this chapter mapped the legal landscape in New Zealand. It found that the law in New Zealand is the least developed (amongst the jurisdictions analysed in this book) to address class and social background discrimination. Discrimination based on 'family status', which is defined to include being a relative of a person, is, however, prohibited in this country.

In mapping the legal landscapes in each of these four countries, the analysis in this chapter shows how the law in each differs in its ability to address class and social background discrimination. Chapters 4, 5 and 6 will now apply these laws to the use of certain technology and other practices in employment, to give examples of possible applications of these laws in the digital age. These chapters build on this author's previous work which argues how class discrimination may arise in modern workplaces, such as through the use of cultural fit when hiring[405] or through 'post-code discrimination'.[406] The chapters therefore focus on exposing risks of this type of discrimination from the use of technology and in the post-pandemic workplace.

Chapter 4 will examine an employer's use of social media, in particular for cybervetting, detailed job advertisement targeting, and, terminating an employee's employment for social media posts. For reasons that will be outlined here and elaborated upon in Chapter 4: cybervetting creates opportunities for discrimination based on a candidate's family and relatives, thus its use may create risks of 'social origin' discrimination (under the Australian AHRC Act and South African EEA), 'family status' discrimination (in the laws of certain Canadian jurisdictions and New Zealand, in which the ground includes relative status), and association discrimination based on certain protected attributes; detailed job advertisement targeting may permit the exclusion of job seekers from certain geographic origins or localities, thus its use may create risks of discrimination based on 'social origin' under the *AHRC Act* and *EEA*; and terminating an employee's employment for certain social media posts, depending on the nature of those posts, may be based on the employee's embodied cultural capital and family background, thus exposing employers to potential liability under the *FW Act* (for unlawful termination of employment) and *LRA* (for unfair dismissal).

Chapter 5 will examine an employer's use of automated candidate screening technologies, in particular contextual recruitment systems (CRS), asynchronous video interviewing (AVI) AI, and gamification in recruitment.

---

[405] See, for example, Capuano, 'Giving Meaning to "Social Origin"' (see Chapter 1, n 72), 124–127.

[406] See, for example, Capuano, Ibid, 124. See also The Law Reform Commission of Western Australia, 'Review of the Equal Opportunity Act 1984 (WA)' (Project 111, Discussion Paper, August 2021), 123.

For reasons that will be outlined here and elaborated upon in Chapter 5: the use of CRS involves, or creates risks of, making adverse distinctions based on a job candidate's socio-economic background, where they grew up and went to school, locality and geographic origins, social capital and/or economic capital, thus its use creates risks of discrimination based on 'social origin' under the *AHRC Act* and *EEA*; the use of AVI disadvantages job candidates based on embodied cultural capital, thus its use creates risks of discrimination based on 'social origin' under the *AHRC Act* and *EEA*; and, the use of gamification in recruitment disadvantages job candidates at the intersection of class, social background and disability, thus whilst its use creates risks of both 'social origin' and disability discrimination at the single-axis, an intersectional lens helps to more clearly bring into focus resulting discrimination.

The analysis in Chapters 4 and 5 will, in particular, show how a Bourdousian view of class has much more relevance and application in the digital age than Marxian, Weberian, Durkheimian, and other views. Whilst 'social origin' (in ILO jurisprudence, Australian and South African law) and 'social condition' (in the law of Quebec, New Brunswick and the Northwest Territories in Canada) both refer to 'class', the law in Canada is ill equipped to address class discrimination as it arises in the digital age. This is because 'social condition' in Canadian legislation and jurisprudence is, as noted above, defined by reference to Weberian market capacities. The failure of this Canadian law to take into account the way Bourdieusian class analysis built upon that of Marx and Weber means that laws in Canada which prohibit 'social condition' discrimination cannot capture risks of discrimination based on Bourdieu's species of capital which may arise from an employer's use of social media,[407] AI and algorithms.[408] This Canadian law therefore has little contemporary relevance to addressing class discrimination in the digital age.

Chapter 6 will examine the use of platform work and the post-pandemic shift to remote working. For reasons which are outlined here and elaborated upon in Chapter 6: in light of the decision of the Quebec Court of Appeal in *Bécancour*, the *Quebec Charter's* protections from 'social condition' discrimination may have particular applications in wage theft, modern slavery and underpayment cases; and, remote and hybrid work may disadvantage employee's at the convergence of home dynamics, family wealth and certain other attributes, thus it may not only create risks of 'social origin' discrimination under the *AHRC Act* and *EEA* at the single-axis, but its capacity for discrimination is clearer when analysed through an intersectional prism.

---

[407] See Chapter 4.
[408] See Chapter 5.

4

Social Media in Recruitment, Hiring and Firing Decisions

Introduction

Social media is part of the everyday lives of many people. Facebook is used by this author to connect and stay in touch with family and friends, share pictures and videos of holidays and life achievements, and engage with hobby groups and communities. Whilst Facebook is considered to be a private space, colleagues may make friend requests which opens up this personal space to those in the workplace. Other, more public, platforms are used for a different purpose. Twitter is used by this author to share a personal hobby and interest in whisky through microblogging and sharing content such as distillery tours in Scotland. Whilst Twitter is used to engage with the whisky community, colleagues in the legal sector have followed and subscribed to blog posts. This demonstrates how activities on Facebook and Twitter, though largely intended for private use, are quite easily opened up and come to the attention of those in our work lives. It also demonstrates how others, such as recruiters and potential future employers, can peer into our private lives through a computer screen.

This blurring of the lines between personal life and work life, and the capacity of employers and recruiters to infiltrate this personal life as it is shared in cyber space, may create significant opportunities for discrimination based on class and factors reflective of social background. This chapter will focus on examining three uses of social media by employers and/or recruiters which may create risks of this type of discrimination: (1) cybervetting; (2) job advertisement targeting; and (3) termination of employment for an employee's social media posts.

Part I will examine the use of social media to vet or screen job candidates (cybervetting), to expose how this creates opportunities for adverse distinctions to be made based on a job candidate's class (social and cultural capital), family or relatives. Part II will then examine the use of job advertisement targeting on platforms such as Facebook and LinkedIn, to show how its use can exclude job seeker's based on their locality and geographical location. Finally, Part III will examine the use of social media to terminate an employee's employment for social media posts, to highlight how this may, in certain circumstances, be based on factors reflective of the employee's class such as embodied cultural capital. In all these three parts of the chapter, the law analysed in Chapters 2 and 3 will be applied to consider whether these practices may involve or create risks of discrimination in international labour law, and the laws of Australia, South Africa, Canada and New Zealand.

I. Cybervetting

This chapter will now turn to critically assess the use of social media to screen or vet job candidates, a practice known as 'cybervetting'[1] which has become the norm in hiring and recruitment.[2] The analysis in this part of this chapter will show how cybervetting creates significant risks of discrimination based on class and social background for three main reasons which will be outlined here, and elaborated upon in Part I(A)-(D) of this chapter. First, cybervetting both private and public social media profiles gives employers access to the personal lives of candidates including various digitized indicators of a candidate's class and social background. Second, to determine candidate suitability for a job the cybervetting process may involve distinctions being made based on these indicators, such as social capital or lack thereof, family and associations (through assessing a candidate's social media connections) and cultural capital (through assessing candidate social media profiles for 'cultural fit'). Third, the practice may involve or create risks of discrimination based on a number of protected attributes, such as 'social origin' in international labour law, Australian law and South African law, 'family status' in laws within Canada, 'family status' in New Zealand law, and others.

---

[1] See, eg Christel Backman and Anna Hedenus, 'Online privacy in job recruitment processes? Boundary work among cybervetting recruiters' (2019) 34(2) *New Technology, Work and Employment* 157; Jillian R Yarbrough, 'Is cybervetting ethical? An overview of legal and ethical issues' (2018) 11 *Journal of Ethical and Legal Issues* 1 http://www.aabri.com/manuscripts/172677.pdf.

[2] See Anatoliy Gruzd, Jenna Jacobson and Elizabeth Dubois, 'Cybervetting and the Public Life of Social Media Data' (2020) *Social Media + Society* 1, 2. See also Linda Skates, "Job applicants' social media profiles now checked by companies as 'common practice'" (15 November 2014, ABC News) http://www.abc.net.au/news/2014-11-15/social-media-profiles-of-job-applicants-checked/5888908.

A. Cybervetting gives employers and recruiters access to the personal lives of candidates, including digitized indicators of class and social background

In the 2020s social media, such as Facebook, Linkedin, Instagram and Twitter, have become an integral part of the lives of many people. This social media includes websites or applications that allow people to network online and share their thoughts or media. On Facebook, people can create personal profiles and then connect with other people who use the platform by 'friending' them. This often involves 'friending' family, friends and colleagues and generally Facebook is used by people as a personal space where they can share updates about travel, or hobbies, or life achievements with or without media such as photographs and video. Facebook can also be used to create more public 'pages', such as a page for a business or a hobby (such as where enthusiasts who share a particular passion might meet). On Instagram, people can share photographs and videos which their 'followers' and others (if the profile is public) can 'like'. On Twitter, people can share their thoughts in the form of a written 'tweet' (which may or may not be accompanied by media), and similarly their 'followers' can like or share the tweet. Finally, LinkedIn tends to be used as a professional networking site where people create profiles that set out education, professional experience and achievements. As such, LinkedIn is often used as a professional online space. Facebook, Instagram, Twitter and LinkedIn are only four examples of social media, and people may also use other platforms (such as YouTube, TikTok, and many others).

The screening of a job candidate's social media can be done in two ways:

- Firstly, an employer or recruiter may request access to a candidate's password protected private social media accounts. An employer or recruiter may get access to a candidate's password protected social media in the following ways: (1) they may ask for the login information; (2) they may ask the candidate to add them as a friend or contact; (3) they may ask the candidate to provide print outs of their accounts; or (4) they may ask the candidate to change the privacy settings on social media to public.[3]

---

[3] See, for example, Elana Handelman, 'The Expansion of Traditional Background Checks To Social Media Screening: How To Ensure Adequate Privacy Protection in Current Employment Hiring Practices' (2021) 23(3) *Journal of Constitutional Law* 661, 688; James B Mattson, 'Social Media and Employment Law' in *Social Media and the Law* (2016, 2nd ed, Lexis Nexis), 31. See also Patrick Williams, 'Employer asks interviewee for Facebook page, but many see it as an invasion of privacy' (10 October 2017, ABC News) https://www.abc.net.au/news/2017-10-10/facebook-employers-ask-to-see-profile-page-for-interview/9033722.

- Secondly, an employer or recruiter may screen the publicly available social media data of the candidate.

An employer gaining access to password protected social media profiles which were intended for private use would likely give the employer access to the user's private life and numerous digitized indicators of class and social background. This may include connection lists (social capital and family), evidence of a person's likes, interests, tastes and hobbies (cultural capital), media of the family home and life circumstances (economic capital and social background), location or 'check-in' tags (locality), etc. This is particularly true for private Facebook profiles, which, like the home, tend to be repositories of personal and life information (which may contain updates, photographs and other media about life milestones such as births or buying a home, birthdays, cultural and religious milestones or sacraments such as baptisms or weddings, social gatherings, family holidays and travel, sporting interests and achievements, the home, etc).

In contrast to private social media accounts, it may seem intuitive that public social media accounts will not contain private information about a person. However, the results of recent empirical research into cybervetting (which will now be outlined) calls this into question, and supports the position that even public social media accounts may be a haven of information about a person's private life.

In one study by Gruzd, Jacobson and Dubois, 429 participants from India (113 participants) and the United States (319 participants) were surveyed to analyse comfort levels with cybervetting from a job seeker's perspective.[4] The study found that even where social media information is available publicly, individuals still have 'context and data-specific privacy boundaries'.[5] Gruzd, Jacobson and Dubois conclude that, overall, their research identifies that just because social media information is 'public' 'does not mean people do not have context-specific and data-specific expectations of privacy'.[6] In another study by Jacobson and Gruzd 482 participants from a Canadian university (92.9 per cent were under 25 years of age)[7] were surveyed to investigate concerns about the use of their publicly available social media data in job hiring.[8] Previous studies did not distinguish between social media data which was public or private.[9] They found that just over one quarter (or 26.3 per

---

[4]   Gruzd, Jacobson and Dubois (n 2), 2–3.

[5]   Gruzd, Jacobson and Dubois (n 2), 2, 9.

[6]   Gruzd, Jacobson and Dubois (n 2), 10.

[7]   Jenna Jacobson and Anatoliy Gruzd, 'Cybervetting job applicants on social media: the new normal?' (2020) 22 *Ethics and Information Technology* 175, 182.

[8]   Jacobson and Gruzd, Ibid, 175–176.

[9]   Jacobson and Gruzd, Ibid, 178.

cent) 'did not know the privacy setting on at least one of their social media accounts'[10] and about half (or 49.6 per cent) 'were not comfortable with their publicly available social media data being used for social media screening'.[11] These findings suggest that young people may post information on publicly available social media which is not targeted for an employer, or they may post such information not knowing whether it is public or private.

In light of the above empirical findings just outlined, public social media posts may contain private or intimate content because the poster either expects an appropriate level of privacy or they may not know that the post is public. Cybervetting, even of public profiles, therefore 'affords prospective employers an unprecedented opportunity to examine the personal lives of job applicants'.[12] This creates risks of discrimination based on numerous grounds[13] including, for reasons that will now be explained further below, class and social background.

Based on the above analysis, vetting both private and public social media can 'reveal' or 'uncover' a candidate's less conspicuous attributes that are not self-evident from a job application or interview, such as attributes which reflect class or social background. However, will an employer's access to these attributes lead them to make distinctions based on class and social background? This chapter will now turn to answer this question. The below text will show that, in addition to posing theoretical risks of discrimination, an employer's access to digitized indicators of class and social background through cybervetting may lead them to make distinctions on the basis of these indicators, specifically social capital, family, associations and cultural capital.

B. Cybervetting may involve distinctions based on social capital, family and associations

A key feature of social media platforms such as Facebook or Twitter is that they list a person's social media connections, such as, for example, their 'friends' (on Facebook) or 'followers' (on Twitter). This means that, through cybervetting, an employer or recruiter not only has access to content created by a job candidate but they will likely see the candidate's social media connections and the content which those connections have created. A profile

---

[10] Jacobson and Gruzd, Ibid, 183.

[11] Jacobson and Gruzd, Ibid, 184.

[12] Gruzd, Jacobson and Dubois (n 2), 10.

[13] See, for example, James B Mattson, 'Social Media and Employment Law' in *Social Media and the Law* (2016, 2nd ed, Lexis Nexis), 32–3; Jillian R Yarbrough, 'Is cybervetting ethical? An overview of legal and ethical issues' (2018) 11 *Journal of Ethical and Legal Issues* 1; Helen Lam, 'Social media dilemmas in the employment context' (2016) 38(3) *Employee Relations* 420. See also Jacobson and Gruzd (n 7), 185.

will often contain content from friends or connections – comments, user names, profile and other pictures, media, 'likes', interactions, etc. Where employers quickly cybervet profiles to save time in recruitment (as they are very likely to do) 'they could' also 'easily mistake friend content for profile content'.[14]

With this in mind, and given that redacting all friend or connection lists and content from profiles may presently be a costly, time-consuming and likely unviable option for employers, it seems that cybervetting creates the risk that the identities and content of a candidate's social media connections will be taken into account. Such connections, particularly on Facebook, are likely to include the candidate's friends and family. An important question, therefore, is whether cybervetting involves making distinctions between job candidates on the basis of their social media connections, and, in turn, creates opportunities for discrimination on the basis of social capital, family and associations.

Until recently, there has been limited understanding of the way a person's social media connections ('friends' or 'contacts') influence the views or perceptions of an employer or recruiter who engages in cybervetting.[15] For reasons that will now be explained, studies of cognitive biases and heuristics in psychology shed light on the way these perceptions may be formed and suggest that a job candidate can be 'tainted' by having negatively perceived social media connections.

Walther conducted five experiments to test attitude formation and the 'spreading attitude effect', a phenomenon whereby pairing a person with someone who is liked or disliked affects the way the person is perceived.[16] Across the five studies Walther found that the spreading attitude effect was not only 'reliable' and 'robust', but also 'resistant to extinction'.[17] The spreading attitude effect may therefore make cybervetters prone to paint job candidates with the same brush as their negative social media connections.[18] The 'negativity bias', which tends to make people attribute

---

[14] Dustin Kaleb Hightower, 'Me or My Friend? Examining SNS Friend Activity's Impact on Applicant Perceptions' (Thesis, Submitted in partial fulfillment of the requirements for the degree of Master of Science in Psychology at The University of Texas at Arlington, August 2020), 11.

[15] See, for example, Hightower (n 14), 1.

[16] Eva Walther, 'Guilty by Mere Association: Evaluative Conditioning and the Spreading Attitude Effect' (2002) 82(6) *Journal of Personality and Social Psychology* 919, 919–920. See also Eva Walther, Rebecca Weil and Jessica Dusing, 'The Role of Evaluative Conditioning in Attitude Formation' (2011) 20(3) *Current Directions in Psychological Science* 192, 194.

[17] Walther, 'Guilty by Mere Association' (n 16), 930.

[18] On the spreading attitude effect, see, Ibid, 930.

more weight to negative information, personal traits, etc,[19] likely means that a candidate's negative social media connections will be more salient to a cybervetter.[20]

The findings of an empirical study by Hightower, which was supervised by Professor Amber Schroeder at the University of Texas at Arlington,[21] supports the contention that a person's negative social media connections can adversely influence a cybervetter's evaluation of that person. The study involved 338 participants (half of whom reported to have varying experience evaluating job applicants)[22] who were divided into smaller groups to complete a cybervetting evaluation of manipulated versions of a person's Facebook profile.[23] The findings 'indicated that when compared to a profile with positive or neutral friend content, a profile with negative friend content demonstrated lower suitability ratings'.[24] As such, consistent with the negativity bias, the study's findings suggest that 'negative friend content' (such as 'unprofessional elements' including the 'use of profanity') 'can lower perceptions of the applicant' by a rater.[25]

Given that the negative social media connections of a job candidate may likely lead a cybervetter to adversely evaluate that candidate, can employers or recruiters simply ignore this information when cybervetting? Consistent with research which 'has repeatedly shown that people make judgments based on information they should ignore',[26] studies of cybervetting suggest that negative social media connections will not likely be ignored in the process. Hightower's hypothesis that instructing raters to ignore negative friend content would result in higher suitability ratings[27] 'failed to garner statistical support'.[28] Whilst results suggested that raters had the ability to ignore positive content,[29] instructing raters to ignore negative friend content

---

[19] Paul Rozin and Edward B Royzman, 'Negativity Bias, Negativity Dominance, and Contagion' (2001) 5(4) *Personality and Social Psychology Review* 296.

[20] See, for example, Hightower (n 14), 7.

[21] See Hightower (n 14).

[22] Ibid, 17.

[23] See Ibid, 18–20, 26.

[24] Ibid, 36.

[25] Ibid, 36.

[26] Berkeley J Dietvorst and Uri Simonsohn, 'Intentionally "Biased": People Purposely Use To-Be-Ignored Information, But Can Be Persuaded Not To' (2019) 148(7) *Journal of Experimental Psychology* 1228, 1228. Whilst findings by Dietvorst and Simonsohn suggest that a person's *desire* to ignore information may be a *necessary condition* for doing so, it is not always a *sufficient condition*; there are instances where people may be unable to ignore information even if they *want* to ignore the information: at 1236.

[27] Hightower (n 14), 12.

[28] Ibid, 28.

[29] See, for example, Ibid, 28, 36.

made no significant difference in ratings of an applicant's suitability when compared to the condition where no instructions were given.[30]

In another study by Zhang et al, 39 recruiters were asked to assess 140 Facebook profiles of job seekers to determine whether social media information is related to recruiter evaluations.[31] The results showed that recruiter judgments of hireability correlated not only with social media data which may be legitimate job criteria (education, work-related training or skills, and written communication skills) but also with data which *should not* be taken into account – age (older job seekers were rated higher than younger ones), marital status (job seekers who were married, engaged or in a relationship were rated higher than single job seekers), religion (job seekers whose profiles had religious information were rated lower) and sex (females were rated more highly than males).[32] This further supports the position that cybervetters may take into account the negative social media connections of candidates, even if they are instructed to ignore the information or know they should not take it into account.

Based on the above analysis, it can be argued that in the process of cybervetting assessing *negative* connection or friend content will often be unavoidable, and access to this information may engage a cybervetter's tendency to paint a candidate with the same brush as their social media connections (as a result of the spreading attitude effect) and place particular weight on negative content (as a result of the negativity bias). The practice of cybervetting therefore involves real risks of making distinctions on the basis of a person's social media connections, who on Facebook for example are often the person's family and relatives. This, in turn, means that cybervetting creates significant opportunities for adverse distinctions to be made on the basis of a job candidate's social capital or lack thereof, family, parents, spouses and other relatives.

C. Cybervetting may involve distinctions based on cultural capital

A 2018 survey of 1,012 hiring and human resources managers from the United States found that social media content which led them to hire a candidate included, amongst other things, content which showed that the candidate had a wide range of interests (31 per cent) or they were a cultural

---

[30] Ibid, 28.

[31] Zhang et al, 'What's on Job Seekers' Social Media Sites? A Content Analysis and Effects of Structure on Recruiter Judgments and Predictive Validity' (2020) 105(12) *Journal of Applied Psychology* 1530, 1538–1539.

[32] See Ibid, 1538.

'fit' (31 per cent).[33] This author has argued elsewhere that employers often measure 'cultural fit' by reference to tastes, hobbies, interests, and other factors that reflect a person's cultural capital, so assessing 'cultural fit' by reference to such factors involves risks of class discrimination in hiring.[34] The use of social media (such as Facebook or Instagram) by employers to assess the 'cultural fit' of candidates may therefore create similar risks of class and social background discrimination, depending on how 'cultural fit' is measured. Cybervetting may also create more opportunities for in-group favouratism (which is explained in chapter 1) to play out, which may in turn lead to adverse treatment of candidates whose profiles exhibit less prototypical characteristics (for example, unfamiliar forms of cultural capital).

Until recently, little was known about how employers use cybervetting in hiring decisions. A recently published empirical study, which involved interviews with 61 human resources professionals, has found that cybervetting involves the making of moral judgments about a job candidate's character and 'red flags' included signs or evidence of certain lifestyle choices from a candidate's online presence (such as signs of alcohol consumption, partying, and looking 'Goth').[35] Some of the human resources professionals made assumptions about the moral character and behaviour of candidates from pictures of them which were posted on social media, to determine whether they were a cultural fit and to deny them work.[36] This supports the argument that cybervetting creates significant new opportunities for discrimination based on a job candidate's embodied cultural capital (for example, lifestyle such as working-class drinking culture), where it is not viewed to align with the employer's perceptions of morality or suitable behaviour.

D. Cybervetting may involve or create risks of discrimination in international labour law, and the laws of Australia, South Africa, Canada and New Zealand

Cybervetting not only creates inequalities based on class and social background, but employers who use this practice in recruitment may also expose themselves to potential liability for discrimination under the laws of Australia, South Africa, Canada and New Zealand.

---

[33] CareerBuilder Press Release (9 August 2018) https://press.careerbuilder.com/2018-08-09-More-Than-Half-of-Employers-Have-Found-Content-on-Social-Media-That-Caused-Them-NOT-to-Hire-a-Candidate-According-to-Recent-CareerBuilder-Survey.

[34] See Capuano, 'Giving Meaning to 'Social Origin" (see Chapter 1, n 72).

[35] See Steve McDonald, Amanda K Damarin, Hannah McQueen and Scott T Grether, 'The hunt for red flags: cybervetting as morally performative practice' (2022) 20(3) *Socio-Economic Review* 915, 922, 930.

[36] See McDonald et al, ibid, 923–925.

First, an employer's use of cybervetting may create risks of discrimination based on 'social origin' under the *AHRC Act* (in Australia) and the *EEA* (in South Africa), which both extend to cover discrimination in recruitment stages before hiring and access to employment.[37] 'Social origin' in these laws, for reasons that are explained in Chapter 2, should be interpreted in a manner that is consistent with the way the term is understood in ILO jurisprudence. Based on the analysis of ILO jurisprudence in Chapter 2, 'social origin' discrimination appears to include discrimination which is based on, amongst other things, a person's cultural capital, family and relatives (such as parents and spouses).[38] Given that, as explained above, cybervetting may involve the making of adverse distinctions in recruitment based on a job candidate's cultural capital, or their family and relatives, employers in both Australia and South Africa who use this practice may therefore risk engaging in 'social origin' discrimination.[39]

These risks are particularly clear when recalling the comments of the ILO Committee of Experts on the 'home visit' recruitment phase used in Colombia, which is explained in Chapter 2. This practice involved ascertaining the social background of job applicants through visiting their homes,[40] and the Committee of Experts called for the practice to be abolished because of its capacity to result in 'social origin' discrimination.[41] Cybervetting the social media profiles of job candidates may be tantamount to an online or digitized form of the 'home visit' recruitment phase, particularly where the profiles provide digitized markers or evidence of content or dynamics in the home (such as from content which is available on many private Facebook profiles, for example). Cybervetting may therefore involve similar risks of 'social origin' discrimination as would arise from using the 'home visit' recruitment phase.

In addition, cybervetting could amount to association discrimination where the practice involves discrimination which is based on, for example, the religion or politics of a job candidate's family member.[42] As explained in Chapter 3, this type of discrimination is prohibited in certain state and territory anti-discrimination laws in Australia, and, in certain Canadian provincial laws. Therefore, where an employer refuses to employ a job

---

[37] See Chapter 3.

[38] See Chapter 2.

[39] See Chapter 3 for the definition of discrimination in the AHRC Act and the legal tests needed to establish unfair discrimination under the EEA.

[40] Observation (CEACR) – adopted 2008, published 98th ILC session (2009) (ILO 111) – Colombia.

[41] Observation (CEACR) – adopted 2008, published 98th ILC session (2009) (ILO 111) – Colombia.

[42] On association discrimination in certain state and territory anti-discrimination law in Australia, see further Chapter 3.

applicant because the employer discovered that the person's family member on Facebook has certain political or religious views, then, this may amount to association discrimination.[43]

Second, given that, as explained above, an employer's use of cybervetting creates opportunities for adverse distinctions to be made on the basis of the identity of a job candidate's family members or relatives, it may expose the employer to potential liability for 'family status' discrimination in Canadian and New Zealand law. This is because, as explained in detail in Chapter 3, in the *Canadian Charter* and the human rights legislation of certain Canadian provinces 'family status' has been defined or interpreted to include not only absolute status but also relative status (that is, the identity of certain family members).[44] In New Zealand the protected ground of 'family status' in the *NZ HRA* includes being a relative of a particular person.[45] As such, where cybervetting exposes that a job candidate has a certain family member or relative, and an employer refuses to hire the candidate based on that relationship, then, this may create risks of 'family status' discrimination in certain jurisdictions in Canada (where 'family status' includes relative status) and in New Zealand.

Risks of unlawful 'family status' discrimination from cybervetting seem particularly high in New Zealand and the Canadian province of Ontario.

Under the *NZ HRA* it is, as explained in Chapter 3, not only unlawful for employers to refuse to employ a qualified applicant for employment by reason of their family status,[46] but it is also unlawful for a person to make an inquiry about a job applicant which could reasonably be understood to indicate an intention to engage in such conduct. By Cybervetting certain platforms (such as Facebook), for reasons which are explained above, employers make inquiries which can be reasonably expected to reveal a candidate's relatives. Making such an inquiry (which is reasonably expected to yield these results) could, depending on the facts of a case, therefore be used as evidence to help support a claim that the employer intended to discriminate on this basis.

In Ontario, as also explained in Chapter 3, an employer which elicits information relating to the 'family status' of a job candidate (by asking them questions or making written or oral inquiries) may infringe the province's human rights legislation.[47] It is arguable that cybervetting may be viewed as a process which elicits such information about a job candidate. For example,

---

[43] See further Chapter 3.
[44] See further Chapter 3.
[45] See Chapter 3.
[46] *NZ HRA*, s 22(1)(a).
[47] Human Rights Code, RSO 1990, c H.19, s 23(2). See also *Yildiz v M.A.G. Lighting*, 2012 HRTO 2232, para [16]–[24].

where an employer inputs the job candidate's name into a Facebook search this may be a written inquiry which could, and most likely will, elicit information about the candidate's family members.

II. Job advertisement targeting

A number of online and social media platforms, including Facebook and LinkedIn, allow employers to advertise available jobs. These platforms allow job advertisements to be targeted so that they are seen by individuals who meet certain criteria. This capacity to target job advertisements for a specific audience is sometimes called 'detailed targeting'. This chapter will now turn to analyse the use of job advertisement targeting through Facebook and LinkedIn to assess whether it creates risks of class and/or social background discrimination. The below analysis will reveal that the job targeting capabilities of Facebook can permit employers to hide advertisements from job seekers who come from certain localities and geographic origins, whilst the job targeting capabilities of LinkedIn can permit employers to exclude job seeker's based not only on locality, but also their economic and cultural capital.

A. Facebook

Facebook allows employers to advertise jobs using its 'Jobs on Facebook' service.[48] Meta (formerly Facebook, Inc) claim that this platform has been used to help people find over 1 million jobs.[49] On 22 February 2022 the Jobs on Facebook service ceased to operate outside of the United States and Canada.[50] It appears that outside the United States and Canada, employers can still use Facebook Marketplace and business pages to advertise job openings (for example, Australian employers post jobs on their business pages[51]). Whilst the Jobs on Facebook service is presently only available in the United States and Canada,[52] it may be made available again in other

---

[48] Meta, 'Post a Job' https://www.facebook.com/business/pages/post-job; Meta, 'About Jobs on Facebook' https://www.facebook.com/business/help/2294865670556540?id= 939256796236247.

[49] Meta, 'About Jobs on Facebook' https://www.facebook.com/business/help/229486567 0556540?id=939256796236247.

[50] Meta, 'Update on the Jobs on Facebook Product' https://www.facebook.com/business/ help/982945655901961.

[51] See, for example, Flight Centre Australia Facebook page https://www.facebook.com/ flightcentreAU/.

[52] It would be interesting to see whether such practices are challenged in Canadian courts. As explained in Chapter 3, *Bates* (see Chapter 3, n 325) appears to support the position that 'social condition' may include locality or where a person lives but this was only

countries sometime in the future. As such, the analysis in this part of this chapter, whilst presently relevant to the United States and Canada, has potential global significance.

A key feature of the Jobs on Facebook service is that it allows employers to target certain job seekers based on specified criteria, such as their interests and locality. The targeting, which is known as 'Detailed Targeting', is made possible through job advertisement preferences of an employer. It appears that people who do not meet a Facebook advertisement's target criteria will not see the advertisement because detailed targeting allows an advertiser to refine the group of people to which Facebook shows the ad.[53]

Case studies published by Meta reveal the extent to which detailed targeting permits employers to exclude people from certain areas being able to view job advertisements:

- a Cuban Guys Restaurants case study stated that, in relation to the restaurant's hiring strategy, it 'filters for people living within 3 miles of the hiring restaurant' in order to 'reach … ideal candidates', adding that its 'worker demographic often doesn't own a car)';[54]
- a Cumberland Farms case study stated that 'Cumberland can attract interested candidates who live near the stores that are hiring – and because workers with short commutes tend to stay in their jobs longer, this helps to lower turnover';[55]
- a Princeton Golf Course case study, under the heading 'Attracting local candidates', stated that 'Facebook helps' it to 'compete for local talent by showing the company's job openings to people who are likely to be interested in them' and '[i]n deciding which posts people see, Facebook weighs factors such as proximity to the employer and previous jobs people have applied to'.[56]

Meta has recognized that the targeting options of Facebook ads have potential to be abused by advertisers. From 19 January 2022 Meta removed certain

---

inferred from the decision in that case and it is not definitive or clear from the adjudication panel's reasoning.

[53] See Meta, 'About Detailed Targeting' https://www.facebook.com/business/help/1823 71508761821?id=176276233019487.

[54] Meta, 'Cuban Guys Restaurants: Case Study' https://web.archive.org/web/20220411062 623/https://www.facebook.com/business/success/cuban-guys-restaurants.

[55] Meta, 'Cumberland Farms: Case Study' https://web.archive.org/web/20220330070600/ https://www.facebook.com/business/success/cumberland-farms.

[56] Meta, 'Princeton Golf Course: Case Study' https://web.archive.org/web/20220330113 555/https://www.facebook.com/business/success/princeton-golf-course.

'detailed targeting' options that have potential to target or exclude people on the basis of health conditions, race, ethnicity, political affiliation, religion or sexual orientation:

> Starting January 19, 2022 we will remove Detailed Targeting options that relate to topics people may perceive as sensitive, such as options referencing causes, organizations, or public figures that relate to health, race or ethnicity, political affiliation, religion, or sexual orientation. Examples include:
>
> - Health causes (e.g., 'Lung cancer awareness', 'World Diabetes Day', 'Chemotherapy')
> - Sexual orientation (e.g., 'same-sex marriage' and 'LGBT culture')
> - Religious practices and groups (e.g., 'Catholic Church' and 'Jewish holidays')
> - Political beliefs, social issues, causes, organizations, and figures
>
> It is important to note that the interest targeting options we are removing are not based on people's physical characteristics or personal attributes, but instead on things like people's interactions with content on our platform.[57]

Despite these concerns, moving into 2022 location targeting is still a key targeting option.[58] However, 'where required, advertisers running housing, employment and credit opportunity ads must continue to identify as a corresponding 'Special Ad Category' and use restricted targeting options'.[59] In relation to job ads in the United States, according to Meta, '[t]hese ads will not allow targeting by age, gender, ZIP code, multicultural affinity, or any detailed options describing or appearing to relate to protected characteristics'.[60]

Importantly, '[a]ge, gender, ZIP code or postal code' targeting is now limited or unavailable for employment campaigns which target audiences

---

[57] Meta, 'Removing Certain Ad Targeting Options and Expanding Our Ad Controls', (9 November 2021) https://www.facebook.com/business/news/removing-certain-ad-targeting-options-and-expanding-our-ad-controls.

[58] Meta, 'About Location Targeting' https://www.facebook.com/business/help/202297959811696?id=176276233019487

[59] Meta, 'Simplifying Targeting Categories' (11 August 2020) https://www.facebook.com/business/news/update-to-facebook-ads-targeting-categories.

[60] Meta, 'Updates To Housing, Employment and Credit Ads in Ads Manager' (26 August 2019) https://www.facebook.com/business/news/updates-to-housing-employment-and-credit-ads-in-ads-manager.

in the United States and Canada.[61] In relation to location targeting for employment campaigns Facebook explains:

> You can target your ads to people by geographic location (such as country, region, state, province, city or congressional district), but not by ZIP code or postal code. You also can't exclude locations.
>
> Specific audiences based on a city, address or pin drop locations will include an expanded radius. For example, if you want to reach people in the US who live in the city of Seattle, your audience will also include people within a 15-mile radius of Seattle's city center.[62]

Whilst Meta has expanded the radius of location targeting, such targeting would, for reasons that will now be argued, still invariably exclude people who may live in ethnically diverse, indigenous, rural, and/or working-class areas of a city, county, or state. For example, a radius expanding 15 miles from Seattle would exclude people who live in southern areas of Kings County which have relatively high indigenous (for example, Muckleshoot) and Latino or Hispanic populations.[63] By way of another example, a radius expanding 15 miles from Melbourne (Victoria, Australia) would exclude people who live in traditionally working-class suburbs such as Dandenong, Frankston and Werribee.[64] The same argument can be made about the use of location targeting in other major cities around the world, and how it invariably would exclude people from a city's outer suburbs and state's regions. Given that many outer suburbs of cities and regions tend to have high poverty rates,[65] it can be argued that location targeting can exclude people who live in undesirable or poor parts of a city.

Opportunities for discrimination which arise from location targeting become more apparent when an intersectional lens is used to consider disadvantages at the intersection of locality, background, race and ethnicity. The above analysis directed attention to the disadvantaging effect which

---

[61] Meta, 'About audiences for credit, employment or housing campaigns' https://www.facebook.com/business/help/2220749868045706?ref=FBBBlog_UpdatesTo Housing.

[62] Meta, 'About audiences for credit, employment or housing campaigns' https://www.facebook.com/business/help/2220749868045706?ref=FBBBlog_UpdatesTo Housing.

[63] University of Washington, 'Mapping Race Seattle/King County 1940–2020' https://depts.washington.edu/civilr/maps_race_seattle.htm.

[64] To measure radius the 'KM from Home' online tool was used: https://2kmfromhome.com/25km

[65] See, for example, Robert Tanton, Dominic Peel and Yogi Vidyattama, 'Every suburb Every town: Poverty in Victoria (November 2018, NATSEM, Institute for Governance and Policy Analysis (IGPA), University of Canberra. Report commissioned by VCOSS), 13.

detailed location targeting may have on Muckleshoot, Hispanic and Latino populations from certain areas in the United States. In Australia, a disproportionate number of First Nations Peoples live in rural areas – as at 2016, little over a third lived in major cities compared to 'three-quarters of the Non-Indigenous population'.[66] Detailed location targeting (such as for inner city jobs) therefore has capacity to exclude job seekers based not only on their locality, but it may also disadvantage people at the convergence of locality, race and ethnicity.

The use of location targeting in 2022 and beyond also seems unnecessary or unjustified. Whilst Meta attempts to point to a business case for using detailed targeting, they appear to be based on poorly made assumptions. For example, in relation to the Cuban Guys restaurants case study mentioned above the assumption appears to be that because the worker demographic tends not to own a car then candidates who live close to the workplace are ideal. This assumption attempts to justify the use of location targeting, but it seems to overlook that people may be willing to relocate closer to employers or use public transport. Additionally, since the outbreak of COVID-19 some employers also allow employees to work remotely with the use of the internet, applications such as Zoom, etc where the requirements of the job can be performed in such a way. Detailed location targeting which permits employers to not make job advertisements visible to people in parts of cities or outer locations therefore not only has capacity to disadvantage people on the basis of locality and social background, but it seems very unlikely to be relevant to the requirements of most jobs (given access to public transport, etc).

B. LinkedIn

Like Facebook, LinkedIn also allows employers to advertise through its platform and use targeting options in order to achieve certain objectives including converting advertising campaigns to job applicants.[67] At present, only location is a mandatory targeting option so advertisers must specify the location of the user they wish to reach, and LinkedIn infers such location

---

[66] Australian Bureau of Statistics, 'Estimates of Aboriginal and Torres Strait Islander Australians' (Ref period: June 2016, Release date: 31 August 2018, Latest release as at 8 August 2022) https://www.abs.gov.au/statistics/people/aboriginal-and-torres-strait-islander-peoples/estimates-aboriginal-and-torres-strait-islander-australians/latest-rele ase#:~:text=Remoteness%20Areas,-At%2030%20June&text=The%2053%2C500%20re maining%20Aboriginal%20and,0.5%25%20in%20very%20remote%20Australia.

[67] LinkedIn, 'Mastering Targeting on LinkedIn', 9 https://business.linkedin.com/content/ dam/me/business/en-us/marketing-solutions/cx/2020/namer-pdfs/linkedin-marketing-solutions-updated-targeting-playbook-2020.pdf ('Mastering Targeting on LinkedIn'), 6.

from the user's profile and IP address.[68] Some users have the option to include not only a city but also a post code as their location.[69] Other options include schools targeting which allows advertisers to reach alumni of certain schools[70] and traits targeting which allows advertisers to reach users with distinguishing characteristics such as being a 'frequent traveler'.[71] The use of such targeting options infers that the ads will be visible to, or reach, those who meet the targeting criteria (and thus not be visible to, or not reach, those who do not meet the criteria). Otherwise, there would appear to be little point in targeting the ads.

These targeting options, like detailed location targeting used through Facebook, have potential to create inequalities not just on the basis of locality but also economic and cultural capital. By using schools targeting employers can exclude those whose lack of life opportunities led them to attend low socio-economic schools and 'universities of access' (which tend to not be prestigious or 'elite'). By engaging in traits or travel targeting, employers would exclude the poor and those who cannot afford to travel frequently based on their lack of access to economic capital (for example, money) and social capital (for example, parents who can pay for travel) as well as cultural capital (for example, interest and tastes in travel).

C. Risks of discrimination in Australian and South African law from job advertisement targeting

Based on the above analysis, the job advertisement targeting capabilities of Facebook and LinkedIn create significant inequalities in access to employment based on class and social background. The targeting capabilities of Facebook permit detailed location targeting in job advertisements which may create inequalities in access to employment based on where a person lives or grew up. The targeting capabilities of LinkedIn are broader, and permit not only detailed location targeting but also targeting based on schools a person attended and traits such as whether they are a frequent traveler. This may create inequalities in access to employment based not just on where a person lives or grew up, but also where they had the opportunity to go to school, whether they can afford travel (economic capital), or whether their parents can afford travel (social capital), or whether they cultivated taste in travel (cultural capital).

---

[68] Mastering Targeting on LinkedIn, 9.
[69] LinkedIn, 'Change the location of your profile' https://www.linkedin.com/help/linkedin/answer/a564134/change-the-location-on-your-profile (accessed 6 December 2022).
[70] Mastering Targeting on LinkedIn, 18.
[71] Mastering Targeting on LinkedIn, 20.

All these factors fall within the meaning of 'social origin' as it is understood in ILO jurisprudence[72] and in a developing body of Australian case law.[73] This ILO jurisprudence may also be useful in South Africa because the term 'social origin' within the *EEA* should be interpreted consistently with the way the term is understood in this jurisprudence.[74] The use of job advertisement targeting through both Facebook and LinkedIn may, therefore, have capacity for significant new risks of indirect discrimination based on 'social origin' in Australia and South Africa.

In Australia, the practice could create risks of indirect discrimination based on 'social origin' under the *AHRC Act*.[75] Detailed location, school and travel/trait targeting (if made available and used in Australia by employers) could be seen to be a practice which results with unequal treatment or a 'disproportionately harsh impact' on job seekers based on their 'social origin'. Provided that it is not closely related to the inherent requirements of a job, then, the practice may fit within the meaning of indirect discrimination in *ILO 111* and therefore the *AHRC Act*.[76]

In South Africa, the practice could also create risks of unfair discrimination based on 'social origin' under the *EEA*.[77] If detailed location, school and travel/trait targeting is made available and used in South Africa by employers it could introduce unfair discrimination into job advertisements (which, pursuant to section 5 of the *EEA*, employers would have a duty to take steps to eliminate). It does appear that the use of such detailed targeting could satisfy the three-stage *Harksen* test because it: (1) differentiates between those who live in certain targeted areas and those who do not (where location targeting is used), those who went to certain schools and those who did not (where schools targeting is used), and those who can afford to travel and those who cannot (where traits targeting is used); (2) appears to fit within the definition of indirect discrimination based on 'social origin' as it is understood in South African jurisprudence; and (3) may be presumptively unfair, in which case the burden would fall on an employer to establish that its use is fair.[78]

It follows that the use of social media recruitment tools such as detailed location, school and travel/trait targeting, if made available and used by employers in Australia and South Africa, not only creates inequalities but may carry real risks of indirect discrimination based on 'social origin'.

---

[72] See Chapter 2.

[73] See Chapter 3.

[74] See Chapter 2.

[75] See Chapter 3 for a discussion of the legal framework.

[76] See further Chapter 3.

[77] See Chapter 3 for a discussion of the legal framework.

[78] See further Chapter 3.

III. Termination of employment for social media posts

In addition to being used as a tool for recruitment and job advertising, social media can also reveal information about current employees which may lead to them being fired by an employer. This chapter will now turn to consider the types of social media posts which have resulted with termination of an employee's employment, to show that, in certain circumstances, these posts may be expressions of class or social background.

The media contains many reports of people being fired from their job for posts which they make on social media ('self posts'), or which others have made about them on social media ('third party posts'). In a study of 312 news media articles about people being fired for social media posts Robards and Graf found that, whilst most related to racism and queerophobia, 18 concerned political content and 1 concerned pre-COVID-19 anti-vaccination.[79] Political content included content which expressed 'controversial political viewpoints or non-partisanship with the employer'.[80] For example, in a third-party post, a government contractor was filmed 'flipping off' the motorcade of president Donald Trump and was subsequently fired.[81]

On social media the boundaries between work life and personal life are therefore increasingly blurred. This is because, as the study referred to above suggests, people have lost their jobs because social media posts indicate they have political or personal views with which an employer disagrees. The difficulty with such action taken by employers is that these views could, for reasons which will now be explained, reflect class and/or social background.

A person's moral views about the world (whether dressed as political, religious or personal) may be strongly related to their class and social background. For Dewey, morality is not an individual trait that can be severed from external forces such as politics or economics, but, rather, it is social.[82] Whilst Bourdieu views taste is an indicium of class,[83] Halewood asks whether there is also a moral element.[84] He concludes that 'morality is pivotal to both social class and to judgements about social class'.[85] Taste,

---

[79] Brady Robards and Darren Graf, '"How a Facebook Update Can Cost You Your Job": News Coverage of Employment Terminations Following Social Media Disclosures, From Racist Cops to Queer Teachers' (2022) *Social Media + Society* 1, 7.

[80] Robards and Graf, Ibid, 6.

[81] Robards and Graf, Ibid, 8.

[82] Michael Halewood, 'Class is Always a Matter of Morals': Bourdieu and Dewey on Social Class, Morality, and Habit(us)' [2022] *Cultural Sociology* 1, 10 citing Dewey, Human Nature and Conduct (1935 [1922], Henry Holt, New York), 9, 319.

[83] See Chapter 1.

[84] Halewood (n 82), 11.

[85] Ibid, 14.

like morality, is a way of acting *and* a way of thinking that reflects 'habitus', something which both Bourdieu and Dewey agree is 'a sedimentation of the environment within us and our bodies'.[86] A person may therefore, in assessing habits or habitus which reflect tastes and moral judgments about what is better or worse for society, make distinctions which reinforce social divisions such as class (aesthetic judgments).[87] Aesthetic, for Bourdieu, may be considered to be masked expressions 'of moral disgust to ways of life of the working class'.[88]

When an employer sees and assesses social media posts, it is important for them to consider the possibility that they may be assessing habits which have been formed and cultivated during upbringing and in social settings. This includes the expression of both tastes and morality which are each social products rather than created in a vacuum separate from one's environment. Such moral views may be reflected in social media posts on a number of topics, such as vaccination hesitancy, opinions against same sex marriage or homosexuality, skepticism about climate change, etc. These views may attract the disapproval of many, including employers, but they may also have a classed and social dimension as they could, depending on the circumstances, have a genesis in class and upbringing. Put another way, certain views may be a sedimentation of a person's environment within them over time, and, therefore, such views could reflect embodied cultural capital and habitus. Assessments will need to be made on a case-by-case basis as to whether a person's views are a genuine product of class or upbringing, religion, political opinion, or a combination of all these things.

In *Cook*, which is discussed in Chapter 3, the Australian Fair Work Commission held that the protected attribute 'social origin' in the *FW Act* includes notions of class, and it measured class by reference to embodied cultural capital including 'dispositions of the mind and body'.[89] The complainant's stance as an 'anti-vaxxer' therefore fell within the meaning of 'social origin'. Whilst the complainant was unsuccessful in establishing the elements of indirect discrimination, this decision suggests that people who lose their job or are fired because of their strongly held beliefs which reflect embodied cultural capital may be able to bring a claim under section 772 of the *FW Act*, which prohibits termination of employment based on 'social origin'. It may follow, therefore, that a worker may be able to bring such a claim where their employment is terminated because they express a

---

[86] Ibid, 14.
[87] See Ibid, 7, 14.
[88] See Ibid, 10.
[89] See further Chapter 3.

strongly held view in a social media post which reflects embodied cultural capital and habitus.

People may, as the examples below will attempt to show, lose their jobs for views which can be argued to reflect 'social origin' (for example, embodied cultural capital and habitus), or a combination of this ground and other grounds such as religion, political opinion or sexual orientation. Whilst each case must be determined on their individual facts on a case-by-case basis, these below examples may shed light on conduct which could potentially amount to termination of employment based on 'social origin', and the intersections between this ground and other grounds.

In one example, a business in Canberra claimed that it had fired a worker after the worker had expressed opposition to same-sex marriage.[90] Whilst it is not possible to comment on the specific facts of this case, generally speaking employers who fire an employee for such a reason may risk doing so because of a combination of the worker's religious views and 'social origin' (for example, where the person is raised in the Catholic faith in circumstances where their family took a strict reading of canon law on marriage[91]). Opposition to same-sex marriage in these circumstances may therefore not only reflect religion but also family background.

Protections from 'social origin' discrimination may also go both ways. For example, in the United States a person who was employed as a minister claimed that the Catholic Diocese of Cleveland fired him for 'liking' his friend's post on Facebook about same-sex marriage.[92] Whilst it is also not possible to comment on the specific facts of this case, generally speaking an employer in Australia who fires an employee for a such reason may risk doing so because of a combination of the person's political views, sexual orientation, religion and 'social origin' (for example, where a same-sex attracted person is raised in the Catholic faith but the family adopts a view of scripture which is accepting of homosexuality). Supporting same-sex marriage in these circumstances may therefore not only be a product of sexual orientation, political opinion, and religion, but it depends on the way a family, or its parish priest, interprets scripture. As such, it could be viewed to reflect 'social origin' where a person has adopted the position over time as a result of their environment.

---

[90] Paul Karp, 'Company that 'fired' woman for saying 'it's OK to vote no' may have broken law' (The Guardian, 20 September 2017) https://www.theguardian.com/australia-news/2017/sep/20/company-that-fired-woman-for-saying-its-ok-to-vote-no-may-have-bro ken-law.

[91] See *Code of Canon* Law, Title VII.

[92] Mark Osborne, 'Catholic minister says he was fired over Facebook post about friends' gay marriage' (ABC News (United States), 30 September 2018) https://abcnews.go.com/US/catholic-minister-fired-facebook-post-friends-gay-marriage/story?id=58183269.

Then there may be examples of termination of employment based on 'social origin' which do not seem related to any other attributes. For example, suppose a young impressionable worker has anti-vaccination views as a result of the sedimentation of their family environment within them (because their parents and older siblings hold such views). Suppose, further, that the worker shares this anti-vaccination view on social media and is subsequently fired. There may, in these circumstances, be scope for the worker to claim that the termination of their employment is based on their embodied cultural capital and habitus, and therefore 'social origin'.

The decision in *Cook*, and the analysis of ILO jurisprudence on which it appears to be based,[93] may also be useful in South Africa. As explained in detail in Chapter 2, 'social origin' in certain South African laws (such as the *LRA*) should be interpreted consistently the way the term is understood in ILO jurisprudence. As such, employers in South Africa who dismiss employees for social media posts should take care to ensure the posts do not reflect 'social origin' (as the above examples may show), or else they may risk facing a dismissals dispute and legal action under section 191 of the *LRA*.

Conclusion

This chapter set out to investigate the extent to which the use of social media by employers and recruiters creates inequalities and risks of discrimination based on class and social background. The chapter examined the use of cybervetting, job advertisement targeting through platforms such as Facebook and LinkedIn, and social media to terminate an employee's employment. This chapter found that all of these three practices create inequalities and certain risks of discrimination based on class and social background.

First, the above analysis of cybervetting reveals how the practice creates significant opportunities and likelihood for adverse distinctions to be made on the basis of a job candidate's family or relatives. Cybervetting could therefore involve or create risks of discrimination based on a job candidate's 'social origin' in international labour law (under *ILO 111*), Australia (under the *AHRC Act*) and South Africa (under the *EEA*), 'family status' in Canada (under the *Canadian Charter* and the human legislation of various provinces) and New Zealand (under the *NZ HRA*). Where it is based on the job candidate's association with people who have, for instance, certain religious or political views, then, it could also create risks of association discrimination which is prohibited in the laws of various Australian states and territories and in various Canadian provinces. The practice of cybervetting therefore exposes employers to possible liability for discrimination under a

---

[93] See further Chapter 3.

number of legislative schemes in all four of the jurisdictions analysed in this book. The practice may, for reasons explained above, also involve making distinctions between job candidates on the basis of their embodied cultural capital to determine cultural fit, thus creating further opportunities for 'social origin' discrimination.

Second, the above analysis of job advertisement targeting reveals how an employer's use of this tool to engage in location, schools or traits targeting creates inequalities based on class and social background. The use of the tool to target potential hires from certain localities or schools or with certain traits, and in turn exclude those who are not from such localities or schools or who do not possess the targeted traits, could, for reasons explained above, create risks of indirect discrimination based on 'social origin' in international labour law (under *ILO 111*), and in Australia (under the *AHRC Act*) and South Africa (under the *EEA*).

Third, the above analysis highlights how an employer's act in terminating an employee's employment for certain social media posts could potentially, depending on the nature of the posts, be based on the employee's embodied cultural capital or habitus. Such termination of employment or dismissal could be argued to be based on an employee's 'social origin', thus exposing employers to possible claims under section 772 of the Australian *FW Act* (which prohibits termination of employment based on this ground). Such acts may also possibly expose employers in South Africa to risks of legal action under the *LRA*, for reasons explained above.

The analysis in this chapter also exposes how the law of each of the four jurisdictions examined in this book offer very different levels of coverage from class and social background discrimination which may arise from an employer's or recruiter's use of social media. Whilst all these jurisdictions appear equipped to address risks of such discrimination from cybervetting, it appears that only the law in Australia and South Africa has capacity to address the inequalities and risks of this type of discrimination which arise from job advertisement targeting and termination of employment for certain social media posts. This reveals a void in the ability of both Canadian and New Zealand law to address such discrimination from social media, which could be filled through legislative reform by enacting laws which prohibit discrimination and termination of employment based on 'social origin' consistently with *ILO 111* and *ILO 158* respectively.

Automated Candidate Screening, Algorithms and Artificial Intelligence in Recruitment

Introduction

Employers and recruiters make use of a number of automation technologies to screen job candidates. With advances in technology, and in particular developments in algorithms and AI, employers and recruiters now have access to sophisticated new job candidate screening tools which can help to automate recruitment in ways that were once only imaginable. Algorithms can now be used to filter candidates based on socio-economic data to assist in bolstering an employer's claims that recruitment is fair. AI now has the ability to analyse a job candidate's use of words or facial expressions with the result that robots, rather than humans, now increasingly determine the candidates that should, and should not, proceed in recruitment processes. Digital games can now be used to assess job candidates to determine their suitability for a job or employer. These are examples of the technologies that will be examined in this chapter.

Put simply, an algorithm follows a computerization procedure to transform inputted information into a desired output.[1] For example, the Australian government's use of an Online Compliance Intervention Program (commonly known as 'Robodebt') automated the issuing of debt notices to welfare recipients who were, based on the use of an algorithm, deemed to have been overpaid.[2] This algorithm averaged a

---

[1] See, Florian Jaton, *The Constitution of Algorithms: Ground-Truthing, Programming, Formulating* (2021, The MIT Press), 48–50.

[2] See University of Queensland, 'How to avoid algorithmic decision-making mistakes: lessons from the Robodebt debacle' (Momentum) https://stories.uq.edu.au/momentum-magaz ine/robodebt-algorithmic-decision-making-mistakes/index.html.

person's earnings which were reported to the Australian Taxation Office over a series of fortnights, and then compared them with the welfare payments a person received, to calculate whether the person was overpaid welfare.[3] However, the formula's use of fortnightly averages (as opposed to actual earnings) meant that the algorithm outputted exaggerated or incorrect debt figures.[4]

AI refers to the ability of a computer or robot to perform or 'execute cognitive tasks with minimal or no human interaction'.[5] It refers to the way computers can simulate human learning and decision-making through the use of mathematics and logic, and it can also be interconnected with a process called machine learning whereby the computer learns from its experience without the need for direct instruction from humans.[6] For example, a machine learning model developed by Amazon sought to automate recruitment decisions (that is, vet applicants) by observing patterns in resumes that were submitted over a 10-year period (most of which came from men), but, problematically, the system had learned to prefer male candidates.[7]

The failings of Robodebt and Amazon's AI recruitment tool are examples of the way the use of automation technologies can lead to certain harms. In the case of Robodebt, the algorithm's formula resulted with bills being issued to welfare recipients for debts they did not owe, and almost $2 billion was unlawfully claimed from 433,000 people.[8] In the case of Amazon's AI, the machine learning model learned to prefer male job candidates. The use of algorithms and AI to automate processes, whilst having capacity to save

---

[3] Ibid.

[4] See University of Queensland, 'How to avoid algorithmic decision-making mistakes: lessons from the Robodebt debacle' (Momentum) https://stories.uq.edu.au/momentum-magaz ine/robodebt-algorithmic-decision-making-mistakes/index.html.

[5] Mona Ashoka, Rohit Madana, Anton Johaa and Uthayasankar Sivarajahb, 'Ethical Framework for Artificial Intelligence and Digital technologies' (2022) 62 *International Journal of Information Management* 1, 2.

[6] See, for example, Microsoft, 'Artificial intelligence (AI) vs machine learning (ML)' https:// azure.microsoft.com/en-gb/solutions/ai/artificial-intelligence-vs-machine-learning/ #process.

[7] Jeffrey Dastin, 'Amazon Scraps Secret AI Recruiting Tool that Showed Bias Against Women' in *Ethics of Data and Analytics: Concepts and Cases* (2022, Auerbach Publishers), 296; Roberto Iriondo, 'Amazon Scraps Secret AI Recruiting Engine that Showed Biases Against Women' (News, 11 October 2018, Carnegie Mellon University, Machine Learning Department) https://www.ml.cmu.edu/news/news-archive/2016-2020/2018/october/ amazon-scraps-secret-artificial-intelligence-recruiting-engine-that-showed-biases-agai nst-women.html.

[8] See 'A Robodebt royal commission has been announced. Here's how we got to this point' (ABC News, 26 August 2022) https://www.abc.net.au/news/2022-08-26/robod ebt-royal-commission-explained/101374912.

time and costs for humans, may also therefore create potential for injustice and discrimination. Whilst research considers how algorithms and AI may reproduce, or result with, gender bias[9] and racial bias,[10] it overlooks problems of class and social background discrimination which may result from the use of these technologies.[11]

The use of algorithms and AI to screen job candidates in, and out, of a job interview or recruitment process gives rise to the question whether the workings of these algorithms and AI create structural barriers on the basis of class and factors reflective of social background. Put another way, it can be asked whether the way these algorithms and AI assess or screen job candidates disadvantage, or involve the making of adverse distinctions, based on the class and/or social background of candidates. This chapter will examine three automated job candidate screening tools: (1) Contextual Recruitment Systems ('CRS'); (2) Hiretech including the use of Asynchronous Video Interviewing ('AVI'); and (3) Gamification.

Part I will examine an employer's use of CRS, to show how it may involve the making of adverse distinctions between candidates based on socio-economic background, family wealth and background, locality, where a person grew up, and also economic and social capital. Part II will examine the use of AVI, to expose how it can create inequalities and disadvantage candidates on the basis of factors reflective of class such as embodied cultural capital. Finally, Part III will examine the use of gamification, to illuminate how it can disadvantage candidates at the convergence of class and disability. In all these three parts of the chapter, the law analysed in Chapters 2 and 3 will be applied to consider whether these practices may involve, or create risks of, discrimination under laws in Australia, South Africa, Canada and New Zealand.

While algorithms and AI may, as noted above, contain the biases of those who develop them, this chapter will focus on exposing structural barriers or adverse distinctions which may arise from the workings of CRS, AVI and gamification.

---

9   See, for example, Marc Cheong, Reeva Lederman, Aidan McLoughney, Sheilla Njoto, Leah Ruppanner and Anthony Wirth, 'Ethical Implications of AI Bias as a Result of Workforce Gender Imbalance' (Report, CIS & The Policy Lab, The University of Melbourne) https://www.unibank.com.au/-/media/unibank/about-us/member-news/report-ai-bias-as-a-result-of-workforce-gender-imbalance.ashx.

10 See, for example, Nicol Turner Lee, 'Detecting racial bias in algorithms and machine learning' (2018) 16(3) *Journal of Information, Communication and Ethics in Society* 252.

11 See, for example, Australian Human Rights Commission, 'Using artificial intelligence to make decisions: Addressing the problem of algorithmic bias' (Technical Paper, 2020).

I. Contextual Recruitment Systems (CRS)

A number of employers now use an algorithm and tool named a 'contextual recruitment system' ('CRS') which has been developed by the UK company Rare.[12] Rare's list of clients includes major employers in Australia and the United Kingdom. In Australia this includes law firms Allens Linklaters, Ashurst, Clayton Utz, DLA Piper and Herbert Smith Freehills.[13] In the United Kingdom Rare's list of clients includes dozens of employers in a range of sectors, including the legal, banking and professional services sectors.[14] The CRS, as a recruitment algorithm, also has potential applications in other markets and thus the use of this algorithm may have international implications.

The CRS 'uses data insights to cast light or give "context" about potential hires, allowing firms to identify candidates who have outshone their peers against the odds'[15]. The law firm Allens explains:

> CRS Australia works by combining publicly available information with candidates' responses asked as part of their application process. This is combined with information from two databases – the first contains bespoke information on more than 2000 high schools nationally; the second contains 2482 residential postcodes. The result delivers two outputs to graduate employers: one a measure of disadvantage and the other a measure of performance.[16]

A 'set of factors that form[s] the contextual data points of the CRS' can be broadly 'grouped into home environment and personal circumstances'.[17]

'Home environment' can include a candidate's 'financial background, whether they worked during the semester, whether they are the first in

---

[12] See, for example, Melissa Coade, 'Firms mine data to profile clerkship talent pool' (Lawyers Weekly, 6 September 2016) http://www.lawyersweekly.com.au/news/19513-firms-mine-data-to-profile-clerkship-talent-pool; 'Allens Adopts a Rare Approach to Grad Recruitment' (Allens, 15 June 2016) https://www.allens.com.au/med/pressreleases/pr15jun16.htm.

[13] Rare Contextual Recruitment System Australia (accessed 29 July 2022) https://web.archive.org/web/20220729003418/https://au.contextualrecruitment.com/.

[14] See Rare Contextual Recruitment System Australia (accessed 29 July 2022) https://web.archive.org/web/20220729003418/https://au.contextualrecruitment.com/.

[15] Melissa Coade, 'Firms mine data to profile clerkship talent pool' (Lawyers Weekly, 6 September 2016) http://www.lawyersweekly.com.au/news/19513-firms-mine-data-to-profile-clerkship-talent-pool.

[16] Allens Linklaters, 'Allens adopts a Rare approach to grad recruitment' (15 June 2016) https://web.archive.org/web/20220728095219/https://www.allens.com.au/insights-news/news/2016/06/allens-adopts-a-rare-approach-to-grad-recruitment/.

[17] Gjeta Gjyshinca, 'Contextual Recruitment in Australia: Why recruiters have a role to play in promoting social mobility, and how contextual data can help to identify hidden talent' (June 2016, Report, Rare/Allens Linklaters), 13.

their family to attend university, and the general level of economic and educational advantage of the candidate's home postcode'.[18] It seems that indicators of geographic disadvantage are likely to be most relevant to contextual recruitment, such as 'the Index of Relative Socio-economic Advantage and Disadvantage (IRSAD), which summarises information about the economic and social conditions of people and households within an area, and the Index of Education and Occupation (IEO), which reflects the educational and occupational level of communities'.[19] The CRS is therefore 'able to identify candidates living either in poor areas, or in areas with low levels of qualifications and lacking employment opportunity'.[20]

Both Rare and Allens recognize that 'using a postcode alone as a proxy for financial disadvantage (or otherwise) can never be completely accurate'.[21] This may be because not all people who live in certain localities are 'disadvantaged'. Therefore, a candidate's 'personal circumstances' appear to be relevant. For Rare and Allens, it seems that relevant 'personal circumstances' indicative of disadvantage include whether 'a candidate's family received government benefits', whether 'the candidate consistently worked long hours during semester', and whether the candidate entered Australia as a refugee or spent time in government care.[22]

In a Lawyers Weekly story concerning the use of the CRS by Allens, it is noted that the CRS 'draws on information provided by candidates and mines demographic and educational data to evaluate a candidate's social, economic and human capital'.[23] According to Allens, the CRS 'enables businesses to view a candidate in context by offering a more complete picture of the candidate's background including considerations such as socio-economic background'.[24] International law firm Hogan Lovells, one of Rare's UK clients, adds that the CRS will enable firms 'to take the economic background and personal circumstances of a candidate into account for the first time'.[25]

---

[18] Ibid.

[19] Ibid.

[20] Ibid, 17.

[21] Ibid, 17.

[22] Ibid.

[23] Melissa Coade, 'Data-driven tool shakes up clerkship application process' (*Lawyers Weekly*, 15 June 2016) http://www.lawyersweekly.com.au/news/18785-data-driven-tool-sha kes-up-clerkship-application-process.

[24] 'Allens Adopts a Rare Approach to Grad Recruitment' (15 June 2016) https://web.arch ive.org/web/20220728095219/https://www.allens.com.au/insights-news/news/2016/ 06/allens-adopts-a-rare-approach-to-grad-recruitment/

[25] Hogan Lovells, 'Hogan Lovells to Pioneer Ground-Breaking Contextual Recruitment Tool' (Press Release, 21 May 2015) https://web.archive.org/web/20220728101014/ https://webcache.googleusercontent.com/search?q=cache%3AgOh6pJ4yytoJ%3Aht tps%3A%2F%2Fwww.hoganlovells.com%2Fen%2Fnews%2Fhogan-lovells-to-pioneer-gro undbreaking-contextual-recruitment-tool+&cd=2&hl=en&ct=clnk&gl=au.

To reiterate what has been stated above, it appears that the CRS identifies candidates who live in certain areas, evaluates the *social and economic capital* and relative 'disadvantage'/'advantage' of candidates, gives a more complete picture of a candidate's *socio-economic background*, and enables employers to take into account a candidate's *economic background*. This demonstrates that the CRS is a tool that is available to be used by employers to gain a picture or a metric of a job candidate's class or social background, making this information available for use in recruitment decisions.

A. Risks of 'social origin' discrimination from an employer's use of CRS

The CRS, as explained above, introduces data about a job candidate's locality (for example, where they live), upbringing (for example, where they went to school), family wealth and circumstances, socio-economic background, as well as economic and social capital into recruitment processes. All these factors, for reasons that are explained in Chapters 2 and 3, appear to be indicia of the protected attribute 'social origin' in ILO conventions, Australian law (under the *AHRC Act* and the *FW Act*) and South African law (under the *EEA* and *LRA*). Whilst the use of the CRS would clearly seem to introduce considerations of 'social origin' into recruitment processes, the question arises whether its use involves *discrimination* on this basis under *ILO 111*, the *AHRC Act* and the *EEA* (which each extend to cover recruitment processes before hiring and access to employment).[26]

To address this question, the way the CRS filters candidates in and out of the running for interviews needs to be examined. A report by both Allens and Rare explains the CRS in more detail, and clarifies:

> Imagine that two students in New South Wales apply to a commercial law firm for a graduate role. Both achieved an ATAR of over 85, securing them places on Law courses at the University of Wollongong (UOW). One – let's call him James – achieved an average GPA of 72, performing well consistently throughout university and the other – Jessica – achieved a GPA of 68, massively improving on her first year grades. James has work experience in a law firm, and Jessica doesn't.
>
> So at first glance, although the candidates are similar, James seems the obvious choice for selection to interview. However, James completed Year 12 at a school in the top one per cent of schools in NSW and Jessica at a school in the bottom one per cent. Both achieved HSC

---

[26] See Chapter 3 for a discussion of the legal frameworks concerning discrimination under the AHRC Act and unfair discrimination under the EEA.

scores of around 82 in all their Year 12 subjects, but James's school cohort averaged 80, and Jessica's just 50. When we look at the school context, Jessica outperformed by over 60 per cent. And then we learn that she could only afford to go to UOW thanks to a scholarship. Further, we learn James's law firm experience was secured by an uncle, and Jessica couldn't afford an unpaid role because she had to support herself through university.

With the *extra, contextualising, information, Jessica is more likely to merit at least an interview* [emphasis added]. She might easily have been overlooked by firms that routinely require legal work experience from their candidates, and that – in fact – means that these firms are missing out. Allens, however, looks for candidates from a broader pool of diverse backgrounds – those who can balance study with work and extra-curricular activities.[27]

First, it seems that, based on this explanation, the processes of the CRS differentiates between and treats job candidates differently on the basis of 'social origin'. In the example provided by Allens and Rare, 'Jessica' *is more likely to merit at least an interview with the extra contextualising information* obtained from the CRS. It was explained further above that the CRS mines for a range of 'contextualising information' in order to perform its work, including socio-economic indicators which are connected with an applicant's post-code, high school, where he or she grew up and went to school, financial situation and home environment, amongst other things. It therefore seems that the CRS highlights certain candidates as meriting an interview, not based on indicators of performance, but rather because of contextualizing information that go to 'social origin'. Put another way, the algorithm seems to help an employer determine that a candidate more likely merits at least an interview based on factors reflective of the candidate's particular 'social origin' which shows that the candidate out-performed in his or her specific social setting.

Second, not only does the CRS appear to differentiate between candidates or treat them differently because of factors that reflect 'social origin', but this distinction may lead to the impairment of equality of opportunity in recruitment and selection for those candidates who are filtered out by the algorithm. It seems likely that a candidate's inclusion in the (finite) interview pool or list of interviewees (for example, Jessica) would be compensated for by the exclusion of somebody else. It also seems that other job applicants

---

[27] 'Contextual Recruitment in Australia: Why recruiters have a role to play in promoting social mobility, and how contextual data can help to identify hidden talent' (Report, Rare/Allens), 12.

who share Jessica's grades and educational characteristics, but not 'social origin' (that is, contextualizing information that shows out-performance in context), will likely not merit an interview. Based on their distinct 'social origins', these applicants have not out-performed in their specific social settings. To include them in the interview pool, despite them not out-performing their context, would defy the purpose of the CRS. Even when giving the benefit of the doubt, and assuming these candidates would not have been offered an interview anyway, the tool seems to make 'social origin' a relevant consideration in deciding who to interview, as it appears to confer a preference on candidates based in their 'social origin'.

If a person is interviewed and then employed (based on his or her contextualizing information from the CRS) when they previously would not have been employed, then a candidate who would otherwise have been employed will not be (because there will be finite places at the law firm).

Whilst it cannot be definitively determined that an employer who uses the CRS will base hiring decisions (as opposed to decisions about who to interview) on a candidate's 'social origin', it should be recalled (as explained in Chapter 3) that both the Australian *AHRC Act* and the South African *EEA* extend to cover discrimination in recruitment stages before hiring. The definition of 'discrimination' in the *AHRC Act*, consistently with the definition in *ILO 111*, covers access to employment. These laws, unlike the *FW Act* for example, are not only concerned with discrimination in hiring or in the employment relationship, but they also, for reasons explained in detail in Chapters 2 and 3, apply to discrimination against job applicants.

As a result, therefore, for reasons which will be explained, there does seem to be a risk that the use of the CRS may satisfy the meaning of 'discrimination' in the *AHRC Act* (as well as *ILO 111*, which has the same definition of 'discrimination') and 'unfair discrimination' in the *EEA*.[28]

In relation to 'discrimination' in section 3 of the *AHRC Act*, it could be argued that the use of the CRS appears to: (1) make distinctions, preferences (by filtering in candidates) and exclusions (by filtering out candidates) on the basis of 'social origin' which; (2) result with the nullification or impairment of equality of opportunity in employment and occupation (which, as just noted and for reasons explained in Chapters 2 and 3, extends to access to employment and recruitment stages before hiring). It follows that the use of the CRS may also create risks of 'social origin' discrimination under *ILO 111*, which may have implications (for example, reputational) for employers internationally.

In relation to section 6(1) of the *EEA*, bearing in mind the three-stage *Harksen* test, the CRS could be seen to: (1) differentiate between candidates

---

[28] For a discussion of the legal frameworks relevant to the *AHRC Act* and the *EEA*, see Chapter 3.

on the basis of 'social origin' by treating them differently; and (2) discriminate against candidates who are filtered out based on factors that go to 'social origin'. Given that 'social origin' is a listed ground on which discrimination is prohibited in both the *EEA* and the South African constitution unfairness will be presumed, thus it will turn on an employer to show that it is fair.[29] It also follows that, if the CRS is seen to involve unfair discrimination, employers in South Africa which use the algorithm may risk not being in compliance with the positive duty in section 5 of the *EEA* to eliminate such discrimination in recruitment procedures.

As such, not only does the use of the CRS result with inequalities and distinctions based on 'social origin', but its use could involve or create risks of discrimination on this basis as well.

B. The use of the CRS may detrimentally affect those who face, or have faced, adversity

Whilst the CRS may be used by employers in good faith to enhance workplace diversity, the *AHRC Act* does not contain a 'special measures' exception which would permit favourable treatment based on 'social origin'.[30] Additionally, although the *EEA* contains an affirmative action exception to 'unfair discrimination', such measures must apply to specifically designated groups (black people, women and people with disabilities).[31] 'Social origin' in both of these Acts appears to be a symmetrical attribute.[32]

Even if a law permits substantive equality based on 'social origin' and the use of special measures to achieve this equality, it is questionable whether the CRS will achieve such equality. For reasons which will now be explained,

---

[29] See, for example, *University of South Africa v Reynhardt* (JA36/08) [2010] ZALAC 9, para [21].

[30] For the sake of completeness it should be noted here the *FW Act* was recently amended to permit 'special measures to achieve equality' in enterprise agreements in certain circumstances (The *Fair Work Legislation Amendment (Secure Jobs, Better Pay) Act* 2022 (Cth) amends the *FW Act* to, amongst other things, now permit 'special measures to achieve equality' in enterprise agreements in certain circumstances: Pt 9. See also, *Fair Work Legislation Amendment (Secure Jobs, Better Pay) Bill 2022, Explanatory Memorandum*, vii [16], xvii [73]-[76], xivi [243], xlix [265]–[268], 97 [356], 98 [543], 99 [548]), but it appears that the legislature only intends for such measures to promote substantive equality that is permitted under anti-discrimination law (such as those concerning women and employees with disability). See *Fair Work Legislation Amendment (Secure Jobs, Better Pay) Bill 2022, Revised Explanatory Memorandum*, 97 [556]–[557]; *Fair Work Legislation Amendment (Secure Jobs, Better Pay) Bill 2022, Explanatory Memorandum*, [246]. See also the newly added s 195(2)(c) of the *FW Act*.

[31] See Chapter 3.

[32] See further Chapter 3.

the algorithm's use may have (perhaps unintended) consequences which adversely affect those who have faced adversity.

Identifying 'disadvantage' generally is not as easy or straightforward as identifying disadvantaged groups of a particular sex (for example, women), or age (for example, older and younger people), or race (for example, people of colour), or ability (for example, people with disability). Given that the CRS can only 'mine' and 'assess' information to which there is legal access, and which people volunteer, the CRS may, for the below reasons, create a skewed, distorted or incorrect assessment of 'disadvantage' or 'advantage'.

Job candidates are unlikely to freely volunteer information to an employer which may reveal 'advantage': private tutoring, family connections, family wealth, family finances or income, etc.[33] If they know that the CRS is used to filter candidates, this is even more unlikely. Savvy job candidates will not likely divulge information to employers that will weigh against them, and accordingly, in these circumstances the CRS can only assess an individual's 'advantage' or 'disadvantage' based predominately on available information about his or her environment.

Candidates may also not wish to volunteer information about 'disadvantage' to a potential employer which they may wish to keep private. This may include becoming a single parent, personal or family abuse (such as physical, sexual, emotional or psychological abuse), family substance abuse, domestic violence, personal or family gambling addiction, childhood neglect, poverty, disability, personal or family illness, psychological and psychiatric conditions, carer responsibilities, and other matters that may be of a personal nature, stigmatized and/or reflect negatively on a person. The CRS may therefore not be able to measure many factors that could reflect 'disadvantage'. As a result, it may not develop an accurate picture of candidates who are (in reality as opposed to on 'paper') 'disadvantaged'.

The tool may therefore benefit 'advantaged' members of settings which it adjudges are 'disadvantaged', whilst working to the detriment of 'disadvantaged' members of settings which it decides are 'advantaged'. For example, some people in 'disadvantaged' environments or localities may be 'advantaged', particularly with increased gentrification of historically working class inner-city localities, and so the tool may work to confer a benefit on the 'advantaged' who happen to live in areas which the tool assesses is 'disadvantaged'. The tool may also adversely affect the 'disadvantaged' who live in areas which the tool assesses as 'advantaged'. For example, a young person may live in a particularly desirable suburb of Melbourne, such as

---

[33] People tend to downplay sources of privilege or advantage over others. See, for example, Liz Moor and Sam Friedman, 'Justifying inherited wealth: Between 'the bank of mum and dad' and the meritocratic ideal' (2021) 50(4) *Economy and Society* 618.

Williamstown or Port Melbourne, but he or she may come from a family of blue-collar workers who have lived in the suburb for decades or from a family which relies on public housing. The CRS may therefore disadvantage such persons even more than they already are, because it may not take into account the difficulties of their private and family lives.

The tool therefore has the capacity to disadvantage or disproportionately impact those who have faced adversity based on 'social origin' of the kind which is not able to be detected or measured by the algorithm, or which is not volunteered. This might result from a situation where, whilst two candidates may have the same grades, work experience and tertiary education, for reasons explained above which will be summarized here, the CRS may filter in the one with visible or measurable 'disadvantages' (which may not reflect the candidate's actual disadvantage) but exclude or reject the other with hidden but genuine disadvantages. This distinction between the candidates appears to be made based on the 'social origin' of each candidate, and the algorithm's capacity to measure it. The above assessment of the CRS therefore exposes how the use of the algorithm has capacity to create inequalities and opportunities for (both upward and downward) 'social origin' discrimination in recruitment processes. While the goal of the algorithm is to enhance workplace diversity, such potential consequences of its use may have not been envisaged.

II. 'Hiretech' and Asynchronous Video Interviewing (AVI)

Asynchronous video interviews (AVIs) or 'on-demand' video interviews, which require a job candidate to record answers to set questions without an interviewer present, have increased in use and popularity since the COVID-19 pandemic.[34] There are many providers of AVI or 'on demand' video services for employers, such as HireVue,[35] Modern Hire,[36] Zapid Hire,[37] Knockri,[38] and VidCruiter.[39] One such provider of this 'hiretech', HireVue, will be the focus of the below analysis because it provides some transparency on the workings of its software and it has taken measures to

---

[34] See, for example, Peter Rubinstein, 'Companies are increasingly using automated video interviews to assess candidates. How do you get through this potentially uncomfortable experience?' (BBC, 6 November 2020) https://www.bbc.com/worklife/article/20201 102-asynchronous-video-interviews-the-tools-you-need-to-succeed.

[35] HireVue https://www.hirevue.com/.

[36] Modern Hire https://modernhire.com/platform/screen/.

[37] Zapid Hire https://www.zapidhire.com/.

[38] Knockri https://www.knockri.com/.

[39] Vid Cruiter https://vidcruiter.com/video-interviewing/pre-recorded/.

reduce bias. Yet, as the below analysis will show, even with these measures or 'safeguards' to reduce bias, 'hiretech' is inherently problematic and its use creates risks of 'social origin' discrimination.

HireVue's software has been used in over 12 million interviews by over 700 organisations,[40] including by employers in Australia[41] and South Africa.[42] This includes a number of major employers. HireVue claims that some users of its technology are Pfizer, Alliance Data Systems, Lion, BHP, and Telstra.[43]

The results of an algorithmic audit of the HireVue algorithm, which were made available to the public in 2021, provide data on the workings of its 'hiretech'. According to this audit, HireVue's assessments:

> incorporate algorithms that analyze candidates' responses to interview questions recorded via webcam, and their performance on psychometric games, to generate competency scores in eight areas: Communication, Team Orientation, Problem Solving, Willingness to Learn, Adaptability, Dependability, Drive for Results & Initiative, and Cognitive Ability. In the use case audited, the competency scores are then used to rank the candidates, with the highest-ranked progressing to an in-person interview, the lowest-ranked being rejected, and the remainder referred to a human reviewer.[44]

As such, HireVue's AI automatically ranks candidates based on their recorded responses to set questions. The AI therefore determines which candidates progress to an in-person interview (those with the highest automated competency scores) and which candidates are rejected (those with the lowest automated competency scores).

---

[40] Drew Harwell, 'A face-scanning algorithm increasingly decides whether you deserve the job', online (The Washington Post, 6 November 2019) https://www.washingtonpost.com/technology/2019/10/22/ai-hiring-face-scanning-algorithm-increasingly-decides-whether-you-deserve-job/.

[41] See Andrew Taylor, 'Talk to the robot: How technology is changing the way you find a job' (The Sydney Morning Herald, 14 November 2021) https://www.smh.com.au/national/talk-to-the-robot-how-technology-is-changing-the-way-you-find-a-job-20211112-p598ir.html.

[42] See Alicia Naidoo, 'Job hunting: Six tips to ace that online interview on HireVue' (The South African, 13 August 2020) https://www.thesouthafrican.com/lifestyle/hirevue-job-interview-tips/.

[43] HireVue, 'Congratulations to the Winners of the 2021 HireVue Customer Excellence Awards!' (accessed 9 April 2022) http://web.archive.org/web/20210930191413/https://www.hirevue.com/awards.

[44] O'Neil Risk Consulting & Algorithmic Auditing (ORCAA), 'Description of Algorithmic Audit: Pre-built Assessments' (Report, ORCAA's algorithmic audit of HireVue's pre-built assessments for early career and campus hires, December 15 2020), 1 ('ORCAA algorithmic audit').

The audit of HireVue's algorithms referred to a number of concerns, including the algorithm's scoring of accents[45] and disadvantage faced by people with speech impairment or those who are not technologically savvy,[46] amongst other things. One strategy used by HireVue to address bias is called 'thresholding', which involves human review of applications with responses which do not contain sufficient content for the algorithm to create meaningful competency scores (for example, low-content or short answers which may be used by minority groups, people with speech impairment, etc).[47]

Since the audit HireVue has refined its algorithms with a view to promoting fairness. The algorithms no longer assess visual analysis (a candidate's 'facial expressions, body language, emotions, or their background and surroundings') and speech inputs (such as tone and pauses).[48] The algorithms are also tested for 'adverse impacts' or 'algorithmic bias' to see if one group, such as men or women, pass assessments at a 'significantly different rate' than other groups.[49] HireVue claims that it only releases the algorithms where it is 'confident that race, gender, and age group differences (or adverse impact) have been minimised'.[50] Whilst HireVue claim to test for adverse impact based on characteristics other than race, gender and age (such as 'attractiveness, country of residence, non-native accent, etc'[51]), it appears that these bias minimization efforts overlook potential for bias or discrimination based on class and social background.[52]

Through being refined so as to not take into account visual analysis and speech inputs, HireVue's AI therefore focuses on assessing the substance of a candidate's responses to questions. This may, at first blush, appear to be an intuitive way to remove risks of bias and discrimination from hiring. However, it will now be argued that even if AI is reduced to assessing only the content of a candidate's responses to questions, the asynchronous manner in which the information from the candidate is obtained has potential to disadvantage candidates from certain classes and social backgrounds.

---

[45] ORCAA algorithmic audit, 4.

[46] ORCAA algorithmic audit, 5.

[47] ORCAA algorithmic audit, 5.

[48] Lindsey Zuloaga, 'The latest leap in HireVue's assessment technology' (Hire Vue, 30 September 2021) http://web.archive.org/web/20220814235107/https://www.hirevue.com/blog/hiring/the-latest-leap-in-hirevues-assessment-technology.

[49] Nathan Mondragon, 'Creating AI-driven pre-hire assessments' (Hire Vue, 7 June 2021) http://web.archive.org/web/20220814235357/https://www.hirevue.com/blog/hiring/creating-ai-driven-pre-employment-assessments.

[50] Mondragon, ibid.

[51] Mondragon, ibid.

[52] See also ORCAA algorithmic audit.

A. The use of AVI can disadvantage candidates from certain classes and social backgrounds

Basil Bernstein has directed attention to the relationship between social class and the use of two language code systems, the 'restricted code' and the 'elaborated code'. Bernstein argued that, through socialization, people from the 'middle class' and associated 'strata' are likely to develop the ability to use both the 'elaborated code' and 'restricted code' whereas people from the 'working class' are likely to be confined to developing a 'restricted code'.[53]

Subsequent research has corroborated Bernstein's theory[54] or obtained results which Bernstein predicted.[55] Whilst code theory has been the subject of academic debate and criticisms, there is empirical evidence which supports Bernstein's theory (particularly that there is a relationship between social class and a family's coding orientation).[56] Based on a multi-year study of mother-child interactions, Hasan found that the use of an 'assumptive' semantic feature, which implied more 'reflexivity' between speaker and listener, was not only indicative of 'restricted code' but it was more likely to occur in discourse from 'dominated' groups from lower autonomy professions (whereas an element of 'elaborated code', the 'prefaced' feature, was used more by dominant groups and implied greater 'individuation').[57] Coding orientation may therefore be learned and perpetuate cultural reproduction of class.

For Bernstein, the class system has the effect of limiting a person's access to 'elaborated codes'[58] so, due to lack life opportunity, those from the working

---

53 Basil Bernstein, 'Elaborated and Restricted Codes: Their Social Origins and Some Consequences' (1964) 66(6) *American Anthropologist* 55, 66–7; Basil Bernstein, *Theoretical Studies Towards a Sociology of Language* (2003, Taylor & Francis Group), 106–7.

54 See, for example, Mohammad Aliakbari and Nazal Allahmoradi, 'On the Effects of Social Class on Language Use: A Fresh Look at Bernstein's Theory' (2014) 5(3) *Advances in Language and Literary Studies* 82; Ajayi Temitope Michael and Amaka Linda Ajuonuma, 'Investigation of Computer-mediated Communication Proficiency among Secondary School Students in Ibadan: Testing Bernstein's deficit hypothesis' (2021) 2(1) *Journal of Language and Discourse Practice* 19; Guangbao Fang, Philip Wing Keung Chan and Penelope Kalogeropoulos, 'Social Support and Academic Achievement of Chinese Low-Income Children: A Mediation Effect of Academic Resilience' (2020) 13(1) *International Journal of Psychological Research* 19, 24–5.

55 Argyle (see Chapter 1, n 101), 128.

56 See Ruqaiya Hasan, 'Ways of Meaning, Ways of Learning: Code as an explanatory concept' (2002) 23(4) *British Journal of Sociology of Education* 537, 537–48; Isabel P Neves and Anna M Morais, 'Pedagogic practices in the family socializing context and children's school achievement' in Parlo Singh (ed), *Basil Bernstein, Code Theory, and Education* (Routledge, 2020).

57 Ruqaiya Hasan, Ibid, 543–46. See also Tien-Hui Chiang and Allen Thurston, 'Designing enhanced pedagogy based on Basil Bernstein's code theory' (2022) 111 *International Journal of Educational Research* 1, 1–3, 8.

58 Bernstein, Theoretical Studies Towards a Sociology of Language (n 53), 136.

class can only develop 'restricted code'. Bernstein was not proposing that the working class had a verbal deficit[59] (his use of the term 'restricted code' is unfortunate and may create confusion). Rather, his work pointed out *differences* in the way language codes are used by people from different social classes.[60] One key difference is the role of a listener in the use of each language code. Bernstein explains that people who use an 'elaborated code' take into account the requirements of a listener when formulating speech so they are less dependent on the listener.[61] In contrast, people who use 'restricted code' may take the listener's needs for granted[62] and they may use words when speaking (such as 'you') to engage with a listener so the listener can draw on their experience.[63] The 'elaborated code' therefore appears more universalistic and independent whereas the restricted code relies more on connection and shared experience to convey information. The use of certain end statements, which are most frequently used by people from 'working classes' to confirm or engage with listeners (such as 'you know what I mean', 'aye' or 'hey', etc in Australia) appears to further support Bernstein's position.

Bernstein's theory suggests that working class people, through using 'restricted' code, will rely more on an active listener to articulate information. This has important implications for AVI or on-demand interviewing 'hiretech' generally and the use of AI in hiring. By using an asynchronous one-way interview, this 'hiretech' removes an active listener (a natural person) and replaces it with a passive listener (AI) which lacks a person's ability to comprehend information, detect the need for follow up questions, clarify matters, request elaboration, etc (anyone who has used Amazon Alexa, Apple Siri, Microsoft Cortana, Samsung Bixby, Google Nest, etc would be familiar with the limitations of these dialogue systems in conversational AI[64] and how they, at present, fall short of human conversation). Michael McTear writes:

> The ability to converse in a natural manner, provide relevant responses, and understand the partner's emotional state is one of the high-level cognitive skills that enables social bonding and coordination of actions.

---

[59] See, for example, Gabrielle Ivinson, 'Re-imagining Bernstein's restricted codes' (2018) 17(4) *European Educational Research Journal* 539; Brook Bolander and Richard J Watts, 'Re-reading and rehabilitating Basil Bernstein' (2009) 28 *Multilingua* 143, 170.

[60] See, for example, Gabrielle Ivinson, 'Re-imagining Bernstein's restricted codes' (2018) 17(4) *European Educational Research Journal* 539.

[61] Basil Bernstein, Theoretical Studies Towards a Sociology of Language (n 53), 60, 88.

[62] Bernstein, Ibid, 59.

[63] Bernstein, Ibid, 86. Users of 'restricted code' may also express 'discrete intent' through 'extraverbal' channels such as 'gesture', 'physical set' and 'facial modifications': Bernstein, 'Elaborated and Restricted Codes' (n 53), 57-61.

[64] See further Michael McTear, *Conversational AI: Dialogue Systems, Conversational Agents, and Chatbots* (2020, Morgan & Claypool Publishers), ch 1.

Communication is based on the agent's cognitive capabilities such as memory, perception, and the ability to plan and learn. Modeling these capabilities computationally is a key challenge in Cognitive Science research.[65]

Based on the above analysis, it can be argued that the use of AVIs, 'on-demand' interviews and 'hiretech' generally favours people who have cultivated 'elaborated code' through socialization and life opportunity, a resource which can be described as cultural capital developed from upbringing. It follows that the use of 'hiretech' (even if it incorporates attempts to reduce bias, such as by coding the technology to not assess visual analysis, speech inputs, or, flag applications for 'thresholding' as HireVue has done) may disadvantage people from classes use 'restricted code' and associated 'extraverbal' signals. Other 'hiretech' without these safeguards, such as Zapid Hire which simply requires candidates to submit video responses to questions[66], poses even greater risks of discrimination based on class and social background. This is because, in AVIs or on-demand interviewing without HireVue's 'safeguards', not only is this line of questioning passive but in these recordings a person's accent (for example, a regional or working-class accent), habitus or home is capable of being assessed and it is not filtered out.

In addition to the use of 'hiretech' being inherently problematic in view of its potential to have a disadvantaging effect on people from certain classes or social backgrounds, the value which the technology itself places on certain words may also have a classed dimension. For example, the audit of HireVue's algorithm states:

> HireVue is upgrading the linguistic components of its models so scores are less sensitive to (arbitrarily) specific words. This is a complex issue, since some words are very important. For instance, perhaps saying 'soda' vs 'pop' should not affect scores, but saying 'client' vs 'customer' should.[67]

The position that a candidate's choice between using the word 'client' as opposed to 'customer' should affect scores may, if adopted, result with the technology indirectly penalizing people from certain classes or backgrounds. For example, the word 'customer' may be more frequently used in working-class or blue-collar households due to the nature of work commonly undertaken by people within these households (for example, retail, labouring, trades, etc). In contrast, the word 'client' may be more frequently used in

---

[65] Michael McTear, Ibid, 13.
[66] See Zapid Hire (accessed 1 April 2022) https://www.zapidhire.com/hire-talent.
[67] ORCAA algorithmic audit, 6.

other households due to the nature of work undertaken by people in these households (for example, professionals). This has particular implications for graduates because, at such an early stage of their careers, they may simply repeat the phraseology used at home by parents or family.

B. Risks of 'social origin' discrimination from the use of AVI

With the above analysis in mind, the asynchronous nature of 'hiretech' (even with the many 'safeguards' implemented by HireVue) has potential to disadvantage and disproportionately affect people from certain classes and social backgrounds on the basis of the speech code which they have cultivated from upbringing. The AI may introduce further disadvantages by, as explained above, potentially penalizing the use of words associated with the working class and favouring the use of words associated with professional backgrounds.

The use of such AI may therefore, in addition to creating inequalities amongst applicants based on speech codes, involve risks of indirect discrimination based on an applicant's manner of speech and use of 'restricted code' (which is a form of embodied cultural capital) and therefore class. As argued in Chapter 3, the protected attribute 'social origin' in both the Australian *FW Act* and *AHRC Act* as well as the South African *EEA* and *LRA* includes, consistently with the way the term is understood in ILO jurisprudence, class as measured by factors including embodied cultural capital. The *AHRC Act* and *EEA* are relevant to the use of AVIs and hiretech in recruitment, as these Acts extend to cover discrimination in recruitment stages before hiring[68] (unlike the *FW Act* which only covers adverse action in hiring and the employment relationship as well as unlawful termination of employment, and, the *LRA* which covers dismissals).[69]

The use of this AI in recruitment could therefore fall within the meaning of 'indirect discrimination' for the purposes of the *AHRC Act* and *ILO 111* (the meaning is the same under both[70]), because it is a practice of interviewing candidates which, though apparently neutral on its face, is not closely related to the inherent requirements of a job and may result with unequal treatment of persons on the basis of class (and therefore 'social origin)'.[71]

Given that the use of the AI may have a disproportionate impact on persons on the basis of 'social origin', it may also fall within the definition of 'indirect

---

[68] See Chapters 2 and 3.
[69] See Chapter 3.
[70] See Chapters 2 and 3.
[71] See further Chapters 2 and 3.

discrimination' in South African jurisprudence.[72] However, the inquiry seems to be made somewhat ambiguous and over complicated by the first stage of the *Harksen* test[73] (that there is a practice which 'differentiates' between people). This is because, although the practice may have a disproportionate or disadvantaging effect based on class and therefore 'social origin' (in which case the second and third stages of the *Harksen* test may be satisfied), it is not absolutely clear that it 'differentiates' between people before any assessment of indirect discrimination can be made. This may reflect problems with applying the *Harksen* test to the use of new technologies, particularly those which automate processes.

III. Gamification in recruitment

'Gamification' is increasingly used in recruitment to help screen job candidates, so that human recruiters can save time by not having to undertake this time-consuming process.[74] Instead of assessing resumes or other documents, the use of 'gamification' in recruitment involves inviting candidates to play digital exercises or 'games'.[75] This part of this chapter will now examine the use of gamification in recruitment to expose how it disadvantages people from already vulnerable groups, particularly on the basis of disability, class, social background or at the convergence of these three axes.

A. Pymetrics games

Pymetrics is a leading provider of gamification services to employers.[76] In a case study of pymetrics, Wilson et al explain that 'pymetrics uses gamified psychological measurement and applied ML [machine learning] to evaluate the cognitive and behavioral characteristics that differentiate a role's high-performing incumbents to make predictions about job seekers applying to that role'.[77]

An article published on the Oxford University Careers Service ('OUCS') website provides an overview of Pymetrics 'games', including pictures

---

72 See Chapter 3.
73 For an explanation of the *Harksen* test, see Chapter 3.
74 See, for example, Pymetrics, 'ANZ's Fair & Engaging Candidate Experience' https://www.pymetrics.ai/case-studies/anz-case-study ('Pymetrics ANZ Case Study').
75 See, for example, Pymetrics ANZ Case Study.
76 Pymetrics https://www.pymetrics.ai/
77 Christo Wilson, Avijit Ghosh, Shan Jiang, Alan Mislove, Lewis Baker, Janelle Szary, Kelly Trindel and Frida Polli, 'Building and Auditing Fair Algorithms: A Case Study in Candidate Screening' (FAccT '21, March 1–10, 2021, Virtual Event, Canada), 668.

and demonstrations.[78] Pymetrics have 12 online games which are used by employers as an assessment tool, and these games measure 91 traits which fit into 9 categories: attention, decision-making, effort, emotion, fairness, focus, generosity, learning, and, risk tolerance.[79]

The 12 Pymetrics games include:[80]

- a 'balloon game', which requires candidates to pump balloons with each pump earning the candidate money. The money can be 'deposited' by candidates but the balloons are at risk of exploding at any time (if the balloon explodes before the money is deposited the candidate loses the money[81]). This tests risk taking and decision making.
- a 'tower game', which is '[a] version of the famous Hanoi Towers game' and requires candidates to 'rearrange three towers', which each have differently coloured sections, 'with the least moves'.[82] This tests planning ability.
- two 'money exchange' games, which require candidates to engage in transactions with an AI-based player.
- a 'keypress game', which requires candidates 'to hit a specific key on [their] keyboard as fast as [they] can, until instructed to stop' whilst '[t]he game … constantly alternate[s] between 'start' and 'stop".[83] This tests the ability to follow instructions and impulsivity.
- a 'hard or easy task game', which requires candidates to choose whether they wish to undertake an easy task or a hard task. This tests effort, decision-making and motivation.
- a 'digits memory game', which is 'a basic memory game' that challenges candidates 'to memorize a sequence of given digits quickly flashing on [their] screen'.[84] This tests memory. The OUCS website contains an example of the game and it involves consecutive numbers flashing on a screen and then candidates are asked to type the numbers which had appeared.

---

[78] Oxford University – Oxford University Careers Service, 'The Pymetrics Games – Overview and Practice Guidelines' (21 November 2021) https://www.careers.ox.ac.uk/article/the-pymetrics-games-overview-and-practice-guidelines ('*OUCS Pymetrics Games Overview*').

[79] *OUCS Pymetrics Games Overview.*

[80] *OUCS Pymetrics Games Overview.*

[81] See Hilke Schellmann, 'Auditors are testing hiring algorithms for bias, but there's no easy fix: AI audits may overlook certain types of bias, and they don't necessarily verify that a hiring tool picks the best candidates for a job' (11 February 2021, *MIT Technology Review*) https://www.technologyreview.com/2021/02/11/1017955/auditors-testing-ai-hiring-algorithms-bias-big-questions-remain/.

[82] *OUCS Pymetrics Games Overview.*

[83] *OUCS Pymetrics Games Overview.*

[84] *OUCS Pymetrics Games Overview.*

- a 'stops game', which involves shapes flashing on a screen and candidates are required to hit the space key when a particular colour appears. This tests attention.
- an 'arrows game', in which candidates are required to 'determine the directions of two sets of flashing arrows' after five arrows flash on the screen.[85] There are different rules applied for different colour variations. This tests adaptivity and learning.
- a 'lengths game', in which candidates are 'shown one of two very similar images' which have a specific element that is slightly longer, or shorter, than the other. The example image of this game on the OUCS webpage contains two pictures of a cat and instructions for candidates. The first picture depicts a cat with a short mustache and the second picture depicts a cat with a long mustache. The instructions are: 'when you see the smaller mustache cat press H', 'when you see the larger mustache cat press G', 'Every correct answer will grant you 1 point', 'The differences between the small and big mustaches are very slim, so pay close attention'.[86] This game tests attention to detail and motivation.
- a 'cards game', in which a candidate is required to draw cards.
- a 'faces game', in which candidates are presented 'with multiple facial expressions, sometimes accompanied by a brief description', and they are then 'requested to recognise the emotion conveyed in the person's face'.[87] This tests emotional intelligence.

The games therefore require a high level of visual perception and reaction speed, presume that all candidates will be able to undertake the assessments, and appear to serve as a filter which determines the candidates that will progress to the next stage of the hiring process. The system compares a candidate's scores from the games with those of employees who work in the relevant job, and, if their personality profile reflects 'the traits most specific to people who are successful in the role', they 'advance to the next hiring stage'.[88]

B. Gamification may disadvantage people with disability

Gamified designs may not be accessible for people with sensory (for example, visual and auditory), physical, cognitive, neurological, and speech

---

[85] *OUCS Pymetrics Games Overview.*
[86] *OUCS Pymetrics Games Overview.*
[87] *OUCS Pymetrics Games Overview.*
[88] Hilke Schellmann, 'Auditors are testing hiring algorithms for bias, but there's no easy fix: AI audits may overlook certain types of bias, and they don't necessarily verify that a hiring tool picks the best candidates for a job' (11 February 2021, *MIT Technology Review*)

disabilities.[89] The high level of visual perception and reaction speeds needed to complete Pymetrics games, in particular, may disadvantage job candidates with disabilities that affect visual acuity, perception, and reaction speeds, for reasons that will now be explained.

Whilst all the Pymetrics games may present difficulties for people with disability, a few of the games can be singled out as particularly problematic. The 'lengths game' and 'faces game' each require high levels of visual acuity which many people with disability may not have due to numerous visual conditions which affect different parts of the eye. People with certain visual conditions may have difficulty perceiving minor differences in objects, detail, faces or facial expressions. They may also react more slowly as a result. Numerous eye conditions may present such difficulties, such as those affecting the cornea, retina, optic nerve, lens or those which result from brain injury or affect the way a person's eyes work.[90]

The fact that the games, such as the 'lengths game', attract points for correct answers suggests that candidates with these conditions will be disadvantaged in the process, as their conditions will impact their ability to score these points. The use of gamification may therefore disadvantage, or not accurately assess, people with such conditions because these conditions may alter the way a person perceives content on a computer screen, thus potentially making them slower, more nervous, risk averse, etc than they might otherwise be if they could see the screen clearly.

These disabilities may sometimes not be obvious to onlookers, and job candidates may be reluctant to disclose hidden or invisible disabilities to employers with the result that many job candidates with such disabilities may 'suffer in silence' and not request reasonable adjustments.[91] Given that gamified recruitment tends to be completed remotely and online other, more visible, disabilities will not come to the attention of employers. It therefore seems likely that job seekers with many disabilities, particularly hidden or invisible disabilities, will face significant disadvantages from having to complete certain gamified assessments in recruitment.

The use of gamification in recruitment may, given the way it can disadvantage job seekers with disability as just explained, have a disabling effect. This, for reasons which will now be set out, has implications which

---

https://www.technologyreview.com/2021/02/11/1017955/auditors-testing-ai-hiring-algorithms-bias-big-questions-remain/.

[89] See, for example, Keyonda Smith and Sandra Schamroth Abrams, 'Gamification and accessibility' (2019) 36(2) *International Journal of Information and Learning Technology* 104.

[90] For an overview of common eye conditions, see, for example, National Eye Institute, 'Eye Conditions and Diseases' https://www.nei.nih.gov/learn-about-eye-health/eye-conditions-and-diseases.

[91] Capuano, 'Post-Pandemic Workplace Design' (see Chapter 1, n 154), 880–2.

may result with synergies of disadvantage at the convergence of disability, class and social background.

C. The 'digital divide': how gamification creates disadvantages at the convergence of disability, class and social background

Disability is often interconnected with class and social background, with the result that it may not always be possible to disentangle these factors as causes of disadvantage (and resulting discrimination) experienced by people with disability. Marxist critiques have been used to identify the way capitalism results with the exclusion of people with varying abilities from the means of production[92] thus directly impacting their ability to earn economic capital. This observation reflects how the exclusion of people with disability from workforce participation may lead many of them to experience poverty, thus compounding the disadvantages which they face. In the digital age, the synergy between disability and poverty (that is, lack of economic capital) manifests as a 'digital divide'.

The ILO Committee of Experts, whilst highlighting the many benefits of technology to enhance access for people with disability, has observed 'While digitalization offers greatly increased levels of access to information and communication for persons with disabilities, many of them do not have access to computers or other information technology due to cost. The digital divide is significant'.[93]

Being largely attributable to poverty,[94] the 'digital divide' is, perhaps unsurprisingly, present in a number of already vulnerable groups in society. This includes not just people with disability, but also refugee migrants who may not have access to digital technologies, lack the skills to use them, and/or not be able to afford them.[95] Socio-economic factors may therefore preclude people from 'engaging in digital spaces'[96] because many underprivileged members of society may also not have the money, skills and education to access and use computers, the internet and other devices.

---

[92]   Paul Harpur, *Discrimination, Copyright and Equality* (2017, Cambridge University Press), 36.

[93]   *Promoting Employment and Decent Work in a Changing Landscape*: Report of the Committee of Experts on the Application of Conventions and Recommendations, Report III (Part B) (International Labour Conference, 109th Session, 2020), 258–9 [697] ('General Survey 2020').

[94]   Farooq Mubarak, Reima Suomi and Satu-Päivi Kantola, 'Confirming the links between socio-economic variables and digitalization worldwide: the unsettled debate on digital divide' (2020) 18(3) *Journal of Information, Communication and Ethics in Society* 415.

[95]   Khorshed Alam and Sophia Imran, 'The digital divide and social inclusion among refugee migrants: A case in regional Australia' (2015) 28(2) *Information Technology & People* 344.

[96]   Smith and Abrams (n 89), 110.

The 'digital divide' may also result from inequalities not just in access to computers, but also from the manner in which computers are *used* by people with different socio-economic backgrounds. Based on a survey of 1,351 school-aged participants from Perth (Western Australia), Harris, Straker and Pollock found that:

> Young people from high NSES [neighborhood socioeconomic status] neighbourhoods had more opportunity for developing their academic skills given the greater use of school computers, the type of computer activities performed, and the variety of other activities they participate in. It is therefore evident that the digital divide issue is not only to do with access to computers but also the nature of their use. ... Young people from low NSES, were found to not be using home computers for learning programs and academic related activities, but for multimedia and chat room activities. ... Increased social use of computers by young people from low NSES neighbourhoods was also reflected in the different types of IT used. These young people were found to have increased use of non-educational IT including TV/DVDs, mobile phones and electronic games.[97]

People from more privileged schools and backgrounds may therefore have an education which better prepares them for gamification in recruitment. This reflects the potential for gamified design to disadvantage those who have not cultivated the skills and familiarity in educational digital games, and instead play games simply for 'fun' or enjoyment.

Mock tests and guides for Pymetrics games are available to help prepare for the gamified assessments, but access to such services requires the payment of fees.[98] This not only seems to reinforce how gamification benefits those who have the opportunity to cultivate familiarity with, and skills in using, educational digital games, but it also reveals economic barriers for people who cannot afford such services or a quality education in early life. Gamification may therefore benefit those who have access to economic and social capital (for example, parents who can pay for schooling or coaching) and adversely impact those who lack such capital.

It follows that gamified design in recruitment has potential to disadvantage candidates on the basis of disability, social background and class. This disadvantage may, in certain circumstances, compound. Certain people from

---

[97] Courtenay Harris, Leon Straker, and Clare Pollock, 'A socioeconomic related 'digital divide' exists in how, not if, young people use computers' (2017) 12(3) *PLoS ONE* 1, 9.

[98] See, for example, Job Test Prep, 'Pymetrics Games: The Ultimate Guide & Practice for 2022' https://www.jobtestprep.co.uk/pymetrics-games.

already vulnerable groups (such as people with disability, refugee migrants and those who went to low socio-economic schools) may face disadvantage at the axis of these attributes. For example, a student from a low socio-economic school with a visual disability may be particularly disadvantaged from gamified recruitment. By way of another example, a refugee migrant with a disability that affects reaction speeds may also be especially disadvantaged. People with disability, particularly those from poor, working-class and/or migrant backgrounds, are therefore vulnerable as gamification may have an especially disproportionate impact on people within these groups.

D. Risks of 'social origin' and disability discrimination from gamification

There may be scope for gamification to fall within the meaning of indirect discrimination based on single-grounds, such as 'social origin' and 'disability', within the framework of the *AHRC Act*[99] and the *EEA* (which both extend to cover discrimination in recruitment stages before hiring and access to employment, as explained in Chapters 2 and 3).[100] This is because, as explained above, it is arguable that the use of gamification to filter out candidates may be a practice which disadvantages or has a disproportionate effect on people with disability, or, on the basis of factors that fall within the meaning of 'social origin' (such as poverty, or social background). Whether all the legal tests are satisfied[101] will need to be determined on a case-by-case basis, but it does appear that an employer's use of gamification may create risks of indirect discrimination based on disability and 'social origin'.

The use of an intersectional prism may help to illuminate the disadvantaging effect of gamification on those who face compounding disadvantages as a result of the practice − people with disability who are experiencing poverty, migrant workers with disability, people from low-socioeconomic backgrounds with disability, etc. The 'digital divide' experienced by these groups, which is explained above, may bring intersectional disability and 'social origin' discrimination into focus. Put another way, in South Africa, where the courts use intersectionality as an analytical tool in discrimination cases,[102] these compounding disadvantages on certain people may help to

---

[99] The regulations to the *AHRC Act* declare additional grounds, including 'disability', as grounds of discrimination: *Australian Human Rights Commission Regulations* 2019, Reg 6. The *Disability Discrimination Act* 1992 (Cth) ('*DDA*') does not seem applicable as it would only cover discrimination in hiring/offers of employment and the employment relationship: see s 15, *DDA*. The general protections in the *FW* Act would also not be applicable for the reasons explained in Chapter 3.

[100] See Chapters 2 and 3 for an overview of these legal frameworks.

[101] See Chapters 2 and 3 for a discussion of the legal tests needed to establish indirect discrimination under the *AHRC Act* and the *EEA*.

[102] See Chapter 3.

reveal discrimination at the axis of 'social origin' and 'disability' which may arise from gamified design in recruitment. Employers in South Africa may therefore have greater difficulty (than employers in Australia, for example) in justifying the use of gamification in recruitment processes.

Conclusion

This chapter set out to investigate the extent to which an employer's use of certain automated candidate screening technologies creates risks of discrimination based on class and factors reflective of social background. The use of CRS, AVI and gamification was examined. The analysis in this chapter revealed how the use of each of these technologies in recruitment may involve making adverse distinctions, or create inequalities and barriers, based on class and certain factors that go to social background.

First, the above analysis of CRS exposes how the algorithm's use may result with the making of adverse distinctions based on a job candidate's family background, family wealth, socio-economic background, locality, geographic origins, where he or she grew up or went to school, economic capital and/or social capital. The use of the CRS in recruitment, therefore, appears to involve risks of adverse distinctions being made based on factors that fall within the meaning of 'social origin', which is a protected attribute in international labour law, Australian law and South African law. As a result of using the CRS employers may, for reasons which are explained above, be at risk of engaging in 'social origin' discrimination within the meaning of the *AHRC Act* (in Australia) and the *EEA* (in South Africa).

Second, the above analysis of AVI exposed how the use of this technology in recruitment may create inequalities and disadvantage job candidates on the basis of embodied cultural capital, such as manner of speech including speech codes and the use of certain words. The use of AVI, therefore, may disadvantage job candidates from working class backgrounds and families who may use such speech codes and words as part of the language and lexicon which they acquired and cultivated whilst growing up. In using this technology to screen candidates an employer may, as a result and as explained above, risk indirectly discriminating against job applicants on the basis of their 'social origin' within the meaning of the Australian *AHRC Act* and the South African *EEA*.

Third, the above analysis of gamification highlighted how the use of such screening tools in recruitment may disadvantage job candidates at the synergy of disability, class and social background. The use of this screening tool in recruitment may therefore create risks of not only discrimination based on single-grounds, such as 'social origin' and 'disability', but resulting discrimination or disadvantage at the intersection of these axes may be particularly severe. This may mean that in South Africa, where the courts use intersectionality to help bring 'social origin' discrimination into focus, gamification presents particular risks of unfair discrimination under the *EEA*.

Notable omissions from this analysis include both Canadian and New Zealand laws. This is because these laws do not clearly prohibit discrimination based on the measurements of class and factors reflective of social background upon which the use of CRS, AVI and gamification, as the above chapter argues, creates distinctions or inequalities and disadvantages.

As explained in Chapter 3, whilst certain laws in Canada – those in Quebec, the Northwest Territories and New Brunswick – prohibit discrimination based on 'social condition' and this ground refers to class, it is measured by reference to Weberian market capacities and fails to take into account the way Bourdieu developed class theory. Social and cultural capital are therefore not indicia of a 'social condition' within the meaning of these laws in Canada. As a result of this, and the lack of clarity as to whether intersectionality can be used to bring 'social condition' discrimination into focus in Canadian jurisprudence,[103] the ground 'social condition' appears to have little to no relevance to the problems of discrimination that may arise from the use of CRS, AVI and gamification.

The analysis in this chapter highlights how a Bourdieusian view of class has much more relevance and application in the digital age than one which is based on, or reflects, Weberian (or Marxian, Durkheimian, etc) class theory. Laws which aim to address discrimination based on class will therefore likely be much more applicable and relevant in the digital age where those laws define the concept of class by reference to Bourdieu's class theory. Not only this, but the interconnectedness of class with family and social background may also require a holistic approach similar to the breadth of the ground of 'social origin' (such as in ILO jurisprudence, examined in Chapter 2) for law to be capable of addressing discrimination based on class, which may engage with issues of cultural reproduction. It also highlights how the use of intersectionality can help to reveal 'social origin' discrimination in ways that may not be possible if a single grounds approach is used.

Beyond the meaning of grounds, the law's scope is also significant. The analysis above revealed how various recruitment tools which automate candidate screening have scope for 'social origin' discrimination, yet only the *AHRC Act* and *EEA* have potential applications to address this problem because they extend to cover discrimination in recruitment stages and access to employment before hiring (not just in hiring and the employment relationship). In contrast, whilst the *FW Act* in Australia prohibits adverse action based on 'social origin', numerous limitations of this Act mean this protection has no application, or cannot be relied upon, to address this type of discrimination as it arises in the digital age.[104] It follows that a law

---

[103] See Chapter 3.
[104] See Chapter 3.

needs to cover recruitment stages before hiring (such as candidate screening and selection for interview) in order to address the inequalities and risks of discrimination which may arise from the use of these tools to automate recruitment processes. This may be a particularly important requirement in laws which seek to address discrimination in employment in the digital age and beyond, in light of the increasing role of AI and algorithms in recruitment (particularly for the automated screening of candidates) and the potential for the use of these technologies to result with injustice and discrimination.

6

Platform Work and the
Post-Pandemic Shift
to Remote Work

Introduction

Advances in technology and the outbreak of the COVID-19 virus in 2020 have significantly changed the way people work. The internet and applications ('apps') on smart devices (such as phones and tablets) now allow people to freelance directly with clients in what has been described as the 'gig economy'. People now have access to food delivery apps such as Menulog and Deliveroo as well as ride-hailing apps such as Uber, and these are now used as part of the normal lives of many people. COVID-19 has also substantially disrupted the way many people work. In an effort to contain the outbreak of the virus, a number of governments imposed lockdowns which resulted with employees making a mass migration from working in offices to working from home. Even after lockdowns were lifted, this trend towards homeworking and remote working appears to remain popular and many employees now engage in hybrid working (which involves splitting the working week between the office and the home or another remote location).

The rise of the gig economy and the post-pandemic shift to remote working, whilst giving convenience to many, also, for reasons that will be explained in this chapter, disadvantages certain workers and makes other groups of workers vulnerable to exploitation. This chapter will focus on examining both of these developments, to expose how they create risks of discrimination based on class and/or factors reflective of social background.

Part I will examine platform work in the gig economy, to highlight how digital technology is used to fuel the exploitation and underpayment of certain socially and economically vulnerable migrant workers. This part of the chapter will then apply the recent decision of the Quebec Court of Appeal in *Bécancour* to illuminate how the *Quebec Charter's* prohibition on 'social condition' discrimination may have particular applications in underpayment and wage theft cases. It will also compare this with the legal framework in Australia to show that whilst the decision in *Foot & Thai Massage* highlights the potential of the *FW Act's* prohibition on adverse action based on 'social origin' to have similar applications, the law in Australia needs reform before it may be able to achieve this.

Part II will examine the post-pandemic shift to remote working and homeworking, to show how it has potential to disadvantage workers at the convergence of class, social background, and other attributes. It will also apply the law analysed in Chapter 3 to assess whether such a shift in the way people work creates risks of discrimination.

I. Platform work and modern slavery in the digital age

Digital technology has allowed the 'digital economy', and online applications such as Uber and Uber Eats, Menulog, etc, to flourish. With internet access, a person can now use Menulog to arrange the delivery of food from a restaurant of choice or Uber to arrange transport to a certain location. A person can also use the internet to arrange prostitution services through websites which serve as an interface between the person and a sex worker. This chapter will now turn to expose the role of digital technology in helping to sustain the exploitation of migrant workers in the prostitution industry, in which these workers are forced to work in conditions of modern slavery as a result of their economic and social vulnerability.

The digital economy has given rise to what can be called a 'triangular' work relationship, which can involve three participants – the provider of services (the worker, such as a driver or rider or sex worker), the user of services (the user-client, such as the person ordering the transport or food or sexual services), and the platform which connects these two people (for example, Uber for a driver, Menulog for a rider to bring food or a website for the provision of sexual services).[1] This type of work in which the provider of services engages is often called 'platform work' because an online digital platform is used by people or organizations to connect with a worker to provide these services.[2] The ILO Committee of Experts explains:

---

[1] See *Promoting Employment and Decent Work in a Changing Landscape*: Report of the Committee of Experts on the Application of Conventions and Recommendations, Report III (Part B) (International Labour Conference, 109th Session, 2020), 95 [201], 136 [310] ('*General Survey 2020*').

[2] See, for example, Eurofound, 'Platform work' (25 November 2022) https://www.eurofound.europa.eu/observatories/eurwork/industrial-relations-dictionary/platform-work.

Platform work is an arrangement that uses a digital platform through which organizations or individuals make contact and engage a third party (an individual or an entity) to provide a product or service in exchange for payment. Many different terms are used to describe the activities mediated through platforms. In addition to 'platform work', these include: 'gig work', 'on-demand work', 'work-on-demand via app', 'digital labour', 'digital (gig) economy', 'crowdsourcing', 'piecework' and 'collaborative consumption'.[3]

The worker is usually paid on a 'piecework' basis,[4] and platform workers are often seen as freelancers. The work is therefore often precarious, and these workers usually have no guarantees of further work or minimum hours of work.[5] Whilst there are many issues with platform work,[6] this chapter will only focus on prostitution services because, for reasons that will become clear, this industry gives rise to particular problems of class and social background discrimination for workers.

Digital platforms can either be web-based (which involves work being performed digitally from anywhere in the world) or location-based applications (which involves jobs or work being advertized online to be performed locally).[7] Client-users can access these digital platforms to then obtain a service which is carried out by a worker. Whilst workers may benefit from engaging in platform work (such as by having increased flexibility[8]), they may also face a number of detriments:

> many workers engage in platform work through necessity. Platform work is often perceived as 'dead-end' work that does not lead to lasting employment. Many platform workers are subject to excessive working hours in a highly competitive context that pushes down wages. There are also increased occupational safety and health problems in some sectors, associated in many cases with a lack of training. In addition, platform workers often spend many unpaid hours searching for work. [citation omitted].[9]

Those from economically vulnerable backgrounds, such as migrants, tend to be attracted to platform work due to structural barriers in accessing

---

[3]   *General Survey 2020*, 136 [307].
[4]   *General Survey 2020*, 136 [310].
[5]   *General Survey 2020*, 136–7 [310].
[6]   See generally *General Survey 2020*.
[7]   *General Survey 2020*, 136 [309]–[310].
[8]   See *General Survey 2020*, 138 [313].
[9]   *General Survey 2020*, 138 [314].

other forms of employment (as compared with the relative ease of accessing platform work).[10]

In Australia, recent media coverage of migrant worker exploitation exposes the role of digital technology in connecting client-users with exploited workers, thus serving as a revenue stream which sustains forms of modern slavery. *Trafficked* was a project led by The Age, The Sydney Morning Herald, 60 Minutes and Stan's Revealed which investigated how Australia's visa system allowed thousands of migrant workers to enter Australia. The findings of the investigation, published in October 2022 by The Age, report how smugglers recruit vulnerable women from Asia to work at licensed brothels and other businesses for low pay or as 'indentured labour'.[11] Former Immigration Department deputy secretary, Abul Rizvi, estimated that 'there were at least 30,000 foreign workers remaining in Australia unlawfully, part of a "rapidly expanding permanent underclass, constantly exploited" in the sex industry, on farms and in other occupations'.[12]

According to the report, South Australian police's 'Operation Webpage' had uncovered, amongst other things, websites which were used to sell the services of sex workers from Asia and leaked briefings which state that the vast majority of these workers spoke little to no English.[13] Whilst these workers all came from Asia (for example, South Korea, China and Hong Kong), their exploitation does not appear to be based exclusively on national extraction or race but rather it seems to result largely from the social and economic vulnerability of the workers.

A. Using the prohibition on adverse action based on 'social origin' in the Australian FW Act to address modern slavery?

The experience and exploitation of these workers from Asia has parallels with the experiences of the massage workers in *Foot & Thai Massage* (an Australian case discussed in detail in Chapter 3), particularly exploitation and underpayments stemming from economic, social and educational vulnerability.[14] In *Foot & Thai Massage* Justice Katzmann held that although the massage workers from the Philippines in that case had experienced

---

[10] See, for example, Niels van Doorn and Darsana Vijay, 'Gig work as migrant work: The platformization of migration infrastructure' [2021] *Environment and Planning A: Economy and Space* 1.

[11] Nick McKenzie, Amelia Ballinger and Joel Tozer, 'Trafficked: Women shunted 'like cattle' around Australia for sex work' (30 October 2022, The Age) ('*Trafficked Report*').

[12] *Trafficked Report*.

[13] *Trafficked Report*.

[14] See further Chapter 3.

adverse action based on their 'social origin', the exception in section 351(2)(a) of the *FW Act* applied to defeat the claim.[15]

The protection from adverse action based on grounds including 'social origin' in the *FW Act* could play a role in supplementing and strengthening Australia's legal responses to modern slavery[16] and migrant worker exploitation,[17] though the outcome in *Foot & Thai Massage* shows that reform is needed before this can happen. The exception in section 351(2)(a), for reasons explained in Chapter 3, presently operates to automatically defeat claims of adverse action based on 'social origin' with the result that workers cannot rely on the general protections of the *FW Act* to bring these claims. The result of this is that, whilst adverse action based on 'social origin' appears to be rampant in Australia against vulnerable migrant workers (as noted above and reflected in the facts and reasoning in *Foot & Thai Massage*), the operation of the exception permits this type of discrimination to go unchallenged in Australian workplaces, therefore absolving employers of liability and responsibility for committing this wrong.

To better protect workers in Australia from modern slavery and strengthen Australia's regulatory response to the problem, the legislatures could consider adding 'social origin' as a ground of discrimination in state and territory anti-discrimination law. This would permit vulnerable and exploited workers (or the Fair Work Ombudsman on their behalf) to bring claims of adverse action based on 'social origin' under the *FW Act*, without these claims being automatically defeated (as would presently occur by operation of section 351(2)(a), which applies because this type of discrimination is not presently unlawful under relevant anti-discrimination law).[18] A determination would then be able to be made by a court on its merits, which would also need to resolve any factual issues such as whether the workers are to be considered employees or contractors who can rely on these general protections.[19]

B. Using the prohibition on 'social condition' discrimination in the Quebec Charter to address modern slavery?

The exploitation of workers from Asia, as explained above, also shares some (albeit less than the workers in *Foot & Thai Massage*) similarities with the way

---

[15] See further Chapter 3.

[16] See, for example, *Modern Slavery Act* 2018 (Cth); *Wage Theft Act* 2020 (Vic); Victorian Government, 'Victoria's wage theft laws' (Reviewed 13 December 2022) https://www.vic.gov.au/victorias-wage-theft-laws.

[17] The potential role of the protection from adverse action based on 'social origin' in addressing migrant worker exploitation was not considered in the report of the Migrant Workers' Taskforce. See Allan Fels and David Cousins, *Report of the Migrant Workers' Taskforce'* (Australian Government, March 2019).

[18] See further Chapter 3.

[19] See *FW Act*, s 342.

the student complainants were underpaid in *Bécancour* (a case from Quebec which is discussed in Chapter 3). In *Bécancour* the Quebec Court of Appeal held that 'student status' is a 'social condition' under the *Quebec Charter* because students, as a group, face social and economic disadvantage.[20] It was found that these student workers had been paid less than other workers of the employer because of their student status, and this was therefore held to be discrimination based on 'social condition' and in beach of the Charter's equal pay protections in section 19. Section 19 of the *Quebec Charter* relevantly provides that '[e]very employer must, without discrimination, grant equal salary or wages to the members of his personnel who perform equivalent work at the same place'.

Reasoning by analogy, the Quebec Court of Appeal's conclusion that 'student status' is a 'social condition' could mean that other economically vulnerable groups could also fall within the meaning of 'social condition'. Such groups could arguably include economically vulnerable migrant workers, such as those from Asia discussed above in this chapter. By paying workers in these economically vulnerable conditions and circumstances less than other workers in a business, an employer may be underpaying the workers based on their 'social condition' and thus a risk of breaching section 19 of the *Quebec Charter* may be present. As such, the Charter may have a role to play in addressing modern slavery in Quebec as well. It should be noted that such workers will need to be 'personnel' within the meaning of section 19, and the connection between underpayments and group identity will need to be established on a case-by-case basis.

Whilst the purchase of sexual services is illegal in Canada,[21] a Google search suggests that massage parlours still appear to operate (such as in Montreal) and make use of migrant workers to provide services to clients. Exploitation of these workers may be more hidden than it is in Australia because it is also illegal to advertize sexual services (apart from one's own sexual services) in Canada.[22] This may have the unintended consequence of stigmatizing sex work and driving it underground, so it is less visible and less regulated. This may also mean that, as just noted, worker exploitation could be less visible than it is in Australia.

One issue with the *FW Act* and the *Quebec Charter* is that they are part of complaint-based systems and vulnerable migrant workers are unlikely to have the confidence, education, knowledge or resources to bring complaints. Therefore, to combat modern slavery on various fronts, the use of these laws could be in tandem with efforts to block digital platforms which provide a

---

[20] See further Chapter 3.

[21] See *Protection of Communities and Exploited Persons Act*, SC 2014, c 25 ('*PCEPA*').

[22] *PCEPA*, s 286.4–286.5.

revenue stream for this activity. This is easier said than done, reflecting on the difficulty of policing the seemingly infinite amount of data on the internet and the failings of algorithms to detect offensive or exploitative material. This is, however, an option to work towards as technology develops and it may be an important preventative measure which could further address the problem of class discrimination in the digital age and resulting exploitation against vulnerable workers.

II. The post-pandemic shift to homeworking and remote work

Whilst, for reasons explained in Chapters 4 and 5, the use of certain AI, algorithms and social media by employers may involve or create significant risks of class and social background discrimination, another new and emerging workplace practice presents similar risks. This part of this chapter will turn to examine the post-pandemic shift to hybrid and remote working, to assess the extent to which it may create inequalities or risks of discrimination based on class and factors reflective of social background.

Since the 1980s there has been a significant increase in the percentage of employees in Australia who work from home for most of time, jumping from 3.5 per cent in April 1989 to 23.9 per cent in June 2021.[23] Whilst approximately a quarter of all occupations worked from home in August 2021, '64 per cent of managers and professionals usually worked from home'.[24] As we move into a post-pandemic world, working from home is set to increase even further. The Australian Bureau of Statistics reports that '[a]lmost twice as many employed Australians worked from home one or more times a week in April 2022 compared with before COVID-19 restrictions in March 2020 (46 per cent compared with 24 per cent)'.[25] The future of work is increasingly expected to be 'hybrid' in nature, whereby employees can split their working week between the office and the home.[26] Consistent with this, some large employers are now downsizing real estate footprints and designing workplaces to embrace the new hybrid working model as they adopt mobility strategies to replace traditional office design.[27]

---

[23] Australian Bureau of Statistics, 'Working arrangements' (Released 14 December 2021) https://www.abs.gov.au/statistics/labour/earnings-and-working-conditions/working-arrangements/latest-release.

[24] Ibid.

[25] Australian Bureau of Statistics, 'Household Impacts of COVID-19 Survey' (Released 17 May 2022) https://www.abs.gov.au/statistics/people/people-and-communities/household-impacts-covid-19-survey/latest-release.

[26] See generally Capuano, 'Post-Pandemic Workplace Design' (see Chapter 1, n 154).

[27] See, for example, CBRE Research, 'The Evolution of Australian Law Firms' (Report, June 2022), 11. See also Carolyn Cummins, 'Westpac gives up key Barangaroo office

The increasing normalization of a hybrid working model may pressure employees to adopt this new way of working, even if it is not in their best interests.[28]

Whilst the assumption may be that everyone has the ability or capacity to work productively from home, this is not always true and experiences with working from home can differ based on a number of factors including home dynamics, family, carer responsibilities and disability. For example, working from home often incorporates family members, such as children and spouses, 'into daily work routines'[29] thus experiences with working from home will differ based on the nature of home dynamics such as the age of children and relationships with people in the home.

An important question, therefore, is whether the post-pandemic shift to hybrid and remote working disadvantages employees on the basis of factors which go to social background, such as family and home dynamics.

A. Intersectional disadvantages based on social origin, parental status or carer responsibilities, gender, age and disability

The post-pandemic shift to remote and hybrid working has potential to create disadvantages for certain employees. For example, hybrid working may disadvantage employees with invisible disability in various ways.[30] When considering disadvantages based on 'social origin', however, the argument could be made that requiring or encouraging people to work from home for all or part of the working week may disadvantage those whose home dynamics (or precarious residential status) are not suitable for home working. However, when an intersectional prism is used, it becomes clearer how remote and/or hybrid working can, for reasons that will now be explained, significantly disadvantage:

a) Young parents, at the intersection of social background, parental status or carer responsibilities and age;
b) Young mothers, at the intersection of social background, parental status or carer responsibilities, age, and, gender or sex;

---

space in flexible working tilt' (The Sydney Morning Herard, 16 February 2022) https://www.smh.com.au/business/companies/westpac-gives-up-key-barangaroo-office-space-in-flexible-working-tilt-20220215-p59wnb.html.

[28] See, for example, Capuano, 'Post-Pandemic Workplace Design' (see Chapter 1, n 154), 879–884.

[29] Susan Baines and Ulrike Gelder, 'What is family friendly about the workplace in the home? The case of self-employed parents and their children' (2003) 18(3) *New Technology, Work and Employment* 223, 233.

[30] See, for example, Capuano, 'Post-Pandemic Workplace Design' (see Chapter 1, n 154), 879–84.

c) Young parents with disability, at the intersection of social background, parental status or carer responsibilities, age and disability; and

d) Young mothers with disability, at the intersection of social background, parental status or carer responsibilities, age, gender or sex, and disability.

These compounding disadvantages at these various axes for young parents and mothers as well as young parents and mothers with disability finds support in recent empirical research into working from home, which will now be outlined.

First, two empirical studies from Spain illustrate how working from home can create disadvantages for young parents at the axis of social background (home dynamics), parental status or carer responsibilities and age. In one study the suitability of homes for teleworking was evaluated through 1800 surveys and analysis of images, and it found that over a quarter of the homes were inadequate.[31] More specifically, participants who found their telework spaces 'more inappropriate were, to a greater extent, young people, living with children under 5 years of age, and mainly in rented and smaller houses, flats, without a fixed place to telework, and deficient digital resources'.[32] In another study 256 participants from the municipality of Madrid were surveyed to investigate how people adapted to working or studying from home following a 2020 lockdown during the COVID-19 pandemic. The study found that one third of households surveyed had inadequate telework spaces, and 'inadequacy was related to a lack of dedicated workspaces, [being] … more than one teleworker per household, poor digital resources, or inadequacy of the characteristics of such spaces'.[33]

Second, two studies from Canada and Australia provide further evidence of the synergies between social background and parental status or carer responsibilities.

In one study Statistics Canada sought to investigate, amongst other things, barriers to productivity for people who work from home ('teleworkers').[34] The study, which involved a sample with 2,758 observations, focused on employees aged 15 to 64 years of age who were new to working from home

[31] Teresa Cuerdo-Vilches, Miguel Ángel Navas-Martín and Ignacio Oteiza, 'Working from Home: Is Our Housing Ready?' (2021) 18(14) *International Journal of Environmental Research and Public Health* 1.

[32] Ibid, 22.

[33] Teresa Cuerdo-Vilches, Miguel Ángel Navas-Martín, Sebastià March, Ignacio Oteiza, 'Adequacy of telework spaces in homes during the lockdown in Madrid, according to socioeconomic factors and home features' (2021) 75 *Sustainable Cities and Society* 1, 8–9.

[34] Tahsin Mehdi and René Morissette, 'Working from home: Productivity and preferences' (Report, Statistics Canada, 1 April 2021) https://www150.statcan.gc.ca/n1/en/pub/45-28-0001/2021001/article/00012-eng.pdf?st=Gjsn-gBE.

and usually worked outside home before the COVID-19 pandemic.[35] The study found that barriers to productivity included 'having to care for children or other family members' (reported as a barrier by close to 20 per cent of the employees) and 'having an inadequate physical workspace' (reported as a barrier by 10 per cent of the employees).[36]

In another study from Australia, Allen and Orifici surveyed 61 workers with family responsibilities who were working from home during the COVID-19 pandemic to obtain information about flexible working arrangements.[37] They found that over half (or 54 per cent) of the participants requested flexible working arrangements from their employers so they could balance work and carer responsibilities, with the 'most common type of flexibility requested … around hours of work'.[38] Such requests for flexible hours of work involved changing 'span of hours, spreading part-time hours over additional days or working at night and/or on the weekend to make up hours'.[39] Allen and Orifici concluded that this suggested the participants in the study 'wanted autonomy to complete their work at a time that fitted in with other responsibilities.[40]

These findings by Allen and Orifici demonstrate that, due to the synergies between home dynamics and parental status or carer responsibilities, many parents or carers who work from home are unable to adhere to the 'normative worker' model. The 'normative worker can be described as the "unencumbered worker" who devotes long hours over the full working week without periods of interruption and uses non-working time for rest or relaxation'.[41] Instead, a parent who works from home will often be interrupted by children or family responsibilities, so many must work atypically in order to be productive and also balance work with home duties. Whilst many parents may prefer to work from home given that it permits more time with family and at the home, employers who are rigid with set working hours (such as 'normal' 9 am to 5 pm office hours) may therefore create unnecessary stress and disadvantages for employees who have caring and family responsibilities whilst they work from home.

Although flexibility around hours of work may allow employees to work atypically from home and thus better permit them to balance work with domestic responsibilities, quite problematically even during the COVID-19

---

[35] Ibid.

[36] Ibid.

[37] Dominique Allen and Adriana Orifici, 'What Did the COVID-19 Pandemic Reveal About Workplace Flexibility for People with Family and Caring Responsibilities?' (2022) No 1 *UNSW Law Journal Forum* 1, 8.

[38] Ibid, 10.

[39] Ibid, 13.

[40] Ibid, 13.

[41] Ibid, 13–14.

pandemic some workers did not raise flexibility needs with employers. Allen and Orifici write:

> the survey results highlight that some workers *did not discuss increased flexibility needs with their employers even during this time when increased work/family conflict was highly visible* [emphasis added]. ... 28 participants with caring responsibilities did not discuss their flexibility requirements with their employers but instead balanced their responsibilities without making changes to work arrangements or worked flexibly without approval. It is likely these participants continued to present as 'model workers' and may have worked 'double shifts' to do so, particularly where they worked 'atypically' without approval.[citation omitted][42]

This finding suggests that, as we move into a post-pandemic world, workers who need flexible working arrangements in order to work atypically at home may be even more reluctant to raise these arrangements with employers. This is because the 'work/family conflict' to which Allen and Orifici refer will gradually become less visible as we move out of the pandemic.

The above analysis of empirical studies from Spain, Canada and Australia demonstrates not only that a person's home dynamics (a factor that reflects 'social origin'[43]) can make it difficult for that person to work from home, but also how these factors intersect with parental status or carer responsibilities and age. For example, whilst lack of space at home may cause difficulties when working from home these difficulties are exacerbated or compounded by the presence of children in the household. As such, young (age) parents (parental status) with space limitations at home (home dynamics) are likely to be more disadvantaged by working from home than others without a young family. Of course, those with older children may also face disadvantages but such disadvantages will not likely be to the same extent as those which result from the level of attention and care which younger children, toddlers and babies need at home.

Third, there may also likely be synergies between social background, parental status or carer responsibilities and gender or sex because many women tend to have the lion's share of domestic duties.[44] In a research paper from 2021, the Australian Productivity Commission wrote:

> analysis based on Housing, Income and Labour Dynamics of Australia (HILDA) data from 2019 indicates that working from home was not

---

[42] Ibid, 14.

[43] See Chapter 2.

[44] See, for example, Australian Government, Australian Institute of Family Studies, 'Mothers still do the lion's share of housework' (Research summary, May 2016) https://aifs.gov.au/publications/mothers-still-do-lions-share-housework.

associated with a fairer or more even distribution of unpaid work. Respondents indicated that their employed female partners, regardless of their work-from-home status, did a fair share of unpaid work. In contrast, working men are likely to be rated as doing less than their fair share of household and childcare tasks by their partners, regardless of whether they work from home.[45]

It follows that working mothers may typically have numerous competing responsibilities whilst working from home, and thus far from being an 'unencumbered' or 'normative' worker, they may need to work atypically in order to be productive whilst working from home. The observation that home work is 'highly gendered'[46] further supports how it may disadvantage women in particular.

Finally, there are also clear synergies between social background, parental status or carer responsibilities and disability. This author has argued that hybrid working, as noted above, has capacity to significantly disadvantage employees with invisible disability in various ways, particularly because employees with such conditions will not likely identify with disability and, therefore, may not disclose disability and request reasonable adjustments to make hybrid working more accessible.[47] Parents with these disabilities will also have added responsibilities at home whilst they attempt to work fluidly in a hybrid working model, so disability compounds with parental status or carer responsibilities. Home dynamics which are unsuitable for hybrid working further adds to this disadvantage. Further, because women tend to have the lion's share of domestic duties as noted above, working mothers with such disability may face further disadvantages at the axis of gender or sex, disability, parental status or carer responsibilities and social background.

For the reasons explained above, an employer's implementation of hybrid working and/or remote working strategies has capacity not only to create inequalities based on social background, but it appears to more clearly result with intersectional inequalities at various axes for working parents. More specifically, without appropriate flexibility these models appear to have capacity to create inequalities for young working parents with certain home dynamics. These inequalities are, for reasons which are explained above,

---

[45] Australian Government, Productivity Commission, 'Working from home' (Research paper, September 2021) https://www.pc.gov.au/research/completed/working-from-home/working-from-home.pdf, 80.

[46] *General Survey 2020*, 197 [479].

[47] See Capuano, Post-Pandemic Workplace Design' (see Chapter 1, n 154), 879–84. While certain employees (such as parents of children who are school age or younger, those with disability, those experiencing family violence and other specified employees) can make requests for flexible working arrangements under s 65 of the *FW Act*, many of these employees may also not make such requests for similar reasons.

more pronounced for young working mothers and young working parents with certain disabilities.

B. Risks of 'social origin' and 'accommodation status' discrimination from remote and hybrid working models

The above discussion of inequalities that arise from homeworking and hybrid work has particular relevance to the intersectional nature of 'social origin' discrimination, as it is conceived in ILO jurisprudence[48] and by South African courts.[49] Importantly, section 6(1) of the *EEA* prohibits unfair discrimination based on a number of grounds including 'gender', 'sex', 'pregnancy', 'marital status', 'family responsibility', 'social origin', 'age', and 'disability'. Whilst resulting discrimination from hybrid and/or remote working at the single axis of each of these grounds or attributes may arise, the use of intersectionality as an analytical tool may help to reveal and bring into focus discrimination at the intersections identified above. The transformational dimension of intersectionality, as explained in Chapter 1, makes the argument even stronger in relation to addressing discrimination against working parents with disability, particularly mothers.

The argument that hybrid and remote working practices amount to 'indirect discrimination' under the *EEA*, however, appears to hit two roadblocks at the first and third stage of the *Harksen* test.[50] In relation to the first stage of the test, the implementation of these practices may not always clearly differentiate between employees. Whilst at the second stage such practices could arguably fit within the definition of 'indirect discrimination', with the passage of time the gradual normalization of these practices may make it increasingly easy for employers to establish under the third stage that the discrimination is fair. Alternatively, or in addition, employers may increasingly seek to rely on the inherent requirements defence. This is because job requirements are increasingly being shaped by the environment in which they are undertaken so, as employers adopt hybrid working buildings and design positions to fit within this dynamic, the ability to work in such a dynamic could be argued to be essential to certain jobs.[51] It follows that the utility of the *EEA* to address inequalities which arise from hybrid and remote working may fade with time as these practices become normal, so employers and government should turn their minds to strategies which can help to prevent these inequalities from emerging.

---

[48]　See Chapter 2.
[49]　See Chapter 3.
[50]　See Chapter 3 for an overview of the *Harksen* test.
[51]　See, for example, Capuano, 'Post-Pandemic Workplace Design' (see Chapter 1, n 154), 906–8.

Given that homeworking and hybrid working models may disadvantage people on the basis of home dynamics or precarious residential status (which appear to fall within the meaning of 'social origin'[52]), there may be scope for such models to create risks of indirect discrimination based on 'social origin' under *ILO 111* and the *AHRC Act*.[53] Risks of indirect discrimination based on 'accommodation status' under the anti-discrimination legislation of the ACT[54] may also arise from the use of these working models, because they have capacity to disadvantage employees who are experiencing homelessness. Such claims, however, are likely to be weak in the absence of a court using intersectionality to bring to light discrimination at the convergence of various axes, as explained above. At present, Australian courts do not appear to use intersectionality in discrimination cases to help reveal discrimination.

However, despite these limitations of the law, the above analysis of intersectionality may have moral value for employers (in Australia, South Africa and globally) who may wish to ensure that all employees have equitable and fair working conditions in the post-pandemic world of work.

Conclusion

This chapter examined the changing nature of work in the digital and post-pandemic world. In particular, it examined technologically driven platform work and the post-pandemic shift to remote working. The examination of both of these developments in the way people work revealed significant new risks and opportunities for discrimination based on class and social background.

First, the analysis revealed how digital technology may help to provide a revenue stream for modern slavery. By engaging with platforms to acquire the services of exploited migrant workers (usually socially and economically vulnerable women), client-users provide a revenue stream for modern slavery. Businesses which exploit these migrant workers, by subjecting them to conditions tantamount to modern slavery through underpayment, debt bondage, control, and instilling fear, may be engaging in adverse action based on 'social origin' under the Australian *FW Act* and risk being in breach of the *Quebec Charter*, as explained above in this chapter. However, the operation of the exception in section 351(2)(a) of the *FW Act*, for reasons explained above, means that claims of adverse action based on 'social origin' will at present be automatically defeated and so such businesses in Australia (such as brothels, motels and farms) may continue to engage in such worker

---

[52] See Chapters 2 and 3.
[53] See Chapters 2 and 3.
[54] See further Chapter 3.

exploitation based on 'social origin' and go unchallenged. To make these employers accountable, reform, as explained in this chapter, is needed.

Second, an intersectional prism was used to bring into focus how remote and hybrid working creates disadvantages at the intersection of 'social origin' and other attributes. The above analysis showed how the South African jurisprudence on 'social origin' discrimination, with its use of intersectionality, has most application to addressing these inequalities because it can help to bring to light resulting intersectional social origin-based discrimination. In contrast, a single grounds approach to 'social origin' discrimination may not bring into focus such discrimination as clearly.

7

Making Future Workplaces Fairer and More Equitable

Introduction

Chapters 4, 5 and 6 exposed the inequalities and varying risks of discrimination based on class and social background which result from an employer's use of technology and new practices. Chapter 4 examined an employer's use of social media for cybervetting, job advertising and terminating an employee's employment. Chapter 5 examined an employer's use of algorithms and AI as recruitment tools, focusing on the use of CRS, AVI and gamification. Chapter 6 examined platform work and the post-pandemic shift to remote and hybrid work. Whilst these practices may result with or worsen classism and related problems in modern workplaces, this chapter is solutions focused and it proposes a way forward for employers who may wish to address or prevent these problems to make their workplaces fairer and more equitable.

This chapter therefore proposes a suite of cascading practices which could be utilized by employers to help prevent some of these problems from arising in recruitment and employment. There may be ways to minimize, or eliminate entirely, these problems and yet still achieve the aims or goals of some of the practices.

I. Re-imagining the use and role of algorithms, AI and social media in recruitment

Whilst certain practices, such as the use of cybervetting, CRS and AI 'hiretech', create inequalities and risks of class and social background discrimination, there are important reasons for their use.

In relation to cybervetting, the practice may be used to help identify a 'bad hire' based on social media data. Employers should, however, reconsider whether cybervetting actually achieves these goals. Zhang et al write:

The present research suggests that job seekers' SM sites contain a large amount of equal employment law and other personal information organizations typically cannot access from more traditional selection procedures. Moreover, some of this information relates to recruiter initial evaluations of job seekers, yet appears to be unrelated to future job performance or withdrawal intentions. Further, structuring the assessment of this information does not appear to improve the validity of inferences. As such, organizations should not use SM information during the staffing process, or at minimum, exercise extreme caution in how they use such information.[1]

Where employers insist on using social media to vet job candidates, one strategy may be to avoid cybervetting certain social media platforms which tend to be used for private use (such as Facebook and Instagram) and, instead, vet platforms which tend to be used for professional use (such as LinkedIn). Put another way, to reduce risks of discrimination, workplace policies should ban vetting of personal spaces (for example, Facebook), but instead encourage vetting of professional spaces (for example, LinkedIn). By not vetting social media platforms which tend to be used for private and personal use (for example, Facebook), risks of class and social background discrimination in cybervetting are greatly reduced.

In relation to CRS and AI 'hiretech', both these practices seem to have similar objectives. Firstly, the main goal of CRS is to uncover hidden talent (or 'gems') who outperform their contexts and increase socio-economic diversity in workplaces[2] (though, as explained in Chapter 5, its use in practice may carry risks of 'social origin' discrimination and adversely impact those who have overcome adversity and disadvantage). Secondly, 'hiretech' AI such as the automated hiring system used by HireVue claims to address the problem of discrimination in hiring by, presumably, using AI to try to eliminate human bias (yet, as also explained in Chapter 5, its use can create risks of class discrimination).[3] As such, on paper, an aim of both

---

[1]   Zhang et al (see Chapter 4, n 31), 1544.

[2]   See Rare, 'Contextual Recruitment in Australia: One Year On' (2017, Report), 1 https://www.rarerecruitment.co.uk/static/research/2017_Contextual_Recruitment_in_Australia-One_year_on.pdf; Rare, 'Measures that matter analysing disadvantage, identifying outperformance and increasing diversity in graduate recruitment' (Report, September 2018) https://www.rarerecruitment.co.uk/static/research/2018_measures_that_matter.pdf; Rare, 'Level Playing Field? Super Schools, Social Mobility and Star Outperformers' (Report, 2017) https://www.rarerecruitment.co.uk/static/research/2017_Level_playing_field.pdf.

[3]   See, for example, Javier Sánchez-Monedero, Lina Dencik and Lilian Edwards, 'What does it mean to 'solve' the problem of discrimination in hiring? Social, technical and

the CRS and HireVue's AI 'hiretech' appears to be to improve equality of opportunity in workplaces.

The implementation of these technologies, however, as explained in Chapter 5, results with inequalities and risks of 'social origin' (that is, class and social background) discrimination. As such, it is important to re-imagine workplace policy and practices with a view to identifying those which may achieve similar goals to those of the 'hiretech' and CRS, but which do not result with inequalities or similar risks of discrimination.

A. Enhancing socio-economic diversity in workplaces without creating inequalities and risks of discrimination based on 'social origin'

Enhancing the socio-economic diversity of people in certain workplaces or attempting to reduce discrimination in hiring is an important goal. Yet, using CRS and 'hiretech' AI to try and achieve these goals likely creates bigger problems such as, quite paradoxically, inequalities and risks of discrimination based on 'social origin' (perhaps in ways that may not have been intended or envisaged).[4] It will now be argued that employers may be able to achieve these goals, however, without using the CRS or 'hiretech' AI.

Rather than use algorithms and AI to try and increase diversity in workplaces, employers could instead turn their minds to addressing the biases (both visible and hidden) and systemic barriers in workplaces which fuel or permit classism and other inequalities based on social background. This might be best achieved through either, or a combination of, CV de-identification, blind recruitment, targeted job advertisement methods and bias training (subject to certain qualifications, explained below), for reasons that will now be explained.

The results of the Victorian government's large-scale *Recruit Smarter* pilot provide some particularly important insights into increasing diversity in workplaces. *Recruit Smarter* was 'the first multi-sector initiative of its kind'[5] and it was 'developed and delivered in partnership with 46 organizations across the public, private, community, non-government, and research sectors', with its objective being to 'collaboratively develop and trial innovative approaches to inclusive recruitment'.[6]

---

legal perspectives from the UK on automated hiring systems' (Proceedings of the 2020 Conference on Fairness, Accountability and Transparency, January 2020), 458–9, 461.

[4] See Chapter 5.

[5] *Recruit Smarter: Report of Findings* (Department of Premier and Cabinet Victoria & The Centre for Ethical Leadership, University of Melbourne, 2018) ('*Recruit Smarter Report of Findings*'), 5.

[6] *Recruit Smarter Report of Findings*, 9.

The Minister for Multicultural Affairs launched *Recruit Smarter* on 20 May 2016 (with findings from the pilot submitted to the Victorian Government in September 2018).[7] The pilot ran over a period of 2 years which included trialing 'CV de-identification, unconscious bias training, and strategic use of language in job advertising'.[8] Based on key findings from the Recruit Smarter trial, it seems that CV de-identification, unconscious bias training and use of language in job advertisements can help to facilitate workplace diversity and uncover hidden talent. An important component of *Recruit Smarter* is the awareness of cognitive bias in its design, because the pilot aimed to address unconscious bias[9] which was identified to be 'a key barrier' job candidates from 'diverse backgrounds' face in trying to find employment.[10]

1. CV de-identification and blind recruitment

CV de-identification was intended to level the playing field[11] and it included removing socio-demographic information from a job candidate's CV such as his or her name, place of residence, university, gender and country of birth[12] (thus, explicit evidence of ethnicity from a person's family name, locality from place of residence, and educational prestige from university was removed). It can be argued that as a result of such de-identification assumptions could also not be made about a person's social background from their first name, such as whether the person has a 'working class' or 'bogan' name.[13] The *Recruit Smarter* technical report reads:

> CV de-identification resulted in significant improvements to recruitment of applicants who were born in an overseas country (VicRoads), who lived in lower socioeconomic suburbs (Department of Premier and Cabinet), and whose gender was under-represented in the targeted role (Department of Treasury and Finance). These results suggest that CV de-identification can increase access and equity of outcomes for applicants from specific social groups.[14]

---

[7] *Recruit Smarter Report of Findings*, 9.

[8] *Recruit Smarter Report of Findings*, 6.

[9] *Recruit Smarter: Technical Report* (The Centre for Ethical Leadership, Ormond College, The University of Melbourne) ('*Recruit Smarter Technical Report*'), 2.

[10] *Recruit Smarter Report of Findings*, 3.

[11] *Recruit Smarter Technical Report*, 20.

[12] *Recruit Smarter Technical Report*, 21, 46.

[13] These names would be the equivalent to 'Chav names' in the United Kingdom or 'ghetto names' in the United States, which are commonly misspelled derivatives of traditional names.

[14] *Recruit Smarter Technical Report*, 46.

Specifically, it was found that, as a result of the CV de-identification, '[a]pplicants from lower socioeconomic suburbs ... were 9.4% more likely to progress through the selection process and receive a job offer'.[15] As such, through having their CV's de-identified, talent from lower socio-economic suburbs were more likely to get a job offer. Selecting candidates based on de-identified criteria seemed to enhance socio-economic diversity in the candidate pool and resulting job offers, which suggests that it may achieve the same goals of CRS and AVI, but without their accompanying risks of 'social origin' discrimination (as explained in Chapter 5).

Whilst the results of another government trial (by the Australian public service) indicated that 'de-identifying applications at the shortlisting stage does not appear to assist in promoting diversity ... in hiring',[16] 'diversity' in this trial was restricted to gender and ethnicity, with only gender, ethnicity and race being de-identified.[17] It therefore does not seem relevant to the broader question of increasing social and socio-economic diversity in workplaces.

2. Bias training

Whilst algorithms such as CRS aim to 'filter in' candidates who have outperformed their context and other AI claims to remove bias from recruitment, they do not take into account biases which may occur further down the recruitment process such as at interviewing and hiring stages. In-group bias (which is explained in Chapter 1) could therefore still play a role in recruitment, with the result that interviewers or hiring managers may prefer candidates who reflect certain prototypical cues that reflect class and social background.

Based on a number of studies, not only is this in-group bias based on class and social background possible but it is very likely to occur. Studies by Kraus, Torrez, Park and Ghayebi from the Yale School of Management found that, firstly, the social class of speakers may be discerned from speech patterns which they use, and, secondly:

---

[15] *Recruit Smarter Report of Findings*, 6.

[16] Australian Government Department of Prime Minister & Cabinet, 'Going blind to see more clearly: unconscious bias in Australian Public Service (APS) shortlisting processes' https://behaviouraleconomics.pmc.gov.au/projects/going-blind-see-more-clearly-unconscious-bias-australian-public-service-aps-shortlisting.

[17] Michael J Hiscox, Tara Oliver, Michael Ridgway, Lilia Arcos-Holzinger, Alastair Warren and Andrea Willis, 'Going blind to see more clearly: unconscious bias in Australian Public Service shortlisting processes' (June 2017, Behavioural Economics Team of the Australian Government) https://behaviouraleconomics.pmc.gov.au/sites/default/files/projects/unconscious-bias.pdf.

people with prior hiring experience use speech patterns in preinterview conversations to judge the fit, competence, starting salary, and signing bonus of prospective job candidates in ways that bias the process in favor of applicants of higher social class. Overall, this research provides evidence for the stratification of common speech and its role in both shaping perceiver judgments and perpetuating inequality during the briefest interactions.[18]

This supports the position that in face-to-face interactions during recruitment, applicants with speech patterns that reflect higher social class are viewed upon more favourably than those whose speech patterns reflect lower social class. It may also support the position that during interview processes, depending on the interviewer, embodied cultural capital (such as accent and speech patterns) may be a cue for determining in-group status and discrimination (that is, in-group favouritism) may result from such group categorization.

One possible solution to this problem may be bias training. In relation to unconscious bias training, the *Recruit Smarter* technical report reads:

> a trial of unconscious bias training across seven organisations found that training improved perceptions of self-efficacy for diversity-supportive behaviour and behavioural intentions to support diversity, which lead to an increase in diversity-supportive behaviours back on the job; for example challenging a colleague who makes a biased comment or initiating conversations about diversity in the workplace. These findings are in accordance with previous research that shows beneficial results from unconscious bias and diversity training (Bezrukova, Spell, Perry, & Jehn, 2016). Though the improvements from this training are relatively small, these can accumulate over time, especially if a large proportion of staff members in an organisation are provided with training.[19]

Carefully designed and long-term bias training may therefore help to mitigate conscious and unconscious bias, such as in-group bias, in circumstances where a job candidate's characteristics come to light, such as at the interview stage.

However, unconscious bias training appears to carry some risks which need to be addressed for the training to have the best chances of success.

---

[18]   Michael W Kraus, Brittany Torrez, Jun Won Park and Fariba Ghayebi, 'Evidence for the reproduction of social class in brief speech' (2019) 116(46) *Proceedings of the National Academy of Sciences* 22998.

[19]   *Recruit Smarter Technical Report*, 2.

The training may, through highlighting bias, make people 'more likely to express their bias'.[20] The training may create tensions between employees who are in target groups and those who are not in target groups, but this 'can largely be mitigated through the structure, design and approach of the training, so that it is cooperative rather than combative in nature'.[21] For example, 'older' diversity training which has focused on the legal consequences of discrimination may 'backfire' as managers may 'resent' that they may be 'singled out for punishment'.[22] Bias training may also give the false impression that the system is fair because people within the system have participated in training.[23]

In a report dated July 2022 and authored by five academics[24] the British Psychological Society ('BPS') recently considered the problem of classism and class-based bias in employment and suggested that 'workplace classism could be tackled by increasing awareness and literacy around class-based inequalities via bias reduction interventions'.[25] The BPS report, however, noted that recent studies demonstrate that biases may not always be 'unconscious' or 'automated' but, rather, people may be aware of these biases.[26] Results of four studies by Daumeyer, Onyeador, Brown and Richeson suggest that, quite problematically, when discrimination is attributed to automatic or unconscious (as opposed to conscious and identifiable) biases it carries less accountability and is seen to warrant less punishment.[27] Bias training which is framed around unconscious bias

---

[20] Calvin K Lai, 'What's unconscious bias training, and does it work?' (28 May 2018, The Conversation) https://theconversation.com/whats-unconscious-bias-train ing-and-does-it-work-95277.

[21] *Recruit Smarter Technical Report*, 50.

[22] Lai (n 20).

[23] *Recruit Smarter Technical Report*, 50.

[24] The authors of the report are: Dr Bridgette Rickett (Leeds Beckett University), Dr Matthew Easterbrook, (University of Sussex), Dr Jennifer Sheehy-Skeffington (London School of Economics), Professor Paula Reavey (London South Bank University) and Dr Maxine Woolhouse (Leeds Beckett University).

[25] Bridgette Rickett, Matthew Easterbrook, Jennifer Sheehy-Skeffington, Paula Reavey, Maxine Woolhouse, 'Psychology of social class-based inequalities: Policy implications for a revised (2010) UK Equality Act' (The British Psychological Society, Report, July 2022) ('BPS Report'), 40.

[26] BPS Report, 40 citing A Hahn and B Gawronski, 'Facing one's implicit biases: From awareness to acknowledgment (2019) 116(5) *Journal of Personality and Social Psychology* 769–94.

[27] Natalie M Daumeyer, Ivuoma N Onyeador, Xanni Brown and Jennifer A Richeson, 'Consequences of attributing discrimination to implicit vs. explicit bias' (2019) 84 *Journal of Experimental Social Psychology* 1, 1, 9.

may therefore 'reduce accountability'[28] and it may also 'give credence to stereotypes'.[29]

In order for bias training 'to be impactful', therefore, the BPS report suggests that:

> training may be better focused on raising awareness of class-based prejudice as emanating from the organisationally shared and embedded norms and values that a person draws upon, sometimes actively, [citation omitted] and increasing knowledge of organisational efforts to address social class-based inclusion and diversity. However, success will depend on structural change whereby organisations reinforce individual training with the implementation of structures and processes both aimed at fostering organisational responsibility for inclusion and blocking decision-maker prejudice and discriminatory practice [citation omitted].[30]

As such, bias training should be offered in a way that not only navigates the problems that may arise from framing bias as 'unconscious' (such as reduced accountability for resulting discrimination), but it should also address organizational norms and values which may perpetuate classism and inform or be reinforced by structural change.

3. Targeted job advertisements

Targeted job advertisements in recruitment can also play an important role in motivating people from certain social groups to apply for particular roles[31] (such as motivating law students with low socio-economic backgrounds to apply for roles in large prestigious law firms), thus increasing the changes of uncovering hidden talent within these groups. Strategies might involve advertising which includes 'success stories' about graduates from low socio-economic backgrounds (which might inspire existing students from similarly low socio-economic backgrounds). Though, care should be taken to ensure that such targeted advertising does not create the same or similar risks of discrimination as the use of social media detailed targeting, which is examined in Chapter 4.

The solution is not, however, as simple as implementing CV de-identification, bias training and targeted job advertisements and expecting

---

[28] BPS Report, 40 citing Daumeyer et al.

[29] BPS Report, 40 citing MM Duguid and MC Thomas-Hunt, 'Condoning stereotyping? How awareness of stereotyping prevalence impacts expression of stereotypes' (2015) 100(2) *Journal of Applied Psychology*, 343.

[30] BPS Report, 40–1.

[31] *Recruit Smarter Technical Report*, 47.

immediate results. The strategy, as noted above, needs to be envisaged as a long-term plan.

Recruit Smarter is perhaps the most large-scale trial of the effectiveness of CV de-identification, bias training and targeted job advertisements in increasing socio-economic diversity within both public and private workplaces in Australia, and the results of the trial are very promising. They indicate that CV de-identification, bias training and targeted job advertisements, when carefully designed, can each play a valuable role in increasing socio-economic diversity in a job candidate pool and eventual job offers. Additionally, bias training may in the long term have mounting benefits in combatting cognitive biases but, for reasons that have been explained, it needs to be designed with care to avoid the pitfalls discussed earlier.

II. Improving post-pandemic workplace design

In addition to the risks of 'social origin' discrimination which arise from the use of certain algorithms and AI as recruitment tools, the analysis in Chapter 6 argued that the post-pandemic shift to hybrid and remote working also creates risks of discrimination based on 'social origin'. These inequalities and risks of discrimination are particularly pronounced and evident when an intersectional prism is used. Through this intersectional lens, inequality and disadvantage appears to be particularly evident at the intersection of four axes: (1) social origin, parental status/carer responsibilities and age (for example, young working parents); (2) social origin, parental status/carer responsibilities, age and gender (for example, young working mothers); (3) social origin, parental status/carer responsibilities, age and disability (for example, young working parents with disability); and (4) social origin, parental status/carer responsibilities, age, gender and disability (for example, young working mothers with disability).

To reduce these compounding disadvantages, it seems necessary to address disadvantages which arise as a result of either, or both, of two characteristics which are common at each of these four axes (social origin and/or parental status/carer responsibilities). Disadvantages based on 'social origin' (that is, home dynamics), which are explained in Chapter 6, could be addressed through workplace policy which supports (such as through subsidizing or paying for) the use of coworking spaces, hubs or making permanent desks available to employees. Disadvantages based on parental status/carer responsibility, which are also explained in Chapter 6, could be addressed through not only such policy, but also practices and policy which normalizes 'atypical' work arrangements to encourage requests for flexible arrangements from employees who need these arrangements. Practices which reinforce the 'normative' worker model (such as emphasis on the use of an employee's accrued leave to provide flexibility)[32] should be addressed to drive cultural change, and the development of policy which encourages the normalization of flexibility should be encouraged.

By addressing disadvantages which result from social origin and/or parental status/carer responsibilities, the compounding and disadvantaging effects of remote and/or hybrid working will likely be lessened on those with characteristics at the four intersections referred to previously.

Conclusion

The analysis in this book shows that the use of certain AI and algorithms which are designed to enhance workplace diversity may, in practice, have an inverse effect and create bigger problems such as various inequalities and risks of discrimination based on class and social background. This chapter argued that employers have at their disposal other strategies which may achieve workplace diversity without creating inequalities or similar risks of discrimination. For instance, there is evidence that a combination of CV-deidentification, bias training and targeted job advertising, as explained above, may help enhance workplace diversity and address discrimination based on class and social background. These practices not only carry fewer risks of discrimination, but bias training addresses an important issue that these recruitment AI and algorithms do not: discrimination beyond initial screening processes, such as at in-person or face-to-face interviews. As such, even if these AI or algorithmic tools were effective, they may simply delay discrimination until later stages of recruitment processes.

Whilst certain AI may cause inequalities and discrimination, AI (when re-imagined and depending on its design) can help employers to implement CV-deidentification and bias training in cost effective ways. Effort could be invested in the development of de-identification AI (similarly to the situation in health care research, for example[33]) for the pseudonymization and removal of sensitive data from job applications. Existing AI could be used to screen for keywords that, rather than reflecting class or social background (for example, 'customer' versus 'client'), reflect objective criteria relevant to a job or position (such as skills, qualifications and experience). Finally, AI and software development could assist with the roll out of cost-effective bias

---

[32] Dominique Allen and Adriana Orifici, 'What Did the COVID-19 Pandemic Reveal About Workplace Flexibility for People with Family and Caring Responsibilities?' (2022) No 1 *UNSW Law Journal Forum* 1, 13–14.

[33] See, for example, Louis Mercorelli et al, 'A framework for de-identification of free-text data in electronic medical records enabling secondary use' (2022) 46(3) *Australian Health Review* 289.

training. This could include computer game–based bias training[34] which have advanced interactive features, goals, provide feedback, and adapt to users to provide education in an environment that is 'immersive' (for example, 'serious games').[35]

Beyond problems posed by certain AI and algorithms, the shift to remote and hybrid working in a 'COVID-normal' world creates inequalities and disadvantages based on social origin, and these are particularly pronounced when an intersectional prism is used. Addressing these problems will not be simple, but a starting point for employers may be to adopt a default position of flexibility which permits the use of coworking spaces, hubs or fixed places of work (depending on employee preferences). Technology (such as internet, videoconferencing, applications or software such as Microsoft Teams and Zoom, and cloud computing) can also play an important role in achieving this flexibility.

Whilst the present use of certain technologies may create inequalities and risks of discrimination in recruitment and employment, they can be reimagined and repurposed to not only reduce these risks but also help to proactively make workplaces of the future fairer.

---

[34] See, for example, Benjamin A Clegg et al, 'Game-based Training to Mitigate Three Forms of Cognitive Bias' (2014, Interservice/Industry Training, Simulation, and Education Conference).

[35] Rebecca E Rhodes, et al, 'Teaching Decision Making with Serious Games: An Independent Evaluation' (2017) 12(3) *Games and Culture* 233, 234.

References

International instruments

- *Convention on the Rights of Persons with Disabilities*
- *ILO Constitution*
- *ILO Convention (No. 111) concerning Discrimination in respect of Employment and Occupation*, done at Geneva on 25 June 1958
- *ILO Convention (No. 158) concerning Termination of Employment*, done at Geneva on 22 June 1982
- *Vienna Convention on the Law of Treaties*
- *Statute of the International Court of Justice*

Reports of ILO supervisory bodies

- *1985 Report of the Commission of Inquiry appointed under article 26 of the Constitution of the International Labour Organisation to examine the observance of the Discrimination (Employment and Occupation) Convention, 1958 (No. 111), by the Federal Republic of Germany*
- 1989 *Report of the Commission of Inquiry appointed under article 26 of the Constitution of the International Labour Organisation to examine the observance by Romania of the Discrimination (Employment and Occupation) Convention, 1958 (No. 111)*
- *Application of International Labour Standards 2014 (I)* (Report of the Committee of Experts on the Application of Conventions and Recommendations, REPORT III (Part 1A), International Labour Conference, 103rd Session, 2014)
- Australia: Direct Request (CEACR) - adopted 2010, published 100th ILC session (2011), Discrimination (Employment and Occupation) Convention, 1958 (No 111)
- Australia: Observation (CEACR) - adopted 2011, published 101st ILC session (2012), Discrimination (Employment and Occupation) Convention, 1958 (No 111)
- Australia: Observation (CEACR) - adopted 2013, published 103rd ILC session (2014), Discrimination (Employment and Occupation) Convention, 1958 (No 111)

- Australia: Observation (CEACR) - adopted 2019, published 109th ILC session (2021), Discrimination (Employment and Occupation) Convention, 1958 (No 111)
- Austria: Direct Request (CEACR) - adopted 2009, published 99th ILC session (2010), Discrimination (Employment and Occupation) Convention, 1958 (No 111)
- Bangladesh: Direct Request (CEACR) - adopted 2012, published 102nd ILC session (2013), Discrimination (Employment and Occupation) Convention, 1958 (No 111)
- Canada: Direct Request (CEACR) - adopted 2006, published 96th ILC session (2007), Discrimination (Employment and Occupation) Convention, 1958 (No 111)
- Canada: Observation (CEACR) - adopted 2010, published 100th ILC session (2011), Discrimination (Employment and Occupation) Convention, 1958 (No 111)
- Canada: Observation (CEACR) - adopted 2013, published 103rd ILC session (2014), Discrimination (Employment and Occupation) Convention, 1958 (No 111)
- Colombia: Observation (CEACR) - adopted 2008, published 98th ILC session (2009), Discrimination (Employment and Occupation) Convention, 1958 (No 111)
- Colombia: Observation (CEACR) - adopted 2009, published 99th ILC session (2010), Discrimination (Employment and Occupation) Convention, 1958 (No 111)
- Colombia: Observation (CEACR) - adopted 2011, published 101st ILC session (2012), Discrimination (Employment and Occupation) Convention, 1958 (No 111)
- Colombia: Observation (CEACR) - adopted 2012, published 102nd ILC session (2013), Discrimination (Employment and Occupation) Convention, 1958 (No 111)
- Congo: Direct Request (CEACR) - adopted 2011, published 101st ILC session (2012), Discrimination (Employment and Occupation) Convention, 1958 (No 111)
- Egypt: Direct Request (CEACR) - adopted 2007, published 97th ILC session (2008), Discrimination (Employment and Occupation) Convention, 1958 (No 111)
- *Equality in Employment and Occupation: General Survey by the Committee of Experts on the Application of Conventions and Recommendations,* Report III (Part 4B) (International Labour Conference, 75th session, 1988)
- *Equality in Employment and Occupation: Special Survey on Equality in Employment and Occupation in respect of Convention No. III, Report of the Committee of Experts on the Application of Conventions and Recommendations,* Report III (Part 4B) (International Labour Conference, 83rd Session, 1996)

- Eritrea: Direct Request (CEACR) – adopted 2010, published 100th ILC session (2011), Discrimination (Employment and Occupation) Convention, 1958 (No 111)
- Eritrea: Direct Request (CEACR) – adopted 2011, published 101st ILC session (2012), Discrimination (Employment and Occupation) Convention, 1958 (No 111)
- Fiji: Direct Request (CEACR) – adopted 2020, published 109th ILC session (2021), Discrimination (Employment and Occupation) Convention, 1958 (No 111)
- *General Survey on the fundamental Conventions concerning rights at work in light of the ILO Declaration on Social Justice for a Fair Globalization, 2008:* Report of the Committee of Experts on the Application of Conventions and Recommendations, Report III(1B) (International Labour Conference, 101st Session, 2012)
- Ghana: Direct Request (CEACR) – adopted 2006, published 96th ILC session (2007), Discrimination (Employment and Occupation) Convention, 1958 (No 111)
- Ghana: Direct Request (CEACR) – adopted 2008, published 98th ILC session (2009), Discrimination (Employment and Occupation) Convention, 1958 (No 111)
- Guinea: Observation (CEACR) – adopted 2012, published 102nd ILC session (2013), Discrimination (Employment and Occupation) Convention, 1958 (No 111)
- Guinea: Observation (CEACR) – adopted 2013, published 103rd ILC session (2014), Discrimination (Employment and Occupation) Convention, 1958 (No 111)
- Honduras: Direct Request (CEACR) – adopted 2009, published 99th ILC session (2010), Discrimination (Employment and Occupation) Convention, 1958 (No 111)
- Honduras: Direct Request (CEACR) – adopted 2011, published 101st ILC session (2012), Discrimination (Employment and Occupation) Convention, 1958 (No 111)
- Hungary: Direct Request (CEACR) – adopted 2012, published 102nd ILC session (2013), Discrimination (Employment and Occupation) Convention, 1958 (No 111)
- Ireland: Direct Request (CEACR) – adopted 2008, published 98th ILC session (2009), Discrimination (Employment and Occupation) Convention, 1958 (No. 111)
- Ireland: Direct Request (CEACR) – adopted 2010, published 100th ILC session (2011), Discrimination (Employment and Occupation) Convention, 1958 (No 111)

- Ireland: Direct Request (CEACR) - adopted 2011, published 101st ILC session (2012), Discrimination (Employment and Occupation) Convention, 1958 (No 111)
- Latvia: Direct Request (CEACR) - adopted 2008, published 98th ILC session (2009), Discrimination (Employment and Occupation) Convention, 1958 (No 111)
- Latvia: Direct Request (CEACR) - adopted 2010, published 100th ILC session (2011), Discrimination (Employment and Occupation) Convention, 1958 (No 111)
- Latvia: Direct Request (CEACR) - adopted 2013, published 103rd ILC session (2014), Discrimination (Employment and Occupation) Convention, 1958 (No 111)
- Mauritius: Direct Request (CEACR) - adopted 2013, published 103rd ILC session (2014), Discrimination (Employment and Occupation) Convention, 1958 (No 111)
- Mauritius: Observation (CEACR) - adopted 2020, published 109th ILC session (2021), Discrimination (Employment and Occupation) Convention, 1958 (No 111)
- Netherlands: Direct Request (CEACR) - adopted 2001, published 90th ILC session (2002), Discrimination (Employment and Occupation) Convention, 1958 (No 111)
- Netherlands: Observation (CEACR) - adopted 2008, published 98th ILC session (2009)
- Norway: Direct Request (CEACR) - adopted 2020, published 109th ILC session (2021), Discrimination (Employment and Occupation) Convention, 1958 (No 111)
- Pakistan: Observation (CEACR) - adopted 2010, published 100th ILC session (2011), Discrimination (Employment and Occupation) Convention, 1958 (No 111)
- Pakistan: Observation (CEACR) - adopted 2011, published 101st ILC session (2012), Discrimination (Employment and Occupation) Convention, 1958 (No 111)
- Paraguay: Direct Request (CEACR) - adopted 2009, published 99th ILC session (2010), Discrimination (Employment and Occupation) Convention, 1958 (No 111)
- Paraguay: Direct Request (CEACR) - adopted 2011, published 101st ILC session (2012), Discrimination (Employment and Occupation) Convention, 1958 (No 111)
- Portugal: Direct Request (CEACR) - adopted 2011, published 101st ILC session (2012), Discrimination (Employment and Occupation) Convention, 1958 (No 111)

- *Promoting Employment and Decent Work in a Changing Landscape*: Report of the Committee of Experts on the Application of Conventions and Recommendations, Report III (Part B) (International Labour Conference, 109th Session, 2020)
- Saint Vincent and the Grenadines: Direct Request (CEACR) – adopted 2009, published 99th ILC session (2010), Discrimination (Employment and Occupation) Convention, 1958 (No 111)
- Türkiye: Observation (CEACR) – adopted 2020, published 109th ILC session (2021), Discrimination (Employment and Occupation) Convention, 1958 (No 111)
- United Kingdom: Direct Request (CEACR) – adopted 2011, published 101st ILC session (2012), Discrimination (Employment and Occupation) Convention, 1958 (No 111)
- Zambia: Direct Request (CEACR) – adopted 2011, published 101st ILC session (2012), Discrimination (Employment and Occupation) Convention, 1958 (No 111)

Other ILO documents
- *International Labour Conference, 'Record of Proceedings' (Forty-Second Session, 1958)*
- International Labour Conference, Fourth Item on the Agenda: 'Discrimination in the Field of Employment and Occupation' (Forty-Second Session, 1958)
- International Labour Conference, Seventh Item on the Agenda: 'Discrimination in the Field of Employment and Occupation' (Report VII(2), Fortieth Session, 1957)
- International Labour Office, *Record of Proceedings* (Ninety-sixth session, Geneva, 2007)
- *Record of Proceedings* (International Labour Conference, Fortieth Session, Twenty-Eighth Sitting, Geneva, 25 June 1957)
- *Record of Proceedings* (International Labour Conference, Fortieth Session, Twenty-Sixth Sitting, Geneva, 23 June 1958)

Legislation and bills: Australia
- *Age Discrimination Act 2004 (Cth)*
- *Anti-Discrimination Act 1977* (NSW)
- *Anti-Discrimination Act 1991* (Qld)
- *Anti-Discrimination Act 1992* (NT)
- *Anti-Discrimination Act 1998* (Tas)
- *Australian Human Rights Commission Act 1986* (Cth)
- *Commonwealth Constitution*
- *Disability Discrimination Act 1992* (Cth)

- *Disability Discrimination and Other Human Rights Legislation Amendment Act* 2009 (Cth)
- *Discrimination Act* 1991 (ACT)
- *Discrimination Amendment Act* 2016 (ACT)
- *Equal Opportunity Act* 1984 (Vic)
- *Equal Opportunity Act* 2010 (Vic)
- *Fair Work Act* 2009 (Cth)
- *Fair Work Amendment Bill* 2014 (Cth)
- *Fair Work Bill* 2008 (Cth)
- *Fair Work Legislation Amendment (Secure Jobs, Better Pay) Act* 2022 (Cth)
- *Human Rights Act* 2004 (ACT)
- *Human Rights and Anti-Discrimination Bill* 2012 (Cth)
- *Human Rights and Equal Opportunity Commission Bill* 1985 (Cth)
- *Modern Slavery Act* 2018 (Cth)
- *Northern Territory National Emergency Response Act* 2007 (Cth)
- *Racial Discrimination Act* 1975 (Cth)
- *Sex and Age Discrimination Legislation Amendment Act* 2011 (Cth)
- *Sex Discrimination Act* 1984 (Cth)
- *Wage Theft Act* 2020 (Vic)
- *Workplace Relations Act 1996* (Cth)

Awards
- *Metal Industries Award* 1984

Government and legislative documents: Australia
- *Australian Human Rights Commission Legislation Bill 2003 Explanatory Memorandum*
- *Fair Work Bill 2008 Explanatory Memorandum*
- *Fair Work Bill 2008, Second Reading, House of Representatives Hansard, 25 November 2008*
- *Fair Work Bill 2008, Second Reading, Senate Hansard, 4 December 2008*
- *Human Rights and Equal Opportunity Commission Bill 1985 Explanatory Memorandum*
- *Human Rights and Equal Opportunity Commission Bill 1985 Explanatory Memorandum*
- *Human Rights Bill 2003 (ACT) Explanatory Statement*
- Official Committee Hansard, Senate Legal and Constitutional Affairs Legislation Committee, Human Rights and Anti-Discrimination Bill 2012 (Wednesday 23 January 2013, Melbourne)
- Official Committee Hansard, Senate Legal and Constitutional Affairs Legislation Committee, Human Rights and Anti-Discrimination Bill 2012 (Thursday 24 January 2013, Sydney)

- Official Committee Hansard, Senate Legal and Constitutional Affairs Legislation Committee, *Human Rights and Anti-Discrimination Bill 2012* (Monday 4 February 2013, Canberra)
- Parliament of Australia, *Dissenting Report by Coalition Senators - Exposure Draft of the Human Rights and Anti-Discrimination Bill 2012* (21 February 2013)
- Parliament of Australia, *Senate Committees - Exposure Draft of the Human Rights and Anti-Discrimination Bill 2012* (21 February 2013)
- Parliament of Australia, *Senate Committees - Exposure Draft of the Human Rights and Anti-Discrimination Bill 2012* (21 February 2013)

Other government documents: Australia
- *Application for approval of The University of Melbourne Enterprise Agreement 2013 [2014] FWCA 1133*
- Australian Government, Fair Work Ombudsman, *FWO Discrimination Policy* (Guidance Note No. 6, 3rd ed, 21 December 2012)

Cases: Australia
- *AB v Registrar of Births, Deaths and Marriages [2007] FCAFC 140*
- *Applicant A v Minister for Immigration and Ethnic Affairs* (1997) 190 CLR 225
- *Australian Rail, Tram and Bus Industry Union v Australian Western Railroad Pty Ltd* [2017] FCCA 1954
- *Bahonko v Sterjov* [2007] FCA 1244
- *Bahonko v Sterjov* [2008] FCAFC 30
- *Bahonko v Sterjov* [2008] HCASL 403
- *Barclay v The Board of Bendigo Regional Institute of Technical and Further Education* [2011] FCAFC 14
- *Board of Bendigo Regional Institute of Technical and Further Education v Barclay* [2012] HCA 32
- *Campbell v Aero & Military Products Pty Ltd* [2015] FCCA 2310
- *Claveria v Pilkington Australia Ltd* (2007) 167 IR 444
- *Commonwealth of Australia v Anti Discrimination Tribunal (Tasmania)* [2008] FCAFC 104
- *Commonwealth v Bradley* (1999) 95 FCR 218
- *Commonwealth v Hamilton* (2000) 108 FCR 378
- *Comptroller-General of Customs v Pharm-A-Care Laboratories Pty Ltd* [2020] HCA 2
- *Evans v Trilab Pty Ltd* [2014] FCCA 2464
- *Fair Work Ombudsman v Foot & Thai Massage Pty Ltd (in liquidation) (No 4)* [2021] FCA 1242
- *Fair Work Ombudsman v Theravanish Investments Pty Ltd & Ors* [2014] FCCA 1170
- *FCS17 v Minister for Home Affairs* [2020] FCAFC 68

- *Howe v QANTAS Airways Ltd* [2004] FMCA 242
- *In Mr Scott McIntyre v Special Broadcasting Services Corporation T/A SBS Corporation* [2015] FWC 6768
- *IW v City of Perth* [1997] HCA 30
- *Janice Shackley v Australian Croatian Club Ltd* [1995] IRCA 475
- *Klein v Metropolitan Fire and Emergency Services Board* [2012] FCA 1402
- *Konrad v Victoria Police* (includes corrigendum dated 9 August 1999) [1999] FCA 988
- *Leach v Burston* [2022] FCA 87
- *McDonald v Civic Disabilities Services Ltd* [2014] FCCA 1464
- *Merlin Gerin (Australia) Pty Ltd v Marion Wojcik* [1994] VicSC 209
- *Ms Karen Lee Cook v St Vincent De Paul Society Victoria* [2022] FWC 1440
- *Nikolich v Goldman Sachs J B Were Services Pty Ltd* [2006] FCA 784
- *O'Hara v Victoria (Department of Education and Training)* [2006] FCA 420
- *Pavolvich v Atlantic Contractors Pty Ltd* [2012] FMCA 1080
- *Qantas Airways Limited v Christie* [1998] HCA 18; *Qantas Airways Ltd v Christie* (1998) 193 CLR 280
- *Registrar of Titles (WA) v Franzon* (1975) 132 CLR 611
- *Rocklea Spinning Mills Pty Limited v Anti-Dumping Authority and D J Fraser* [1995] FCA 1188
- *Roos v Winnaa Pty Ltd* [2017] FWC 3737
- *Rumble v The Partnership trading as HWL Ebsworth Lawyers* [2019] FCA 1409
- *Sapevski v Katies Fashions* [1997] IRCA 219
- *Vergara v Bunnings Group Ltd* [2022] FedCFamC2G 818
- *X v Commonwealth* [1999] HCA 63
- *Yager v R* [1977] HCA 10
- *Zhang v Royal Australian Chemical Institute Inc* (2005) 144 FCR 347

Legislation: South Africa
- *Constitution of the Republic of South Africa, 1996*
- *Constitution of the Republic of South Africa,* 1993
- *Employment Equity Act* 1998
- *Labour Relations Act* 1995
- *Promotion of Equality and Prevention of Unfair Discrimination Act* 2000

Legislative documents: South Africa
- *Constitution of the Republic of South Africa, 1996 Explanatory Memorandum*

Cases: South Africa
- *Allpass v Mooikloof Estates (Pty) Ltd t/a Mooikloof Equestrain Centre (JS178/09)* [2011] *ZALCJHB* 7

- *Anyanwu and Another v 15-On-Orange Hotel (Pty) Ltd* (C39/2012) [2013] ZALCCT 20
- *Avril Elizabeth Home for the Mentally Handicapped v Commission for Conciliation Mediation And Arbitration and Others* [2006] ZALCJHB 19
- *Benyon v Rhodes University and Another* (5351/2016) [2016] ZAECGHC 161
- *Centre for Child Law and Others v Minister of Basic Education and Others* (2840/2017) [2019] ZAECGHC 126
- *Centre for Child Law v Director General: Department of Home Affairs and Others* (CCT 101/20) [2021] ZACC 31
- *City Council of Pretoria v Walker* (CCT8/97) [1998] ZACC 1
- *Damons v City of Cape Town* (CCT 278/20) [2022] ZACC 13
- *Dayimani v National Department of Health and Another* (JS753/18) [2019] ZALCJHB 44
- *De Bruyn v Metorex Proprietary Limited* (JA 40/2020) [2021] ZALAC 18
- *De Klerk v Cape Union Mart International (Pty) Ltd* (C 620/2011) [2012] ZALCCT 22
- *Department of Correctional Services and Another v Police and Prison Civil Rights Union (POPCRU) and Others* (CA 6/2010) [2011] ZALAC 21
- *Head of Department Western Cape Education Department and Others v S* (1209/2016) [2017] ZASCA 187
- *Independent Municipal and Allied Trade Union and Another v City of Cape Town* (LC521/03) [2005] ZALC 10
- *J and Another v Director General, Department of Home Affairs and Others* (CCT46/02) [2003] ZACC 3
- *Kanku and Others v Grindrod Fuelogic* (C602/2014) [2017] ZALCCT 26
- *Khumalo v University of Johannesburg* (JS533/16) [2018] ZALCJHB 31
- *Letta BHE and Others v Magistrate, Khayelitsha and Others* (9489/02) [2003] ZAWCHC 49
- *Mabaso v Law Society of the Northern Provinces* (CCT 76/03) [2004] ZACC 8
- *Mabuza v Mbatha* (1939/01) [2002] ZAWCHC 11
- *Mackay v ABSA Group and Another* (C 487/98) [1999] ZALC 116
- *Magidiwana and Another v President of the Republic of South Africa and Others* (37904/2013) [2013] ZAGPPHC 292
- *Mahlangu and Another v Minister of Labour and Others* (CCT306/19) [2020] ZACC 24
- *Maraba and Others v Tshwane University of Technology* (JS1032/12) [2019] ZALCJHB 209
- *Mbana v Shepstone & Wylie* (CCT85/14) [2015] ZACC 11
- *Mias v Minister of Justice and others* (CA15/00) [2001] ZALAC 6
- *Minister of Constitutional Development and Another v South African Restructuring and Insolvency Practitioners Association and Others* (CCT13/17) [2018] ZACC 20

- *Minister of Constitutional Development and Another v South African Restructuring and Insolvency Practitioners Association and Others* (CCT13/17) [2018] ZACC 20
- *Minister of Finance v Van Heerden* [2004] ZACC 3
- *Mvumvu and Others v Minister of Transport and Another* (7490/2008) [2010] ZAWCHC 105
- *National Union of Metal Workers of South Africa and Others v Bader Bop (Pty) Ltd and Another* (CCT14/02) [2002] ZACC 30
- *Ndlovu v Mondi Kraft a division of Mondi Ltd* (D1060/2000) [2001] ZALC 224
- *Ntai and Others v South African Breweries Limited* (J4476/99) [2000] ZALC 134
- *One South Africa Movement and Another v President of the Republic of South Africa and Others* (24259/2020) [2020] ZAGPPHC 249
- *Osman v Minister of Safety and Security and Others (EC09/2008) [2010] ZAEQC 1*
- *Police and Prison Rights Union and Others v Department of Correctional Services and Another* (C544/2007) [2010] ZALC 68
- *Rafoneke v Minister of Justice and Correctional Services and Others* (3609/2020) [2021] ZAFSHC 229
- *Ramuhovhi and Another v President of the Republic of South Africa and Others* (412/2015) [2016] ZALMPTHC 21
- *Ramuhovhi and Another v President of the Republic of South Africa and Others* (412/2015) [2016] ZALMPTHC 18
- *Ramuhovhi and Others v President of the Republic of South Africa and Others* (CCT194/16) [2017] ZACC 41
- *Reynhardt v University of South Africa* (JS 1061/02) [2007] ZALC 96
- *S v Khanyisile and Another* (CA 12/2012) [2012] ZANWHC 35
- *Social Justice Coalition and Others v Minister of Police and Others* (EC03/2016) [2018] ZAWCHC 181
- *South African National Defence Union v Minister of Defence* (CCT27/98) [1999] ZACC 7
- *South African Transport Allied Workers Union obo Finca v Old Mutual Life Assurance Company (SA) Limited and Another* (C198/2004) [2006] ZALC 51
- *Tharage v Digital healthcare Solutions (Pty) Ltd* (JS386/2008) [2010] ZALC 158
- *Tshwane University of Technology v Maraba and Others* (JA110/2019) [2021] ZALAC 25
- *University of South Africa v Reynhardt* (JA36/08) [2010] ZALAC 9
- *Volks NO v Robinson and Others* (CCT12/04) [2005] ZACC 2

Legislation: Canada

- *Alberta Human Rights Act, RSA 2000, c A-25.5*
- *Canadian Human Rights Act*, RSC 1985
- *Charter of Human Rights and Freedoms*, CQLR 1975, c C-12
- *Human Rights Act*, 2010, SNL 2010, c H-13.1
- *Human Rights Act*, RSNB 2011, c 171
- *Human Rights Act*, RSNS 1989, c 214
- *Human Rights Act*, RSPEI 1988, c H-12
- *Human Rights Act*, RSY 2002, c 116
- *Human Rights Act*, SNu 2003, c 12
- *Human Rights Act*, SNWT 2002 c 18
- *Human Rights Code*, RSBC 1996 c 210
- *Human Rights Code*, RSO 1990, c H.19
- *Protection of Communities and Exploited Persons Act*, SC 2014, c 25
- *The Human Rights Code*, CCSM c H175
- *The Saskatchewan Human Rights Code*, 2018, c S-24.2

Human Rights Commission Guidelines: Canada

- *Lignes Directrices sur la Condition Sociale (Commission des droits de la Personne, March 1994)*
- *New Brunswick Human Rights Commission Guideline on Social Condition* (Adopted on 27 January 2005)

Cases: Canada

- *Aluminerie de Bécancour inc. c. Commission des droits de la personne et des droits de la jeunesse (Beaudry et autres), 2021 QCCA 989*
- *Bates v Northwest Territories*, 2018 CanLII 61920 (NT HRAP)
- *Bates v Northwest Territories (Education, Culture and Employment) (No. 1)*, 2017 CanLII 98893 (NT HRAP)
- *Beaulieu c. Facebook inc.*, 2021 QCCS 3206
- *Bécancour Smelter Inc. vs. Commission des droits de la personne et des droits de la jeunesse (Beaudry and others)*, 2021 QCCA 989
- *Campbell v Yukon Housing Corp.*, 2005 CanLII 94014 (YK HRC)
- *Champagne vs Quebec (Administrative Tribunal)*, 2001 CanLII 24787 (QC CS)
- *Commission des droits de la personne (Leroux) c. J.M. Brouillette inc.*, 1994 CanLII 191 (QC TDP)
- *Commission des droits de la personne (Québec) v Gauthier* (1993) 19 CHRR D/312
- *Commission des droits de la personne et des droits de la jeunesse (Beaudry et autres) v Aluminerie de Bécancour inc.*, [2018] Q.H.R.T.J. No. 12

- *Commission des droits de la personne et des droits de la jeunesse (Miller et autres) c. Ville de Montréal (Service de police de la Ville de Montréal) (SPVM)*, 2019 QCTDP 31
- *Commission des droits de la personne et des droits de la jeunesse (Asmar) c. Ville de Montréal (Service de police de la Ville de Montréal) (SPVM)*, 2019 QCTDP 17
- *Commission des droits de la personne et des droits de la jeunesse (Bia-Domingo) c. Sinatra*, 1999 CanLII 52 (QC TDP)
- *Commission des droits de la personne et des droits de la jeunesse (Mercier et une autre) c. Dion*, 2008 QCTDP 9 (CanLII)
- *Commission des droits de la personne et des droits de la jeunesse (J.S.) c. Montréal (Communauté urbaine de) (Montréal (Ville de))*, 2014 QCTDP 7
- *Couet c. Quebec (Attorney General)*, 1997 CanLII 8766 (QC CS)
- *D'Aoust c. Vallières*, 1993 CanLII 422 (QC TDP)
- *Falkiner v Ontario (Minister of Community and Social Services)* 2002 CanLII 44902 (ON CA)
- *Gorham v Delorey*, [2017] N.B.J. No. 274
- *Johnson & Johnson Products Inc. and Union of Energy and Chemical Workers, Local 115*, 1995 CanLII 15888 (QC SAT)
- *Johnson v Social Affairs Commission*, 1984 CA 61
- *Kin c. McNicoll* 2021 QCTDP 34
- *Lessard v Northwest Territories (Department of Education, Culture & Employment)*, 2018 CanLII 109795 (NT HRAP)
- *Levesque v Quebec (Attorney General)*, 1987 CanLII 964 (QC CA)
- *Lodovici v Wam Development Corporation*, 2015 CanLII 78454 (NT HRAP).
- *Mercer v Northwest Territories and Nunavut (Workers' Compensation Board)*, 2007 NWTHRAP 4 (CanLII)
- *Moore v Northwest Territories Housing Corporation*, 2022 CanLII 13384 (NT HRAP)
- *Newfoundland Dental Board v Human Rights Commission*, et al 2005 NLTD 125 (CanLII)
- *Northwest Territories (WCB) v Mercer*, 2014 NWTCA 1
- *Order of Certified General Accountants of Quebec c. Quebec (Attorney General)*, 2004 CanLII 20542 (QC CA)
- *Ordre des comptables généraux licenciés du Québec c. Québec (Procureur général)*, 2004 CanLII 20542 (QC CA)
- *P.T. c. Mohammad Naqeeb*, 2021 QCCS 1378
- *Portman v Yellowknife (City)*, 2016 CanLII 62610 (NT HRAP)
- *Portman v Yellowknife (City)*, 2017 CanLII 338 (NT HRAP)
- *Portman v Yellowknife (City) (No. 1)*, 2016 CanLII 154167 (NT HRAP)
- *Quebec Human Rights (Commission) v O'Hashi* 31 C.H.R.R D/474 (T.D.P.Q)
- *Québec Poultry Ltée c. Quebec (Commission des droits de la personne) et Devost (No. 2)*, 1978 CanLII 3385 (QC CS)

- *R.L. c. Ministère du Travail, de l'Emploi et de la Solidarité sociale*, 2021 QCCS 3784
- *R.O. c. Ministre de l'Emploi et de la Solidarité sociale*, 2021 QCCA 1185
- *Regina Hospital Center Limited c. Human Rights Commission*, 1985 CanLII 5254 (QC CS)
- *Resource Development Trades Council of Newfoundland and Labrador v Long Harbour Employers Association Inc*, 2013 CanLII 62193 (NL LA)
- *Syndicate of nurses, respiratory therapists, nursing assistants of Cœur-du-Québec (SIIIACQ) (CSQ) v SIUSSS-MCQ*, 2017 CanLII 13636 (QC SAT)
- *Tanudjaja v Attorney General (Canada) (Application)*, 2013 ONSC 5410
- *WCB v Mercer*, 2012 NWTSC 57
- *William Head Institution v Canada (Commissioner of Corrections)*, 1999 CanLII 7643 (FC)

Books

- Argyle, Michael, *The Psychology of Social Class* (1994, Routledge)
- Atrey, Shreya, *Intersectional Discrimination* (2019, Oxford University Press)
- Bartolomei de la Cruz, Hector, Geraldo von Potobsky and Lee Swepston, *International Labor Organization: The International Standards System and Basic Human Rights* (1996, Westview Press)
- Bennett, Tony, David Carter, Modesto Gayo, Michelle Kelly and Greg Noble, *Fields, Capitals, Habitus: Australian Culture, Inequalities and Social Divisions* (2020, Taylor & Francis)
- Bernstein, Basil, *Theoretical Studies Towards a Sociology of Language* (2003, Taylor & Francis Group)
- Boldur-Lățescu, Gheorghe, *The Communist Genocide in Romania* (2005, Nova Science Publishers)
- Bourdieu, Pierre, *Distinction: A Social Critique of the Judgement of Taste* (1984, Richard Nice trans, Harvard University Press) [trans of: *La distinction: Critique sociale du jugement* (first published 1979)]
- Brewer, Marilynn B, *Intergroup Relations* (2003, Open University Press, 2nd ed)
- Clarke, Sandra, *Newfoundland and Labrador English* (2010, Edinburgh University Press)
- Durkheim, Emile, *The Division of Labor in Society* (translated by George Simpson, 1960, The Free Press of Glencoe Illinois)
- Figes, Orlando and Boris Kolonitskii, *Interpreting the Russian Revolution: The Language and Symbols of 1917* (1999, Yale University Press)
- Fitzpatrick, Sheila, *Everyday Stalinism: Ordinary Life in Extraordinary Times: Soviet Russia in the 1930s* (1999, Oxford University Press)
- Fitzpatrick, Sheila, *Tear Off the Masks!: Identity and Imposture in Twentieth-Century Russia* (2005, Princeton University Press)

- Friedman, Sam and Daniel Laurison, *The Class Ceiling: Why it Pays to be Privileged* (2019, Bristol University Press)
- Gaze, Beth and Belinda Smith, *Equality and Discrimination Law in Australia: An Introduction* (2017, Cambridge University Press)
- Gustafson, Ruth Iana, *Race and Curriculum* (2009, Palgrave MacMillan)
- Harpur, Paul, *Discrimination, Copyright and Equality* (2017, Cambridge University Press)
- Jaton, Florian, The Constitution of Algorithms: Ground-Truthing, Programming, Formulating (2021, The MIT Press)
- Kassin, Saul, Steven Fein, Hazel Rose Markus, *Social Psychology* (2014, Wadsworth, 9th ed)
- Kochetkova, Inna, *The Myth of the Russian Intelligentsia: Old Intellectuals in the New Russia* (2010, Routledge)
- Marx, Karl and Freidrich Engels, *The Communist Manifesto* (2018, Lerner Publishing Group Inc, United States; originally authored in 1848)
- Mattson, James B, 'Social Media and Employment Law' in *Social Media and the Law* (2016, 2nd ed, Lexis Nexis)
- McColgan, Aileen, *Discrimination, Equality and the Law* (2014, Hart Publishing)
- McGregor, Craig, *Class in Australia* (1997, Penguin)
- McTear, Michael, Conversational AI: Dialogue Systems, Conversational Agents, and Chatbots (2020, Morgan & Claypool Publishers)
- Molnar, Christoph, Interpretable Machine Learning (2020, Leanpub)
- Paternoster, Henry, *Reimagining Class in Australia: Marxism, Populism and Social Science* (2017, Springer International Publishing AG)
- Pearce, Dennis C and Robert S Geddes, *Statutory Interpretation in Australia* (2014, LexisNexis Butterworths, 8th ed)
- Servais, Jean-Michel, *International Labour Law* (2011, Wolters Kluwer, 3rd ed)
- Sünker, Heinz, *Politics, Bildung and Social Justice: Perspectives for a Democratic Society* (2006, Sense Publishers)
- Threadgold, Steven and Jessica Gerrard (eds), *Class in Australia* (2022, Monash University Publishing)
- Valticos, N and G von Potobsky, *International Labour Law* (1995, Kluwer Law and Taxation Publishers)
- Valticos, N, *International Labour Law* (1979, Kluwer)
- Verdery, Katherine, *National Ideology Under Socialism: Identity and Cultural Politics in Ceausescu's Romania* (1995, University of California Press)
- Weber, Max, *Economy & Society: A New Translation* [1921] (2019, Harvard University Press, edited and translated by Keith Tribe)
- Wright, Erik Olin, *Approaches to Class Analysis* (2005, Cambridge University Press)

- Wright, Erik Olin, *Class Counts* (2000, Cambridge University Press)

Book chapters
- 'Conflict Theory' in George Ritzer (ed), *Encyclopedia of Social Theory*, vol. 1 (2005, Sage Publications Inc)
- Abley, Mark, 'Hoser' (published online 27 June 2019, The Canadian Encyclopedia)
- Bourdieu, Pierre, 'The Forms of Capital' in J G Richardson (ed), *Handbook of Theory and Research for the Sociology of Education* (1986, Greenwood Press)
- Denis, Derek and Sali A Tagliamonte, 'Language Change and Fiction' in Wolfram Bublitz, Andreas H Jucker and Klaus P Schneider (eds), *Handbooks of Pragmatics* (2017, Vol. 12, De Gruyter Mouton)
- Firat, Rengin and Steven Hitlin, 'Morally Bonded and Bounded: A Sociological Introduction to Neurology' in *Biosociology and Neurosociology*, Will Kalkhoff, Shane R Thye and Edward J Lawler (eds) (2012, Emerald Publishing)
- Grusky, David and Gabriela Galescu, 'Foundations of a neo-Durkheimian class analysis' in Erik Olin Wright, Approaches to Class Analysis (2005, Cambridge University Press)
- Grusky, David B and Gabriela Galescu, 'Is Durkheim a class analyst?' in Jeffrey C Alexander and Philip Smith (eds), *The Cambridge Companion to Durkheim* (2005, Cambridge University Press)
- Hogg, Michael A and Deborah J Terry, 'Social Identity Theory and Organizational Processes' in Michael A Hogg and Deborah J Terry (eds), *Social Identity Processes in Organizational Contexts* (2001, Taylor and Francis)
- Hogg, Michael A, 'Social Identity Theory' in *Encyclopedia of Identity* (2010, Sage Publications)
- Hogg, Michael A, 'Social Identity Theory' in Peter J Burke (ed), *Contemporary Social Psychological Theories* (2006, Stanford University Press)
- Kebede, Alem, 'Cultural Capital' in Ronald L Jackson II and Michael A Hogg (eds), *Encyclopedia of Identity* (2010, Sage Publications) vol 1
- Moon, David, 'Late Imperial Peasants' in *Late Imperial Russia: Problems and Prospects: Essays in Honour of R.B. McKean*, Ian D Thatcher (ed) (2005, Manchester University Press)
- Neves, Isabel P and Anna M Morais, 'Pedagogic Practices in the Family Socializing Context and Children's School Achievement' in Parlo Singh (ed), *Basil Bernstein, Code Theory, and Education* (2020, Routledge)
- Print, M, 'Social and Cultural Capital in Education' in Sanna Järvelä (ed), *Social and Emotional Aspects of Learning* (2011, Elsevier)
- Stukuls Eglitis, Diana, 'Means of Production' in George Ritzer (ed), *Encyclopedia of Social Theory*, vol. 1 (2005, Sage Publications Inc)

- Tajfel, Henri and John Turner, 'The Social Identity Theory of Inter-Group Behavior' in S Worchel and WG Austin (eds) *Psychology of Intergroup Relations* (1986, Nelson-Hall Publishers)
- Waglay, Judge B, 'The Impact of the International Labour Organization on South African Labour Law', in Stefan Van Eck, Pamhidzai Bamu and Chanda Chungu (eds), *Celebrating the ILO 100 Years On: Reflections on Labour Law from a Southern African Perspective* (2020, Juta and Company)
- Wright, Erik Olin, 'Social Class' in George Ritzer (ed), *Encyclopedia of Social Theory* (2004, Sage)

Journal articles

- Alam, Khorshed and Sophia Imran, 'The Digital Divide and Social Inclusion Among Refugee Migrants: A Case in Regional Australia' (2015) 28(2) *Information Technology & People* 344
- Aliakbari, Mohammad and Nazal Allahmoradi, 'On the Effects of Social Class on Language Use: A Fresh Look at Bernstein's Theory' (2014) 5(3) *Advances in Language and Literary Studies* 82
- Allen, Dominique and Adriana Orifici, 'What Did the COVID-19 Pandemic Reveal About Workplace Flexibility for People with Family and Caring Responsibilities?' (2022) No 1 *UNSW Law Journal Forum* 1
- Allen, Dominique, 'Adverse Effects: Can the Fair Work Act Address Workplace Discrimination for Employees with a Disability?' (2018) 41(3) *UNSW Law Journal* 846
- Ashoka, Mona, Rohit Madana, Anton Johaa and Uthayasankar Sivarajahb, 'Ethical Framework for Artificial Intelligence and Digital Technologies' (2022) 62 *International Journal of Information Management* 1
- Backman, Christel and Anna Hedenus, 'Online Privacy in Job Recruitment Processes? Boundary Work Among Cybervetting Recruiters' (2019) 34(2) *New Technology, Work and Employment* 157
- Baines, Susan and Ulrike Gelder, 'What is Family Friendly about the Workplace in the Home? The Case of Self-employed Parents and their Children' (2003) 18(3) *New Technology, Work and Employment* 223
- Bekker, Ian and Erez Levon, 'Parodies of Whiteness: Die Antwoord and the Politics of Race, Gender, and Class in South Africa' (2020) 49(1) *Language in Society* 115
- Bernstein, Basil, 'Elaborated and Restricted Codes: Their Social Origins and Some Consequences' (1964) 66(6) *American Anthropologist* 55
- Bleicher, Josef, 'Bildung' (2006) 23(2–3) *Theory, Culture and Society* 364
- Bolander, Brook and Richard J Watts, 'Re-reading and Rehabilitating Basil Bernstein' (2009) 28 *Multilingua* 143
- Bourdieu, Pierre, 'Symbolic Capital and Social Classes' (2013) 13(2) *Journal of Classical Sociology* 292

- Bourdieu, Pierre, 'What Makes a Social Class? On The Theoretical and Practical Existence Of Groups' (1987) 32 *Berkeley Journal of Sociology* 1
- Byun, Soo-yong, Evan Schofer and Kyung-keun Kim, 'Revisiting the Role of Cultural Capital in East Asian Educational Systems: The Case of South Korea' (2012) 85 *Sociology of Education* 219
- Capuano, Angelo, 'Giving Meaning to "Social Origin" in International Labour Organization ("ILO") Conventions, the Fair Work Act 2009 (Cth) and the Australian Human Rights Commission Act 1986 (Cth): "Class" Discrimination and Its Relevance to the Australian Context' (2016) 39(1) *UNSW Law Journal* 84
- Capuano, Angelo, 'Post-pandemic Workplace Design and the Plight of Employees with Invisible Disabilities: Is Australian Labour Law and Anti-Discrimination Legislation Equipped to Address New and Emerging Workplace Inequalities?' (2022) 45(2) *UNSW Law Journal*
- Capuano, Angelo, 'The Meaning of "Social Origin" in International Human Rights Treaties: A Critique of the CESCR's Approach to "Social Origin" Discrimination in the ICESCR and its (Ir)Relevance to National Contexts Such as Australia' (2017) 41(3) *New Zealand Journal of Employment Relations* 91
- Crenshaw, Kimberle, 'Demarginalizing the Intersection of Race and Sex: A Black Feminist Critique of Antidiscrimination Doctrine, Feminist Theory and Antiracist Politics' (1989) 1 *University of Chicago Legal Forum* 139
- Cuerdo-Vilches, Teresa, Miguel Ángel Navas-Martín and Ignacio Oteiza, 'Working from Home: Is Our Housing Ready?' (2021) 18(14) *International Journal of Environmental Research and Public Health* 1
- Cuerdo-Vilches, Teresa, Miguel Ángel Navas-Martín, Sebastià March, Ignacio Oteiza, 'Adequacy of Telework Spaces in Homes During the Lockdown in Madrid, According to Socioeconomic Factors and Home Features' (2021) 75 *Sustainable Cities and Society* 1
- Cullen, Holly, 'Does the ILO Have a Distinctive Role in the International Legal Protection of Child Soldiers?' (2011) 5 *Human Rights and International Legal Discourse* 63
- Cullen, Holly, 'The Collective Complaints System of the European Social Charter: Interpretative Methods of the European Committee of Social Rights' (2009) 9 *Human Rights Law Review* 61
- Daumeyer, Natalie M, Ivuoma N Onyeador, Xanni Brown and Jennifer A Richeson, 'Consequences of Attributing Discrimination to Implicit vs. Explicit Bias' (2019) 84 *Journal of Experimental Social Psychology* 1
- Dietvorst, Berkeley J and Uri Simonsohn, 'Intentionally "Biased": People Purposely Use To-Be-Ignored Information, But Can Be Persuaded Not To' (2019) 148(7) *Journal of Experimental Psychology* 1228

- Durbach, Nadja, ''They Might As Well Brand Us': Working-Class Resistance to Compulsory Vaccination in Victorian England' (2000) 13(1) *Social History of Medicine* 45
- Fang, Guangbao, Philip Wing Keung Chan and Penelope Kalogeropoulos, 'Social Support and Academic Achievement of Chinese Low-Income Children: A Mediation Effect of Academic Resilience' (2020) 13(1) *International Journal of Psychological Research* 19
- Fowler, Bridget, 'Pierre Bourdieu on Social Transformation, with Particular Reference to Political and Symbolic Revolutions', (2020) 49 *Theory and Society* 439
- Fredman, Sandra, 'Substantive Equality Revisited' (2016) 14(3) *International Journal of Constitutional Law* 712
- Gazley, J Lynn et al, 'Beyond Preparation: Identity, Cultural Capital, and Readiness for Graduate School in the Biomedical Sciences' (2014) 51 *Journal of Research in Science Teaching* 1021
- Gruzd, Anatoliy, Jenna Jacobson and Elizabeth Dubois, 'Cybervetting and the Public Life of Social Media Data' (2020) *Social Media + Society* 1
- Halewood, Michael, 'Class is Always a Matter of Morals': Bourdieu and Dewey on Social Class, Morality, and Habit(us)' [2022] *Cultural Sociology* 1
- Handelman, Elana, 'The Expansion of Traditional Background Checks to Social Media Screening: How To Ensure Adequate Privacy Protection in Current Employment Hiring Practices' (2021) 23(3) *Journal of Constitutional Law* 661
- Harris, Courtenay, Leon Straker, and Clare Pollock, 'A socioeconomic related 'digital divide' exists in how, not if, young people use computers' (2017) 12(3) *PLoS ONE* 1
- Hasan, Ruqaiya, 'Ways of Meaning, Ways of Learning: Code as an explanatory concept' (2002) 23(4) *British Journal of Sociology of Education* 537
- Ivinson, Gabrielle, 'Re-imagining Bernstein's Restricted Codes' (2018) 17(4) *European Educational Research Journal* 539
- Jacobson, Jenna and Anatoliy Gruzd, 'Cybervetting Job Applicants on Social Media: The New Normal?' (2020) 22 *Ethics and Information Technology* 175
- Kraaykamp, Gerbert and Koen van Eijck, 'The Intergenerational Reproduction of Cultural Capital: A Threefold Perspective' (2010) 89 *Social Forces* 209
- Kraus, Michael W, Brittany Torrez, Jun Won Park and Fariba Ghayebi, 'Evidence for the Reproduction of Social Class in Brief Speech' (2019) 116(46) *Proceedings of the National Academy of Sciences* 22998
- Kujinga, Tungamirai and Stefan van Eck, 'The Right to Strike and Replacement Labour: South African Practice Viewed from an International Law Perspective' (2018) 21 PER/PELJ 2

- La Hovary, Claire, 'Showdown at the ILO? A Historical Perspective on the Employers' Group's 2012 Challenge to the Right to Strike' (2013) 42 *Industrial Law Journal* 338
- Lam, Helen, 'Social Media Dilemmas in the Employment Context' (2016) 38(3) *Employee Relations* 420
- Lehmann, Wolfgang and Alison Taylor, 'On the Role of Habitus and Field in Apprenticeships' (2015) 29(4) *Work, employment and society* 607
- Lehmann, Wolfgang, 'Habitus Transformation and Hidden Injuries: Successful Working-class University Students', (2013) 87(1) *Sociology of Education* 1
- Lehmann, Wolfgang, 'Working-class students, Habitus, and the Development of Student Roles: A Canadian Case Study' (2012) 33(4) *British Journal of Sociology of Education* 527
- Lewis, Amy C and Steven J Sherman, 'Hiring You Makes Me Look Bad: Social-Identity Based Reversals of The Ingroup Favoritism Effect' (2003) 90(2) *Organizational Behavior and Human Decision Processes* 262
- Maeba, Yusaku, 'A Practical Study on Bernstein's Sociolinguistic Code Theory in Japan: Differences in Linguistic Code in Children in the 1st Year' (2016) 2 Osaka Human Sciences 119
- McDonald, Steve, Amanda K Damarin, Hannah McQueen and Scott T Grether, 'The Hunt for Red Flags: Cybervetting As Morally Performative Practice' (2022) 20(3) *Socio-Economic Review* 915
- Mercorelli, Louis et al, 'A Framework for De-Identification of Free-Text Data in Electronic Medical Records Enabling Secondary Use' (2022) 46(3) *Australian Health Review* 289
- Michael, Ajayi Temitope and Amaka Linda Ajuonuma, 'Investigation of Computer-mediated Communication Proficiency among Secondary School Students in Ibadan: Testing Bernstein's Deficit Hypothesis' (2021) 2(1) *Journal of Language and Discourse Practice* 19
- Molenberghs, Pascal and Samantha Morrison, 'The Role of the Medial Prefrontal Cortex in Social Categorization', (2014) 9(3) *Social Cognitive & Affective Neuroscience* 292
- Molenberghs, Pascal, 'The Neuroscience of In-Group Bias' (2013) 37(8) *Neuroscience and Biobehavioural Reviews* 1530
- Moor, Liz and Sam Friedman, 'Justifying Inherited Wealth: Between 'the Bank of Mum and Dad' and the Meritocratic Ideal' (2021) 50(4) *Economy and Society* 618
- Mubarak, Farooq, Reima Suomi and Satu-Päivi Kantola, 'Confirming the Links Between Socio-Economic Variables and Digitalization Worldwide: The Unsettled Debate on Digital Divide' (2020) 18(3) *Journal of Information, Communication and Ethics in Society* 415
- Nielsen, Henrik Karl, 'The Concept of Discrimination in ILO Convention No. 111' (1994) 43(4) *International & Comparative Law Quarterly* 827

- O'Regan, Kate, 'The Right to Equality in the South African Constitution' (2013) 25 *Columbia Journal of Gender and Law* 110
- Paternoster, Henry John, Deborah Warr and Keith Jacobs, 'The Enigma of the Bogan and its Significance to Class in Australia: A Socio-Historical Analysis', (2018) 54(3) *Journal of Sociology* 429
- Portes, Alejandro, 'Social Capital: Its Origins and Applications in Modern Sociology' (1998) 24 *Annual Review of Sociology* 1
- Rhodes, Rebecca E, et al, 'Teaching Decision Making with Serious Games: An Independent Evaluation' (2017) 12(3) *Games and Culture* 233
- Robards, Brady and Darren Graf, '"How a Facebook Update Can Cost You Your Job": News Coverage of Employment Terminations Following Social Media Disclosures, From Racist Cops to Queer Teachers' (2022) *Social Media + Society* 1
- Rozin, Paul and Edward B Royzman, 'Negativity Bias, Negativity Dominance, and Contagion' (2001) 5(4) *Personality and Social Psychology Review* 296
- Savage, Mike et al, 'A New Model of Social Class? Findings from the BBC's Great British Class Survey Experiment' (2013) 47 *Sociology* 219
- Schoenbaum, Naomi, 'The Case for Symmetry in Antidiscrimination Law' [2017] *Wisconsin Law Review* 69
- Smith, Keyonda and Sandra Schamroth Abrams, 'Gamification and Accessibility' (2019) 36(2) *International Journal of Information and Learning Technology* 104.
- Sorkin, David, 'Wilhelm von Humboldt: The Theory and Practice of Self-formation (*Bildung*), 1791–1810' (1983) 44 *Journal of the History of Ideas* 55
- Tajfel, Henri, 'Experiments in Intergroup Discrimination' [1970] *Scientific American* 96
- Thornton, Margaret, 'Equality and Anti-Discrimination Legislation: An Uneasy Relationship' (2021) 37(2) *Law in Context* 12.
- Thornton, Margaret, 'The Elusiveness of Class Discrimination' (2012) 24(3) *Legaldate* 7
- Tsaousi, Christiana, '"What Underwear Do I Like?" Taste and (Embodied) Cultural Capital in the Consumption of Women's Underwear' (2014) *Journal of Consumer Culture* 1
- Türkmen, Saadet, 'The Story in the Story of Gule' in Solmaz Golsabahi-Broclawski, Ibrahim Özkan and Artur Broclawski (eds), *Transkulturelle Psychiatrie: Erfahrungen von Experten aus der EU* (LIT Verlag, 2014)
- Van Bueren QC, Geraldine, 'Inclusivity and the Law: Do We Need to Prohibit Class Discrimination?' (2021) *European Human Rights Law Review* 274
- van Doorn, Niels and Darsana Vijay, 'Gig Work as Migrant Work: The Platformization of Migration Infrastructure' [2021] *Environment and Planning A: Economy and Space* 1

- Walther, Eva, 'Guilty by Mere Association: Evaluative Conditioning and the Spreading Attitude Effect' (2002) 82(6) *Journal of Personality and Social Psychology* 919
- Walther, Eva, Rebecca Weil and Jessica Dusing, 'The Role of Evaluative Conditioning in Attitude Formation' (2011) 20(3) *Current Directions in Psychological Science* 192
- Yarbrough, Jillian R, 'Is Cybervetting Ethical? An Overview of Legal and Ethical Issues' (2018) 11 *Journal of Ethical and Legal Issues* 1
- Zhang et al, 'What's on Job Seekers' Social Media Sites? A Content Analysis and Effects of Structure on Recruiter Judgments and Predictive Validity' (2020) 105(12) *Journal of Applied Psychology* 1530

Handbooks, reports, papers, submissions and theses

- *Australian Government, Australian Institute of Family Studies, 'Mothers Still Do the Lion's Share of Housework' (Research summary, May 2016)*
- Australian Government, Productivity Commission, 'Working from Home' (Research paper, September 2021)
- Australian Human Rights Commission, 'Using Artificial Intelligence to Make Decisions: Addressing the Problem of Algorithmic Bias' (Technical Paper, 2020)
- Australian Human Rights Commission, *Federal Discrimination Law* (Online Handbook, 2016)
- Bridge Group, 'Who Gets Ahead and How? Socio-economic Background and Career Progression in Financial Services: A Study of Eight Organisations' (Report)
- Calvin K Lai, 'What's Unconscious Bias Training, and Does it Work?' (28 May 2018, *The Conversation*)
- CBRE Research, 'The Evolution of Australian Law Firms' (Report, June 2022)
- Chant, Sylvia and Carolyn Pedwell, 'Women, Gender and the Informal Economy: An Assessment of ILO Research and Suggested Ways Forward' (Discussion paper, International Labour Organization, 2008)
- Clegg, Benjamin A et al, 'Game-based Training to Mitigate Three Forms of Cognitive Bias' (2014, Interservice/Industry Training, Simulation, and Education Conference)
- DLA Piper, 'Guide to Going Global: Employment' (Full Handbook, 2020) https://www.dlapiperintelligence.com/goingglobal/employment/handbook.pdf
- Fels, Allan and David Cousins, *Report of the Migrant Workers' Taskforce'* (Australian Government, March 2019)
- Fredman, Sandra, 'Intersectional Discrimination in EU Gender Equality and Non-Discrimination Law' (May 2016, Report, European Commission)

- Gardiner-Garden, John, 'Defining Aboriginality in Australia' (Current Issues Brief No. 10 2002–03, Parliament of Australia)
- Gjyshinca, Gjeta, 'Contextual Recruitment in Australia: Why Recruiters Have a Role to Play in Promoting Social Mobility, and How Contextual Data Can Help to Identify Hidden Talent' (June 2016, Report, Rare/Allens Linklaters)
- Hightower, Dustin Kaleb, 'Me or My Friend? Examining SNS Friend Activity's Impact on Applicant Perceptions' (Thesis, Submitted in partial fulfillment of the requirements for the degree of Master of Science in Psychology at The University of Texas at Arlington, August 2020)
- Hiscox, Michael J, Tara Oliver, Michael Ridgway, Lilia Arcos-Holzinger, Alastair Warren and Andrea Willis, 'Going Blind to See More Clearly: Unconscious Bias in Australian Public Service Shortlisting Processes' (June 2017, Behavioural Economics Team of the Australian Government)
- Human Rights Commission of Newfoundland and Labrador, Annual Report for 2004/05
- KMPG, 'Social Mobility Progression Report 2022: Mind the Gap' (Report, December 2022)
- KPMG UK, 'Socio-Economic Background Pay Gap Report 2021' (September 2021)
- Law Reform Commission of Western Australia, 'Review of the Equal Opportunity Act 1984 (WA)' (Project 111, Discussion Paper, August 2021)
- MacKay, Wayne and Natasha Kim, 'Adding Social Condition to the *Canadian Human Rights Act*' (Canadian Human Rights Commission, February 2009)
- McKenzie, Nick, Amelia Ballinger and Joel Tozer, 'Trafficked: Women shunted 'like cattle' around Australia for sex work' (30 October 2022, *The Age*)
- Mehdi, Tahsin and René Morissette, 'Working from home: Productivity and preferences' (Report, Statistics Canada, 1 April 2021)
- New Brunswick Human Rights Commission's 'Guideline on Social Condition' (February 2019)
- O'Neil Risk Consulting & Algorithmic Auditing (ORCAA), 'Description of Algorithmic Audit: Pre-built Assessments' (Report, ORCAA's Algorithmic Audit of HireVue's Pre-built Assessments for Early Career and Campus Hires, December 15 2020)
- PwC, Diversity Pay Report
- Rare, 'Contextual Recruitment in Australia: One Year On' (Report, 2017)
- Rare, 'Level Playing Field? Super Schools, Social Mobility and Star Outperformers' (Report, 2017)

- Rare, 'Measures That Matter Analysing Disadvantage, Identifying Outperformance and Increasing Diversity in Graduate Recruitment' (Report, September 2018)
- *Recruit Smarter: Report of Findings* (Department of Premier and Cabinet Victoria & The Centre for Ethical Leadership, University of Melbourne, 2018)
- *Recruit Smarter: Technical Report* (The Centre for Ethical Leadership, Ormond College, The University of Melbourne)
- Rickett, Bridgette, Matthew Easterbrook, Jennifer Sheehy-Skeffington, Paula Reavey, Maxine Woolhouse, 'Psychology of Social Class-Based Inequalities: Policy Implications for a revised (2010) UK Equality Act' (The British Psychological Society, Report, July 2022)
- Sánchez-Monedero, Javier, Lina Dencik and Lilian Edwards, 'What Does it Mean to 'solve' the Problem of Discrimination in Hiring? Social, Technical and Legal Perspectives from The UK on Automated Hiring Systems' (Proceedings of the 2020 Conference on Fairness, Accountability and Transparency, January 2020)
- Social Mobility Commission, 'Changing Gears: Understanding Downward Social Mobility (Research report, November 2020)
- South African Human Rights Commission, 'Achieving Substantive Economic Equality Through Rights-Based Radical Socio-Economic Transformation in South Africa' (Equality Report, 2017/18)
- Tanton, Robert, Dominic Peel and Yogi Vidyattama, 'Every Suburb Every Town: Poverty in Victoria (November 2018, NATSEM, Institute for Governance and Policy Analysis (IGPA), University of Canberra. Report commissioned by VCOSS)
- The Law Reform Commission of Western Australia, 'Review of the Equal Opportunity Act 1984 (WA)' (Project 111, Discussion Paper, August 2021)
- Thomas, Constance, Martin Oelz and Xavier Beaudonnet, 'The Use of International Labor Law in Domestic Courts: Theory, Recent Jurisprudence, and Practical Implications' in Les normes internationales du travail: Un patrimoine pour l'avenir (International Labour Organization, 2004)
- UK Government, 'Levelling Up the United Kingdom' (Presented to Parliament by the Secretary of State for Levelling Up, Housing and Communities, 2 February 2022)
- Wilson, Christo, Avijit Ghosh, Shan Jiang, Alan Mislove, Lewis Baker, Janelle Szary, Kelly Trindel and Frida Polli, 'Building and Auditing Fair Algorithms: A Case Study in Candidate Screening' (FAccT '21, March 1–10, 2021, Virtual Event, Canada)

Surveys

- *World Values Survey Wave 7 (2017–2020; Study #WVS-2017): Australia*
- World Values Survey Wave 7 (2017–2020): Canada
- World Values Survey Wave 6 (2010–2014), 121–122
- PwC, 'Hopes and fears 2021: The views of 32,500 workers' (Survey, PwC)
- Brown, C, R D'Almada-Remedios, K Dunbar, J O'Leary, O Evans and M Rubin, 'Class at Work: Does Social Class Make a Difference in the Land of the 'Fair Go'?' (Sydney, Diversity Council Australia, 2020)

Reference materials

- *Encyclopaedia Britannica*
- MacMillan Dictionary
- Merriam Webster Dictionary

Websites

- https://www.technologyreview.com
- https://www.careers.ox.ac.uk
- https://www.pymetrics.ai/
- http://cpcadcr.presidency.ro
- http://repository.lasalle.edu.co
- http://www.eafit.edu.co
- http://www.ilo.org
- http://www.iwgia.org
- http://www.lawyersweekly.com.au
- https://2kmfromhome.com
- https://about.instagram.com
- https://au.contextualrecruitment.com
- https://depts.washington.edu
- https://modernhire.com
- https://press.careerbuilder.com
- https://regnet.anu.edu.au
- https://resource.capetown.gov.za
- https://socialmobilityworks.org
- https://treaties.un.org
- https://vidcruiter.com
- https://www.abc.net.au
- https://www.abs.gov.au
- https://www.allens.com.au
- https://www.cbc.ca
- https://www.chcf.org
- https://www.facebook.com/business
- https://www.fwc.gov.au
- https://www.gov.za

- https://www.hirevue.com/
- https://www.humanrights.gov.au
- https://www.humanrights.gov.au
- https://www.knockri.com/
- https://www.nytimes.com
- https://www.ohrc.on.ca
- https://www.ons.gov.uk
- https://www.qhrc.qld.gov.au
- https://www.smh.com.au
- https://www.statsnwt.ca
- https://www.thesouthafrican.com
- https://www.wa.gov.au/
- https://www.who.int
- https://www.zapidhire.com/
- www.bbc.com
- www.hoganlovells.com
- www.washingtonpost.com

Index

References to footnotes show both the
page number and the note number (54n131).